Theorizing Bruce Lee

Contemporary Cinema ⬤5⬤

Contemporary Cinema is a series of edited volumes and
single-authored texts focusing on the latest in film culture, theory,
reception and interpretation. There is a concentration on films released
in the past fifteen years, and the aim is to reflect important current
issues while pointing to others that to date have not been given sufficient
attention.

Theorizing Bruce Lee

Film-Fantasy-Fighting-Philosophy

Paul Bowman

Amsterdam - New York, NY 2010

For Keira and Lilly, whose first reactions to seeing Bruce Lee
I will never forget

Institutional support:
The Centre for Cinema Studies, Department of Theatre and Film,
University of British Columbia

Cover illustration: Design by Andrew deWaard, based on Bruce Lee
Action Figure package illustration by Enterbay, based on still from
Game of Death (Copyright Universal Studios).

ISBN: 978-90-420-2777-0
E-Book: 978-90-420-2778-7
ISSN: 1572-3070
©Editions Rodopi B.V., Amsterdam - New York, NY 2010
Printed in the Netherlands

Contents

User Guide: Main Menu

Warning

At the start of *Enter the Dragon* (1973), Bruce Lee delivers one of his most famous lines: 'it is like a finger pointing away to the moon'. The status of this aphorism and indeed the meaning of the lesson that Lee seems to be delivering when he says the words are contentious: is this a platitude or a profundity, a cliché or a koan, a riddle or ridiculousness? Is it mystical philosophy, an intercultural encounter, or a cynical parody – a synthetic simulation? This is a complicated matter to decide. In an analysis of some of the occurrences of the finger pointing to the moon riddle in Zen Buddhist writings (yet without ever mentioning or indicating an awareness of Bruce Lee), Eve Kosofsky Sedgwick observes that Western education largely proceeds by 'assuming that every lesson can be divided into ever more bite-sized, ever more assimilable bits'. The 'wisdom traditions' of Buddhism, on the other hand, principally 'assume that students have already surmounted a fairly high threshold of recognition' (2003: 171-2). The book you are currently reading, *Theorizing Bruce Lee: Film—Fantasy—Fighting—Philosophy*, makes a similar assumption. It assumes that readers have an awareness of Bruce Lee, his films, and probably even some sense of quite how dramatic and significant his entrance was – not just in the realms of film but also in those of cultural fantasies as well as in terms of the proliferation and development of martial arts. Indeed, as we have already seen, his impact may even be felt in philosophy itself. All of this is as much as to say that the assumption organising this book is that to study or theorize Bruce Lee cannot proceed according to 'ever more bite-sized, ever more assimilable bits', because it requires the simultaneous engagement with issues to do not only with film, philosophy, fighting, popular culture, and issues in postcolonialism related principally to ethnic Chinese diasporic consciousness in the 1960s and 1970s, but also to questions of intercultural exchange, encounters, and so on. As this book's subheading and chapter titles announce, the hypothesis organising *Theorizing Bruce Lee: Film—Fantasy—Fighting—Philosophy* is that in the case of a complex object (or field) like Bruce Lee, these coordinates are interrelated and interimplicated; they cannot simply be separated, but must instead be engaged in relation to each other. Of course, things become even more complicated when one realises that each of these coordinates – film, fantasy, fighting, philosophy – exists in not just one but several academic disciplinary languages. At the same time, they are engaged – in multiple and mutually contradictory ways – in popular cultural discourses. So, to state it as directly as possible: this is going to be messy.

Language Selection

Inevitably, there are going to be a huge range of voices and 'languages' involved here. As well as Bruce Lee's films and published writings there are the words of his friends and students. There are films and practices inspired or informed by Bruce Lee. There are academic studies of Lee in several disciplines, and many more which use, mention or involve Lee in a supplementary manner. There are different ways of approaching and engaging with his films, his writings, his martial arts, his epoch, his significance and his legacy. This book cannot speak in all of these languages all of the time. Moreover, it cannot simply let all voices be heard, unfiltered, unedited or unproduced. So, on the one hand, I must inevitably quote from many different 'languages', or texts that use wildly differing frameworks and registers, but on the other hand, I must inevitably prefer certain styles, orientations and registers over others, and translate a cacophony into a coherent utterance, intelligible to certain ears, in terms of particular concerns. This is another way of saying that although not everyone is going to approve, this book is written in the academic language of contemporary cultural studies, and the many voices, perspectives and positions referenced and discussed in it are largely going to be engaged in terms of the questions and issues that circulate within and constitute this messy discursive field. So, as much as non-academics may baulk at such a treatment of Bruce Lee, it remains the case that the academic language of cultural studies is arguably the *lingua franca* of the contemporary Western (and increasingly global) arts and humanities. So, to state it as discursively as possible: this is actually going to be tidy.

Scene Selection

Each of the four chapters is a largely discrete entity which could be read in isolation, and the book could conceivably be read in any order. However, the book has been designed to be read from start to finish, insofar as Chapter One is the most introductory and each subsequent chapter builds on, emphasizes different aspects of, deepens or develops away from arguments and ideas laid down earlier. So the choice of scene selection is yours, although the recommendation is that you 'play all'. However, the book does not deal with Bruce Lee in a linear or biographical manner. Chapters turn and return to several key moments, scenarios, ideas, questions and themes, and they approach them with different emphases, in different styles, according to different optics: the opening scenes of *Enter the Dragon*; the fight with Chuck Norris in *Way of the Dragon*; the nationalism of *Fist of Fury*; the significance of nunchakus; Bruce Lee's historical and cultural 'locations' (1960s Hollywood and Hong Kong, in particular); Lee's *antidisciplinary* critique of martial arts styles and institutions and his *interdisciplinary* approach to martial arts; the 'philosophy' of jeet kune do, the interpellative and subjectivizing force of Lee's image and movements, etc. These scenes and problematics have been selected because of their exemplarity: they exemplify ongoing issues in film studies, postcolonialism, cultural and political theory, and cultural studies. Indeed, this is my primary reason for studying and writing a book about Bruce Lee in the first place. *Theorizing Bruce Lee* raises questions and proposes insights – for film studies, cultural studies, identity studies, postcolonial studies, and beyond – that are both fundamental and ongoing, generative and unresolved, constitutive and contemporary.

Special Features

Given the complex multimedia, multidisciplinary, multicultural and multidimensional nature of the object or topic called 'Bruce Lee', this book necessarily enters into several fields: film, postcolonialism, critical theory, semiotics, poststructuralism, the margins of philosophy, and so on. Not entirely unlike Bruce Lee's approach to martial arts, perhaps, this work has to be both interdisciplinary and antidisciplinary. Inevitably, therefore, there will be those in these fields who are going regard this book as improper through and through – as not doing film studies *properly* or postcolonialism *properly*, etc. This is a criticism which is as inevitable as it is provocative: it suggests a lot about what people regard as 'proper' and it ultimately begs questions about the limits and maintenance of disciplinary borders, conventions, hermeneutical fields, the ways in which disciplines construct their objects and define their limits, their partiality, their investments, orientations, antagonisms and exclusions. This work tries to foreground these often invisible but always active forces which attend *any* discipline. As such, the book tries to reinstate to a high level of visibility that which is often a deleted scene.

Chapter 1
Introduction
Theorizing Bruce Lee:
Sublime Object of Academia

Cross-ethnic representation, then, is not just a matter of discovering more and newer routes to and contacts with other cultures, whether by means associated with Christopher Columbus (caravels) or Bill Gates (modems). Instead, it is a process in which the acceleration and intensification of contacts brought by technology and commerce entail an acceleration and intensification of stereotypes, stereotypes that, rather than simply being false or incorrect (and thus dismissable), have the potential of effecting changes in entire intellectual climates…
- Rey Chow, 'Brushes with the Other as Face' (2002: 63)

Stereotyping Bruce Lee: Trivia, Clichés and Provocations

The topic of Bruce Lee may strike some as trivial – kids' stuff, even: a 1970s celluloid action man who defined a brief moment in a bygone era when 'everybody was kung fu fighting', or briefly wanted to be. Indeed, not only trivial, Bruce Lee might actually exemplify many of the things we might be better off without: silly boys' crazes, faddishness, escapism, nerdiness, fantasies of physical violence, representations reliant on ultimately racist stereotypes, the commodification of oriental alterity. So: trivial, nerdy, fetishistic, violent, orientalist, exploitative, and typifying the western impetus to appropriation. Already this could constitute a fairly damning series of charges, charges which are implicit in the essential thrust of not only certain Marxian views on popular culture, but also a fair few feminist and liberal humanist criticisms too. Thus, if the question is 'What is Bruce Lee?', then one answer might be: a trivial and trivialising, violent, masculinist, orientalist stereotype; a mythologized commodification of alterity packaged for a fetishistic Western gaze; the mythological reduction of ethnicity into posters, t-shirts, nerds' film collections; one which provided bullies, show offs, fighters and fantasists the world over with an entire new lexicon of moves and stances for posturing, parading and pugilism. So, perhaps not even 'kids' stuff', Bruce Lee could ultimately come to strike you as exactly the sort of *putatively* trivial thing that is not actually trivial at all, but is rather the sort of thing you might want to keep very far away from kids: a dangerous supplement, an irredeemably patriarchal and fetishistic commodity, a sublime object of ideology.

Although this may seem like excessive hyperbole and caricature, it is nevertheless the case that precisely such dismissals and denunciations of Bruce Lee do occur – particularly as a first reaction to the suggestion that anything remotely serious or worthy of attention might condense in or around Bruce Lee. Yet even if there is indeed *something* in the sorts of criticism to which I have just gestured, wherein Bruce Lee might be deemed trivial, deleterious or ideological, or in which Bruce Lee is regarded as representing or participating in something to do with capitalist commodification, Western orientalism or patriarchy, then surely this can only mean that there is indeed something serious and worthy of attention here.

This array of thorny issues can be broached through a consideration of the intertwined topics of representation and participation, particularly in this case in the way that they converge in the chiasmus of the cinema. Representation is, of course, not exactly the same topic as that of cinema, but the two are deeply intertwined and interimplicated. Moreover, both are arguably implicated in the very constitution of everyday social and cultural reality – particularly people's beliefs, biases, assumptions, values and prejudices, and in the complex relationships between representation and participation. In the case of Bruce Lee, we are perhaps chiefly or primarily obliged to consider the knotty issue of cross-cultural and inter-ethnic representation. How do we represent others, first of all?

What is the status and significance of the representations that are 'Bruce Lee'? Who or what is being represented and who or what is doing the representing?

As we will see, there is much that can be regarded as stereotypical when it comes to Bruce Lee. Indeed, perhaps it is through a consideration of stereotypes that Bruce Lee may best be approached at the outset. Of course, stereotypes are stereotypically construed as being 'bad' sorts of representation. This is generally because they are understood to objectify the other in a way that is reductive, crude, hostile or simplistic. But, there is a problem with this stereotype of stereotypes. As Rey Chow alerts us, 'any charge that others are stereotyping inevitably involves, whether or not one is conscious of it, one's own participation in the same activity' (1995: 57-8). That is to say, 'in order to criticize stereotypes, one must somehow resort to stereotypical attitudes and presumptions' (57). For, she argues, 'in order to repudiate a certain attitude as racist stereotyping, one would, to begin with, need to have already formed certain attitudes toward that attitude, to have *stereotyped* it or marked it as uniformly possessing a distinguishing set of traits' (57). Chow's point is that rather than trying to expel stereotypes from the realms of representation, perhaps we need to acknowledge that there may well be no getting away from stereotypes – that stereotyping may actually reflect an inevitable aspect of 'culture'.

To explain this possibility, Chow focuses on Fredric Jameson's provocative argument that the 'relationship between groups is, so to speak, unnatural' (qtd. in Chow 1995: 55). Relationships between groups are founded in 'the chance external contact between entities which have only an interior (like a monad) and no exterior or external surface, save in this special circumstance'. In Jameson's words, it is 'the outer edge of the group that – all the while remaining unrepresentable – brushes against that of the other'. This 'outer edge' does not exist as such for those within that group, and only comes into existence through and as the constitutive encounter with the other. 'Speaking crudely then', concludes Jameson, 'we would have to say that the relationship between groups must always be one of struggle and violence' (qtd. in Chow 1995: 55):

> the group as such is necessarily an imaginary entity, in the sense in which no individual mind is able to intuit it concretely. The group must be abstracted, or fantasized, on the basis of discrete individual contacts and ex-

periences which can never be generalized in anything but abusive fashion. *The relations between groups are always stereotypical insofar as they must always involve collective abstractions of the other group, no matter how sanitized, no matter how liberally censored and imbued with respect... The liberal solution to this dilemma – doing away with the stereotypes or pretending they don't exist – is not possible...* (Jameson as qtd. in Chow 1995: 56-7)

Thus, Chow proposes, cross-cultural and inter-ethnic representations will always entail an element of 'the outer edge of one group brushing against that of another' – that is, '*an encounter between surfaces rather than interiors*' (57). As such, this 'cannot really be foreclosed again by the liberalist suggestion that everyone is entitled to her own stereotypes of herself, which others should simply adopt for general use'. This is because 'stereotypes' are now to be understood as 'relations conducted around exteriors' – constitutive limit- or liminal-points of contact, rather than that of 'transparent communication' or communion between equal subjects who are transparent to each other.

In political and cultural contexts, Chow suggests, 'what the successful use of stereotypes by political regimes has proved is not simply that stereotypes are clichéd, unchanging forms but also – and much more importantly – that stereotypes are capable of engendering realities that do not exist' (59). 'Contrary to the charge that they are misrepresentations', Chow states, 'stereotypes have demonstrated themselves to be effective, realistic political weapons capable of generating belief, commitment, and action'; drawing our attention to the 'fantastic figures of the Jew, the Jap, and the wetback [which] have all produced substantive political consequences, from deportation to incarceration to genocide or ethnic cleansing' (59). All of this is as much as to say that visual culture such as film and other forms of representation can be, to say the least, important and consequential. It is the overarching concern of this book to explore these relations engendered between the putatively 'merely' cinematic, fictional, filmic or representational aspects of 'Bruce Lee' and other scenes and contexts – relations between representation and participation, between fantastic figures and substantive political and cultural consequences. Bruce Lee is certainly the former. This book is concerned with the latter.

Brushes with Bruce Lee as Body

Davis Miller captures the moment of his first chance encounter with this fantastic figure very powerfully, in his account of the first time he saw Bruce Lee:

> The picture that night was *Enter the Dragon.* The house lights dimmed, flickered, went out. The red Warner Brothers logo flashed.
> And there he stood.
> There was a silence around him. The air crackled as the camera moved towards him and he grew in the centre of the screen, luminous.
> This man. My man. The Dragon.
> One minute into the movie, Bruce Lee threw his first punch. With it, a power came rolling up from Lee's belly, affecting itself in blistering waves not only upon his onscreen opponent, but on the cinema audience.
> A wind blew through me. My hands shook; I quivered electrically from head to toe. And then Bruce Lee launched the first *real* kick I had ever seen. My jaw fell open like the business end of a refuse lorry. This man could fly. Not like Superman – better – his hands and his feet flew whistling through sky. Yes, better: this wasn't simply a movie, a shadow-box fantasy; there was a seed of reality in Lee's every movement. Yet the experience of watching him felt just like a dream.
> Bruce Lee was unlike anyone I (or any of us) had seen. (Miller 4)

Indeed, such a fantastic figure is Bruce Lee that, in a passionate reflection on his life and significance, Miller proposes that Bruce Lee has a 'face as faceless as God'. To Miller's mind, Lee possesses 'the ultimate, ethicless, unqualified fame' of an order that very 'few people have attained'. 'Among names which come to mind', he suggests, are 'Jesus, Buddha, Muhammad'. Indeed, 'perhaps only four people from the twentieth century can be considered for this list': Adolf Hitler, Muhammad Ali, Elvis Presley and – 'yes, surprisingly' – Bruce Lee (Miller 94).

Many may baulk at the appearance of Bruce Lee on such a list. But, along with many biographers and fans of Lee, Miller invites us to consider the fact that 'everyone' knows the name 'Bruce Lee' and what it has come to stand for: 'his ambiguous reputation as the twentieth-century god of martial art is known in almost every city, town, and village on the planet' (94). Yet, this is first and foremost a familiarity with the *name*, not a *face*. For, in fact, globally-speaking 'relatively few of us have seen Lee or one of his few movies, [yet] his name may be recognized in more places than that of anyone else of our time' (94). This has been the case since the moment of his entrance – which was in many senses also effectively the moment of his exit, since the film which brought him global fame, *Enter the Dragon* (1973), was actually released in some countries the very month that he died.

According to André Bazin, the film icon 'is no longer "human", engaging in the transcendence which characterizes living gods and dead heroes' (qtd. in Chow 1995: 31). The strange 'power of filmic images' is that 'they are *retroactive,* calling for a submission to that which has, in the process of being turned into an image, already become past or dead' (31). For Bazin, 'only the dead is larger than life' (Chow 1995: 31). Bruce Lee's unique visual impact plus the announcement of his death at more or less exactly the moment of many Westerners' first contact with his films surely (over)determined his vast but often unfortunate spectral legacy. 'Lee's death created a crisis', says Leon Hunt, 'and a rush to fill what Kwai Cheung Lo calls the "Hole punched out by (his) body"' (77). Cinema abhors a vacuum. The hole was quickly filled with copies, re-releases, re-edits, re-hashed attempts at recombining old footage into new products and Bruce Lee 'clones' – indeed, a whole subgenre of movies and commerce that has been called 'Bruceploitation'.

Miller acknowledges sadly that 'within two years of Lee's death, his name had become a cliché [...] to be tagged on to every side-kicker in every *dojo,* arena, *dojang,* gym, *kwoon,* movie-studio lot, or back alley' (94-5). Bruce Lee then became less a proper name than a metonym for 'kung fu', or a synecdochic term for a certain kind of action. But, Bruce Lee is also overwhelmingly an *image*: 'his likeness is sold in boutiques in Beverly Hills and in souks in Marrakesh, hangs on apartment walls in Kiev and in Paris, in mud huts in central African nations and in the Australian outback' (94). Lee is indeed *the* image of martial arts – 'his image is the one that's still most common on the cover of martial arts publications world-round' – but in a way that totally *exceeds* martial arts: 'his ambiguous reputation as the twentieth-century god of martial art' is precisely that: ambiguous, uncertain, unsure. What is *certain* is the significance of Lee's visuality. Again, Miller sums it up excellently:

> In *Enter the Dragon* Bruce Lee moved fluidly... with a rhythm distinctly his own. And, *oh!,* was he fast. Even faster than Ali. So explosively quick that the paths of his hand strikes were invisible. You could see techniques begin and end – nothing in the middle. It hardly seemed possible. Yet here he was, right in front of me, right here on this shimmering twenty-foot tall screen.

> Fists flying, feet soaring, punching and kicking bad guys from all an-
> gles. Punches and kicks – and much, much more. Lee's limbs moved in
> such a marvellously precise fashion that, when he was facing the camera,
> his blows seemed to slice the screen into sections. In addition he was the
> only genuinely lithe man I had ever seen, other than Ali. (Women are
> sometimes lithe, I believed; men almost never.) Lee used hands and feet,
> knees and elbows, shoulders and head, *good great God, his entire body!*
> And he did so with just about perfect grace and balance. Even more amaz-
> ing: when he was standing still, something inside him vibrated; something
> continued to move. (Miller 4-5)

Miller recounts Phil Ochs' observations that what was seen for the first time with Bruce Lee was neither 'the vulgarity of James Arness pistol-whipping a drunken, stubbled stage robber', nor 'the ingenious devices of James Bond coming to the rescue, nor the ham-fisted John Wayne slugging it out in the saloon over crumbling tables and paper-thin imitation glass'. Rather, Bruce Lee demonstrates 'the science of the body taken to its highest form, and the violence, no matter how outrageous, is always strangely purifying' (4).

This singularity, this exceptionality, this event, the fact that 'Bruce Lee was unlike anyone I (or any of us) had seen', is the key reason he become 'as faceless as God'. In Deleuze and Guattari's terms, Bruce Lee was a 'sense event' par excellence. In his wake, not only does 'every side-kicker' become (reminiscent of) Bruce Lee by side-kicking; not only does every side-kick henceforth bear the mark of Lee; and not only has Lee has left an indelible mark on every side-kick and arguably every side-kicker since 1973 and, of course, *retroactively* on the entire history of side-kicking; but it is actually *as a consequence of Bruce Lee* that 'side-kicking', AKA martial art, became what it subsequently did in public consciousness and discourse, both East and West. So, as well as the fact that 'there isn't a martial artist on the planet who hasn't been influenced by Bruce', it is perhaps even more significant to note the extent to which it is 'hard to overstate how visible the martial disciplines have become because of Lee. If he had not existed, few of us would have heard of martial art or kung fu' (Miller 148). According to Miller, 'Before Lee's death there were fewer than 500 martial arts schools in the world; by the late 1990s, because of his influence, there were more than 20 million martial arts students in the United States alone' (148).

Of course, Bruce Lee was only one event or moment in a larger history of the western interest in oriental martial arts. So in one sense he cannot be taken to 'be' the entire history of the western interest in oriental martial arts, in and of himself. But, it soon becomes apparent that Lee has a very peculiar place – within and without, part of and more than – that history, as we will see when we undertake a consideration of the history of martial arts in the west (below). In a most immediate and straightforward sense it is possible to observe that in addition to being *name*, *face*, and *action*, or symbol, metaphor and metonym for 'martial arts', the sense-event 'Bruce Lee' refers to and has indelibly marked notions of, fantasies about, aspirations for and practices of *the body*, through and through. According to Miller:

> In addition to Lee's considerable legacy of introducing more Westerners to Asian culture and philosophy than anyone else in history, he served to foreshadow, and be a forebear of, the hyperfitness body culture of the latter portion of our century. Before Lee, none of us had seen anyone with his streamlined, functional, no scrap muscularity. *How can anyone look like that?* I wondered, watching *Enter the Dragon*; in 1999, studying photos of him on my desk, it still seems almost impossible to me. Yet this aesthetic, first encountered in Lee, has since become not only desirable but is regarded as a twenty-first-century, new-evolutionary goal, among both men and women. (Miller 149)[1]

Thus, suggests Miller, even though people who don't practise martial arts often 'regard Lee's movies almost as respectfully as Three Stooges shorts – Larry bonks Moe on his noggin, Moe sticks his fingers in Larry's eyes, Larry stomps on Curly's foot' – nevertheless 'there are others who take Bruce Lee very seriously'. In fact, writes Miller, 'Three decades after his death Lee is revered by martial arts practitioners throughout the world' (94).

Observations like these both acknowledge and yet nevertheless overstep or miss the significance and ramifications of the *cinematic* dimension of Lee's popular cultural impact. His impact 'beyond' the cinematic realm, in the fields of martial arts practice, is *assumed*, and almost goes without saying (even though the precise nature of this impact is arguably quite questionable). But the nature of his intervention is overwhelmingly *cinematically determined*. However, this *cinematic* dimension is both easily overlooked and not something that is easily delimitable.

---

[1] We will return to this theme again in Chapter Four. See also Žižek (2004: 78-9).

The Bruce Lee(s) Cultural Revolution

In order to broach this complex field, perhaps we ought merely to affirm some putatively obvious points about Bruce Lee's cinematic significance – points that may well go without saying but should not pass unremarked. Chief among these, as Miller points out, is the extent to which 'Lee fundamentally changed movie fight scenes: those of us born before 1960 grew up in a culture which considered kicking to be "dirty" fighting; martial arts are now employed in nearly every fight in almost every action movie' (149). Moreover, in addition to 'inspiring many professional athletes, Lee has influenced the way every single action-movie hero and heroine has moved in fights since the mid-1970s' (155). Lee has 'inspired video-game programmers and stunt guys': 'Almost all stunt co-ordinators who came after Bruce were influenced' (155) says George Tan:

> Any movie or TV show with fights in it – *Raiders of the Lost Ark, Star Wars, Buffy the Vampire Slayer,* animated fights in *The Lion King* – it doesn't matter what. If you know what you're looking at, you'll catch camera angles and martial arts techniques from Bruce's scenes, stuff Bruce invented. He contributed so much to the industry that has never been recognized. (qtd. in Miller 156)

All of the practices and fantasies mobilised by Bruce Lee relate directly and ineradicably to the cinematic apparatus. Indeed, even though one might be tempted to rush to the conclusion that it is in the realms of bodily martial arts practice that the absent presence of Bruce Lee continues to be most felt, perhaps it could be said to be considerably more active in other realms than in martial arts practice. As we will see in subsequent discussions, even though we may prefer to think that 'reality', 'history', 'materiality' and 'physical existence', rather than myths and fantasies, are the most important factors on any discussion of reality, materiality and physical existence, such a preference needs to be deconstructed if we are not to be led by the nose by myths and fantasies about what reality, history and physical existence *are*. Bruce Lee's significance, status, and the significance and status of his interventions into any realm are reliant *constitutively* on his cinematic interventions, and not the other way around. This is so even if his actual physical abilities were superlative. This type of deconstructive argument (which inverts and displaces the usual presumptions and hierarchies) will be developed more fully in due course.

The significance and importance of such styles of reading and analysis is not limited to Bruce Lee. Similarly, the significance of Bruce Lee cannot be limited to 'Bruce Lee', or to his fans, or to martial arts. As Miller asks: 'did Lee make a significant contribution to anything more ennobling than the (rather sociopathic) prettification of violence?' His answer is resounding: 'Indeed he did. Perhaps the best, most life-affirming aspect of Lee's legacy is this: a popularization of forward-looking art and philosophy' (156). We shall engage with this 'art and philosophy' extensively in the ensuing pages. Miller himself provides an extremely wide-ranging list of artists, musicians, athletes, obsessives and entrepreneurs who have been influenced significantly by Bruce Lee's contribution. This list demonstrates that Lee's impact extends way beyond the relatively circumscribed fields of martial arts practice and physical culture, and even beyond the often supposedly hermetically-sealed realms of cinema. Rather, Bruce Lee's 'influence' extends right into the complexity of the intertwined tangles, knots, relays, overlaps and interconnections of what can be called 'popular culture' – and thereafter, of course, *the world*. As will be argued in the following chapters, there is no possibility of sustaining such ideas as the existence of independent, autochthonous, hermetically-sealed and discrete 'realms' or 'spheres' of culture that are immune to each other; there is no 'high culture' that is sealed off from 'low culture', no 'philosophical realm' that is immune to or free from the 'ideological realm', and so on. Indeed, such distinctions only exist in the efforts to institute such distinctions *as if* they actually exist.

Enumerating or elaborating more and more contexts in which Bruce Lee is diversely influential is perhaps less important to any study than analysing and examining the reasons *why* something came to be (deemed) influential. Although it is very easy to *look at Bruce Lee* and to come up with subject-centred (psychologistic or psychoanalytic) reasons to do with body, movement, identification, fantasy and desire in order to explain why Bruce Lee became so hugely popular, it is nevertheless equally if not more important to also examine both the contexts and effects of historical and economic forces and the cinematic apparatuses which operate within and as parts of these contexts. As Leon Hunt points out, for instance:

> In 1963, Bruce Lee published *Chinese Gung Fu: The Philosophical Art of Self Defence* in the United States. ... Except to martial arts cognoscenti (and not many of those), 'gung fu' (or 'kung fu') was virtually unknown outside South-East Asia and diasporic Chinese communities. Prior to the 1970s, North Americans and Europeans were more familiar with Japanese and Okinawan martial arts like Karate, Judo and Ju-Jitsu. ... Ten years later, 'kung fu' had permanently entered the transnational imaginary – it was the name of a television show, a genre, a pedagogic industry, the subject of comics, magazines and other merchandising. On 20 July 1973, Bruce Lee died, but was already well on his way to being a 'Legend' – 'part man, part myth, part magic', as the trailer for his final film, *Enter the Dragon* (1973) put it. *Enter the Dragon* was the commercial high-point of a global 'kung fu' craze... (1)

Of course, Bruce Lee did not simply *cause* this 'craze'. Many other larger forces and historical movements paved the way. As Hunt notes, for instance, perhaps primary here is the fact that 'in 1966, Hong Kong cinema set itself the aim of breaking the Western market within five years' (3). It finally broke into the American market in 1972 with the Shaw Brothers film *King Boxer*, and 'between 1971 and 1973, approximately three hundred kung fu films were made for the international market, some of them never released in Hong Kong itself' (3). Moreover:

> The Western interest in Asian martial arts paralleled the United States' shifting relations with South-East Asia. American servicemen 'brought back' Judo and Karate from the post-War occupation of Japan, later incorporating it into training for the Korean War. The 'kung fu craze' of the 1970s overlapped with both the Vietnam War and President Nixon's visit to China. (Hunt 12)

Such less than tangible and less than subject-centred forces – those often-invoked but usually vague, spectral powers of History, War and Economics over what might sometimes be erroneously regarded as the autonomous or independent realms of popular culture – doubtlessly exerted a huge force on sewing the seeds of Bruce Lee's popularity. (Brian Preston, too, connects Bruce Lee's popularity with the impact of the Vietnam War on the American psyche [Preston 2007: 76], which we will discuss at length in the following chapters.) Interestingly, however, Hunt notes that what the 'Asiaphilia' of the kung fu craze actually loved was a certain 'mindlessness' to do with the martial arts. Hence, he suggests, this 'subtly' amounts to yet another kind of orientalist 'encounter marked by conquest and appropriation' (Hunt 2003: 12). Or, as Hunt puts it (following Hamamoto), 'Orientalism' ('a Western style for dominating, restructuring, and having authority over the Orient' (Said 1978: 3)) 'gives way' to an Asiaphilia – or a 'fetishization of all things Asian in popular culture' – that, whilst 'deceptively benign', actually 'naturalizes and justifies the systematic appropriation of cultural property and expressive forms created by Yellow people'. According to Hamamoto:

> The classic colonial system of unequal exchange was based on the theft of human and material resources from the underdeveloped countries of the periphery and its removal to the imperial core society. The politics of cultural appropriation extends the history of exploitation into the 'post-industrial' information economy. (qtd. in Hunt 2003: 13)

Nevertheless, Hunt retorts, any general asiaphiliac drive to 'appropriate' the other culture (cinematically) is ultimately complicated – frustrated, even – by the small matter of *the stars themselves*. 'Stars don't entirely work as others – they are objects of desire and/or identification' (14), he points out; adding: 'As a teenager, I desperately wanted to be Bruce Lee (albeit within limits – the "international" Lee of *Enter the Dragon* rather than the "local" Lee of *Way of the Dragon*)' (14). In other words, Hunt is suggesting that the condition of possibility for desiring 'Chinese'/kung fu – the object-cause of the desire – is also the condition of impossibility for satisfying it – the obstacle. One cannot *be* Bruce Lee. Such a frustrated desire – in Lacanian terms, the work of this particular lack – is of course amplified by the fact of Bruce Lee's irremediable absence. For, through the combination of events which offered *Enter the Dragon* to the world and the announcement of its star's rather mysterious death, this absence, this *lack*, this enigma opened up both desire and its frustration, posed questions and removed the answers. Indeed, says Hunt:

> Given the existence of 'cultic myths surrounding celebrity deaths', it seems fair to say that death gives as well as taking away.... With Bruce, things are rather more complicated because his death was experienced in very different cultural contexts. This is partly a matter of timing. When Lee died, two of his films had opened in the US, *The Big Boss* in May 1973, *Fist of Fury* in June. In the UK, *Fist of Fury* came first, opening on 19 July, the day before he died. In other words, the Western Lee cult was always founded on the paradox of an impossibly athletic and charismatic star who seemed to have burned out on first contact. In this context, Lee's death was always part of his 'aura'. In Hong Kong, Li Siu-lung was already known for his Cantonese films, but had in any case been breaking box office records in South-East Asia for two years. One only needs to look again at the Hong Kong funeral footage to see that when Lee's 'strings' were cut, the effect was rather more traumatic than the curiosity it provoked in the West. (Hunt 2003: 97)

Hence, says Hunt, 'Lee's death created a crisis' and a 'rush to fill' the 'hole punched out by (his) body' (77) at the same time as 'Lee's premature death certainly expedited his elevation to myth' (76), and his name 'became the locus' of what Tony Rayns describes as an 'interlocking network of stories, dreams and fantasies with entirely different levels of veracity, authenticity and credibility' (Rayns 1984: 26). In other words, 'the Lee "Legend" was mass-mediated from the start, and continued to blur the line between real-life exploits and those of his on-screen characters' (76). Hunt notes that 'In low-budget biopics from the mid-1970s, there is often a slippage from "Lee" to *Fist of Fury's* super-patriot Chen Zhen or *Way of the Dragon*'s self-sufficient émigré hero Tang Lun' (76). There is also, of course, an explosion in martial arts films, stars and practices worldwide in the wake of Bruce Lee's simultaneous entrance and departure.

Post-Modern Post-Mortem

At the same time as observing this concrete history, one must be careful to avoid the historical naïveté of assessing Bruce Lee (or anything else for that matter) according to a straightforwardly linear narrative or timeline. For instance, Bey Logan claims that 'the effect of Lee's films on the Hong Kong industry was "negligible", and [that] the "big Chinese hits released the year after his death ... look pretty much as they would had Bruce never returned to Hong Kong"' (qtd. in Hunt 2003: 97). Yet this does not mean that Bruce Lee's impact was in fact negligible. Rather, as Derrida was fond of pointing out (often by quoting from Shakespeare's *Hamlet*), nothing is self-present to itself, 'effects' are often delayed, disjointed, out of step. According to Derrida, for impeccable philosophical reasons, 'the time is out of joint' (1994): the 'significance', 'meaning' or dispersed effects of something are often established quite anarchically, unpredictably and retroactively. To exemplify this, we might even consider the complex position and role of books like this very one. For, a book like this one may purport merely to describe and analyze the impact and importance of Bruce Lee. But it is also a definite part of that impact. It is even, arguably, part of the *production* or *invention* of that very impact. For, such works as this are also actually 'performative' (productive, inventive), rather than merely being 'constative' or descriptive. This book may itself be regarded as a consequence of the impact of Bruce Lee, just as much as it might be regarded as retroactively productive or inventive of that very 'impact'. Thus, 'time', here, could be out of joint. Causality is undecidable. Is this book the *expression of* or *productive of* the ongoing impact and significance of Bruce Lee?

Whether the former or the latter, we surely need to ask ourselves the question posed by Fulbeck: 'Why do we want to keep Bruce Lee alive?' (qtd. in Hunt 2003: 97). Fulbeck relates this desire to the question of whether 'the Chinese man needs a hero', and to Lee's 'potential (or not)' to be 'a hero for Asian-Americans'; and thus to the question of whether 'the Chinese loved him or maybe ... loved America loving him' (Hunt 2003: 97). Or, as Eperjesi recently asked about *Crouching Tiger, Hidden Dragon* (2000): 'Does the West love this movie because it is profoundly Asian, or because it is not?' (2004: 29) As we will see in the following chapters, such issues as these open out onto questions of identity politics and, indeed, in the (Freudian) terms of Rey Chow, a complex theoretical and cultural problematic defined by the psychoanalytic theme of 'narcissism'.

Whether we deliberately 'want' to keep Bruce Lee alive or whether Bruce Lee spectres, clones, copies, infections, allusions and phantasms have not been 'exorcised' for reasons that require further diagnosis is a complex question. The prior question is that of why, how and where Bruce Lee might be said to 'live'. Hunt notes that 'for a "Legend" and local hero, [Lee's] legacy is not always easy to pin down' (2003: 97). Indeed, this, says Hunt, 'brings us back to the conundrum of where the King of Kung Fu's Kingdom actually is. Hong Kong? America? The nomadic space of the émigré?' (97) Enigmatically, he concludes that, quite distinct from the range of filmic developments opened up by other martial arts stars, 'Lee marked a road that seemingly led nowhere without his presence' (98). Yet, what is so significant about this 'presence' is that with Lee, full presence is so entirely permanently deferred. This is exponentially magnified by the fact that so little is actually *known* about him. As Miller puts it:

> If Ali is the most famous fellow of the twentieth century whom we know most about, Lee is the one about whom we know least. Celluloid and print fictions have dramatically marginalized him and his impact on

society. Few of us have a clue what Lee said, felt, dreamed, did, or didn't do. The mist of money-making myth around him is so thick that the truth of his story has been almost entirely obscured. ...

The reality is this: in the three years immediately preceding his death Bruce Lee revolutionized the martial arts and for ever changed action movie-making. He became the first truly international film luminary (popular not only in the United States, Great Britain and Europe, but in Asia, the Soviet Union, the Middle East and on the Indian subcontinent – in those pre-Spielberg days people in most nations were not particularly worshipful of the Hollywood hegemony). Until now Lee has received little credit for these accomplishments. (Miller 2000: 96)

A household name that is immensely well-known and yet unknown, Bruce Lee remains an enigma. However, this enigmatic status is not that of a mysterious Taoist priest or High Plains Drifter. Bruce Lee's life is not shrouded in a mystery that derives from a lack of knowledge or information. Information about Bruce Lee abounds. Archives and records about Bruce Lee have not been lost in the mists of time. Rather, Bruce Lee suffers from what postmodern theorists once called the *legitimation crisis in knowledge* (Lyotard 1984). For, a huge amount of speculation and argumentation has been amassed about Bruce Lee. He lived much of his life openly. He even documented, recorded, took copious notes about and even filmed his own training and teaching. Evermore text is produced about Bruce Lee. Myriad different discourses involve Bruce Lee or are even structured by a figure (or fantasy) of Bruce Lee. And four decades after his 'arrival', Bruce Lee studies, fandom, hagiography and criticism continue to proliferate. Nevertheless, there is a crisis in *knowledge* about Bruce Lee. The 'truth' of Bruce Lee is interminably and vehemently contested. Chiefly, perhaps, this centres on a simultaneous excess and dearth of knowledge about Bruce Lee's martial arts ability. Insofar as this excess and absence relates to the cinematic representation of his image and the difficulty of verification in what was once called 'the society of the spectacle' (Debord 1967), this too is a quintessentially postmodern problematic. Indeed, it is around this latter problematic that many questions condense. As we will see in the analysis that concludes this introductory chapter, when it comes to the verification of knowledge of and about martial arts, the question becomes one of *what* 'knowledge' might actually be. There is an irreducible problem of *establishment* here, to which we will return.

The enduringly controversial status of Bruce Lee has arisen for reasons that are surely overdetermined. First, there is the still-surprising and contentious issue of his premature death. Then this was intensified by the equally surprising and unlikely death of his son, Brandon Lee. For, Bruce Lee died in circumstances that have been regarded as either mysterious or dubious. But his son, Brandon, was shot and killed on a film set, by a gun that was meant to fire blanks, whilst filming the death-scene of the character he was playing in *The Crow* (1994). Brandon's death provided more fuel for and reignited various enduring theories about conspiracies and even curses. The latter took the form of claims that Bruce and Brandon's were deaths by supernatural causes. Indeed, it is bizarre that even Bruce Lee's widow implicitly sanctioned such legends in approving of the story of *Dragon: The Bruce Lee Story* (1993) – a film that Meaghan Morris calls 'a sanitized as well as hagiographic interpretation of Bruce Lee's life as authorized by his widow' (2001: 180), and which Hunt notes 'seems to have drawn its inspiration from the "Bruce Li" films of the 1970s as much as widow Linda Lee Cadwell's credited biography' (2003: 79). From the 'fog of rumour, myth and mystery [that] continues to surround the circumstances of Lee's death', Miller identifies the main theories about it:

> Among the most popular theories: he died from overtraining or from too much sex; he was murdered by angry kung fu masters; by the Chinese 'Mafia'; he was poisoned by an evil herbalist; killed by a secret society of martial arts assassins; by the director of his first two movies (fewer than three weeks before his death, Lee had threatened this director – who'd been goading him for weeks – with a knife hidden in his belt buckle); by the head of the movie studio for which he worked, who, through the remainder of the century, would reap hundreds of millions of dollars from Lee's legend; by rival Hong Kong movie magnates, who were rumoured to be jealous of, and infuriated by, Lee's success; by Lee's lover(s); by his wife; by big mythological dragons angered that he had called himself Small Dragon Lee. Or that he had an unsuspected congenital condition that became lethal because of the intensity with which he lived. And maybe most fabulously, that Lee had not died, but had gone into seclusion, in the Shaolin temple/a cave in the jungles of south-east Asia/a remote mountaintop. And that he'd return at some date… (Miller 2000: 95)

Of course, Bruce Lee did die – and according to both his physician, Dr Donald Langford, and the neurosurgeon who treated his first near-death episode of cerebral oedema, Dr Peter Wu, his death was a result of the fact that he 'was particularly sensitive to one or more of the alkaloids in cannabis' (Miller 2000: 136).[2] Unless curses and vengeful demons work by such proxies as human causes and physical effects, Bruce Lee's death was evidently not a direct result of any of the more 'fabulous' speculations, such as those proposed by *Dragon: The Bruce Lee Story* – although we will have various reasons to visit and revisit that quasi-official, but obviously 'fable-like' text in subsequent chapters. Yet, in a sense, maybe it is the case that the 'most fabulous' story – the idea that Lee would 're-turn' – is not so fabulous after all. For, so to speak, in being struck down Lee nevertheless instantly 'returned' – in a manner not unlike Obi-Wan Kenobi's return after death in *Star Wars* – spectrally, phantasmatically, but also virally, as copies, clones, parodies, pastiches, ideas, fantasies, arguments, texts and discourses.

Of the first cinematic 'returns' which emerged after Lee's death (whether they were wanted or not), Hunt argues that not only did they arise because of and 'contribute to the heterogeneous myth' of Bruce Lee, 'offering variations on apocryphal stories, [and] speculating on the many rumours surrounding his death', they also functioned as interesting ways of 'posing questions about identity and cultural belonging' (2003: 79). For instance, Hunt notes Stephen Teo's argument that 'the mirror reflections of Lee in *Way of the Dragon* and *Enter the Dragon* point not to his narcissism, but to [in Teo's words] "the Chinese masses looking back", the "aspirations of Hong Kong people"' (Hunt 2003: 79). Teo's is an extremely problematic argument, to which we will return in Chapter Three. But, for Hunt, the return of Lee, the efforts to 'keep him alive', the proliferation of his clones and copies, as well as 'the endless recycling of footage of his funeral' and so on 'reflect a body in crisis, overwhelmed by the discourses willed onto it' (2003: 79).

---

[2] Miller writes: '"He would have died in May from severe brain oedema", says Dr Wu, who is renowned for his cerebral oedema research in Asian males. "Bruce was in a very critical condition. It was sheer luck that experienced medical people were there to help him. We removed quite a lot of hashish from his stomach. In Nepal there have been all kinds of neurological problems associated with hashish, especially cerebral oedema. Bruce said that he was chewing the hashish because he was under a lot of pressure. Doing that, he would be exposed to all of the chemicals full strength. We gave Bruce a long talk before he was discharged from hospital, asking him not to eat the stuff again. We told him that his very low percentage of body fat could make him vulnerable to drugs. We said that the effects would be heightened by continued contact. We also told him that his level of stress could dramatically magnify the effects. Since he'd already had a very bad time with the drug, we told him the effects were likely to be worse the next time. [However] He said that it was harmless. He said that Steve McQueen had introduced him to it and Steve McQueen would not take it if there was anything bad about it"' (Miller 2000: 137).

Eastern Orientation, Western Bias

The reading or interpretation of any text is always a process of *reading into* – indeed, arguably, often, of *overwhelming* it, by willing discourses onto it. Bruce Lee exists at a chiasmus of a great many possible discourses – as Hunt says, Lee is a body that is 'both Chinese and "Western", omnipotent and all too vulnerably human, unique and "clonable"' (2003: 79). It is the interplay of these discourses of race, gender, class, ethnicity, nationality, postcoloniality, economic and cultural globalisation, as well as philosophy and pedagogy, and so on, in one site that makes Bruce Lee such an overwhelmingly rich source of discursivity. This remains so even though, as Hunt points out, we should still have absolutely no illusions about the 'intentions' of Bruceploitation films and products (79). For, obviously, the posthumous-Lee and post-Lee proliferation of martial arts films and practices in the West may be regarded as both an obvious and entirely predictable rush to cash-in on the latest craze. However, the speed and trajectory (Westward) of this post-Bruce Lee gold rush deserves some consideration. For, there was not just a Hong Kong-based rush to replicate the success of Lee. There quickly emerged a very specific breed of white western martial arts star, too.

Sean Tierney draws our attention to this issue of *speed* and *direction*, pointing out that the 'speed, efficacy, and unorthodox yet highly efficient means by which Whites learn martial arts is a recurring motif in Western film' (2006: 611). One might also remark the speed and narrative (re)orientation with which white western martial art stars emerged – and indeed the speed with which the very *notion* of 'white western martial arts experts' came to seem *obvious*, *natural*, and *normal*. For, in fact, Tierney's argument about the 'recurring motif in Western *film*' of the 'speed, efficacy, and unorthodox yet highly efficient means by which Whites learn martial arts' can also be seen to be echoed in and to be an echo of very many other 'Western' discursive contexts. Perhaps the most exemplary filmic instance of this, of course, occurs in *The Matrix* (1999), wherein 'the White character Neo is imbued with exemplary martial arts skill in seconds through the use of computers' (611). One also sees something similar in *The Fifth Element* (1997), in which 'the "supreme", "divine", "most perfect" being in the universe, played by White actress Milla Jovovich, literally speed-reads her way to martial arts proficiency in the time it takes her to do a comical imitation of Bruce Lee' (611). At issue here, then, is the matter and manner, first, of the Western appropriation and second the 'Westernisation' (or spurious universalization) of martial arts.

Once again, Davis Miller's recollection of his first contact with the mysterious new/ancient skill of karate is perhaps representative of very many Westerners' introduction to ideas of martial arts. And once again, this happens cinematically and televisually. Miller tells us of another memorable visit to the cinema:

> The movies that night were *Doctor No* and *Goldfinger*. Hours later, *entirely* worked up, I lay wide awake in bed, hearing the movie voices inside me, recalling not women on the screen, but how James Bond had been so screw-everybody-cool, and how he'd disposed of all bad guys, effortlessly and systematically, the power magically vested in him by late-twentieth-century technology and by a strange, mystical Japanese science called 'karate'.
>
> A few weeks later, Daddy told me about a new TV show, *The Man from U.N.C.L.E.* We watched the first episode together. And here they were again, these secret agent types, these coolest of the cool. To me, the hero, Napoleon Solo, was badder than Bond, cooler than zero as he hiply and virtuously battled, and almost effortlessly destroyed, each and every foe. He was seldom, if ever, hurt in return, having been rendered indestructible (and nonchalantly cocky!) by near-magical gadgetry, and by knowledge of that same exotic and miraculous 'karate'. (Miller 2000: 10)

Gary Krug identifies this kind of 'first contact' as exemplary of what he calls 'the first stage of representation' of oriental martial arts in the west: a period of 'discovery and mythologizing' that took place between the 1920s and 1970s. What is dominant during this period is that at this stage 'karate was, in a sense, frozen as a cultural moment, much as rainforests or "primitive" tribes become relatively fixed signifiers in the instance of their discovery' (Krug 2001: 398). In other words, the 'complexity of the thing becomes lost in its representation that exists in ready-made relationships within systems of signification and discourses' (398-9). As Miller's account clearly suggests, a first Western 'meaning' of karate in the west is initially constructed through its dramatic proximity to and easy articulation with the spy genre. Thus, even on first contact, 'karate was removed from the cultural systems that created and defined it and was transplanted into new meaning systems' (399), at the same time as maintaining its fetishistic 'function as signifier of all that Asia was in the

imagination of the beholders' (398). Specifically, of course, karate's alterity and the legends of the

> secret traditions of martial artists and the fabulous stories circulating
> within martial arts circles proved helpful in feeding the popular imagina-
> tion with beliefs about the practices in general as secret, highly advanced,
> deadly, and possessing the ability to make the practitioner virtually invul-
> nerable to physical harm. (398)

As Krug points out, such prejudices were immediately projected onto
'karate' as a result and as a reiteration of 'beliefs about Asia in general as
mysterious, inscrutable, violent, ... with links to unpleasant, illegal, or
immoral activities', beliefs which 'had their roots in early Portuguese,
Dutch, and English writings from the 16th and 17th centuries' and which
'continued to be expressed through the Vietnam War era, revealing the
durability of ignorance and stereotyping' (398). Like Miller (and actually
corroborating the extent to which Miller's recollections might be taken as
representative), Krug also strongly connects the earliest Western popular
cultural occurrences of martial arts with spy films and dramas:

> The genre of spy films allowed for more techniques to appear on screen,
> although these were completely out of context of the larger practices. The
> uncertain allegiance of Asian nations in the East-West cold war allowed an
> ease in the continued representation of all things Asian as politically and
> morally suspect. In 1964, the James Bond film *You Only Live Twice* al-
> leged to show aspects of Japanese culture as well as some martial arts
> techniques. However, these were only used as window dressing to high-
> light the 'exotic' element of the setting and to drive the plot. The most
> prominent representations of martial arts in this film were of evil ninja as-
> sassins. Television shows such as *I Spy* and *The Man From UNCLE* also
> caricatured the martial arts with dramatic throws and techniques, nearly
> always in the hands of Anglo-Americans. Within this genre, Bruce Lee
> made his appearance on American television as Kato in the *Green Hornet*
> in 1967. (Krug 2001: 399)[3]

According to Tierney, it is significant that the filmic, TV and popular cultural tradition of white Western appropriation combined with 'window
dressing' allusions to *orientalness* have persevered. For instance, despite
The Matrix's proposition that martial arts can be thought of as ab-
stractable, objectifiable, standardizable and transferable in the manner of

---

[3] Interestingly, Miller recalls that at the time of *The Green Hornet*'s first TV showing he missed
it completely – and hence had no knowledge of Bruce Lee until seeing *Enter the Dragon* – because *The Green Hornet* was broadcast on a different channel but at the same time as *The Man
From U.N.C.L.E.*

software, the film nevertheless still 'makes a perfunctory nod to the skill's cultural origin by decorating the set where Neo's new skills are first displayed in an Asian motif' (611). Tierney's argument is that 'Neo's whiteness does not keep him from gaining a skill that is aesthetically bound to its own ethnic origins; he can transcend the ethnic specificity that the skill cannot' (611). Indeed, this is the crux of his argument. For, as his title makes clear – 'Themes of Whiteness in *Bulletproof Monk, Kill Bill,* and *The Last Samurai*' – Tierney regards this theme as not only recurrent but arguably almost *compulsory* in Western martial arts films.

Tierney selected these three films (*Bulletproof Monk, Kill Bill* and *The Last Samurai*) simply because they were all released in 2003, and in all of them 'a White protagonist "mastering" an Asian martial art was part of the narrative'. Furthermore, 'In each film, the protagonist's ethnicity is [initially] questioned as an inhibition but found to be irrelevant'. Thus, through textual analyses of the films, Tierney identifies four themes that are extremely common to Hollywood-produced martial arts movies: 'The supraethnic viability of whiteness, the necessary defeat of Asians, the disallowance of anti-White sentiment, and the presence of at least one helpful and/or generous Asian' (607). And Tierney's argument and analysis are persuasive: these films are arguably 'ethnically biased', at least in favour of the white protagonist. To Tierney, this is both noteworthy and problematic because 'martial arts film originated in Asia and first gained widespread popularity in America in the 1970s with the rise to stardom of Bruce Lee'. But, nowadays, the Asian dimension is reduced merely to the status of a motif, or indeed even a fetish:

> During the 1980s, martial arts returned to American theaters but with a significant shift in the ethnic makeup of the martial arts star. In Bruce Lee's absence, White men such as Chuck Norris, Jean Claude Van Damme, and Steven Seagal gained fame as 'martial arts' actors. The shift in the ethnicity is a significant change that demands investigation because in 2003, *Kill Bill, The Last Samurai,* and *Bulletproof Monk* again made a White person 'mastering' Asian martial arts a narrative theme in mainstream American film. (607)

Tierney proposes that such films are best assessed according to what he calls a theoretical approach sensitive to the 'strategic rhetoric of whiteness'. This 'rhetoric' is one which allows for a 'perpetuation of specific ideological constructs of whiteness that include ethnic superiority and recurrent, stringent assignment of roles and functions based on ethnicity'

(607). According to this paradigm, 'the Asian ethnicity of the defeated practitioner is a salient and necessary element in establishing White mastery': after all, 'What better way to illustrate mastery of an Asian martial art than to defeat or kill an Asian practitioner?' (613) Accordingly, this aspect of these films works 'to defend and perpetuate the conflation of White with human, to rationalize and camouflage cultural appropriation as a normal, harmless, natural behavior, and to promote a kind of supra-ethnic viability for Whites that is not equally represented for Others' (609). As such, 'the films are not benign instances of intercultural exchange; they are quite significantly one-sided in nature'. They also 'provide the White audience with filmic reinforcement of underinterrogated assumptions of whiteness' as the unquestionable/unnoticeable norm and universal (609). Accordingly, Tierney concludes:

> American martial arts films provide examples of cultural appropriation undergirded by whiteness ideology rationalized through strategic rhetoric of whiteness. Acquisition of martial arts mastery by White protagonists may be seen as innocuous, entertaining, and enriching, but it constitutes a significant filmic form of cultural colonialism and appropriation that reinforces hegemonic ideas of racial and cultural superiority and inferiority, with consequences that reach far beyond the movie theater. (Tierney 2007: 622)

This is a very provocative and plausible argument. However, instead of following through with an analysis or discussion of the precise characteristics, mechanisms, relations and effects of these 'consequences', Tierney makes a very particular move: his conclusion takes the form of a move *away* from a focus on the textually-produced ethical stances that these texts adopt towards ethnicity, and indeed even away from the question of 'consequences that reach far beyond the movie theater'. Rather, Tierney moves to pose a range of questions about *'the audience'*:

> One obvious consideration for further study is to examine why the White audience wants or needs to have these kinds of ethnically focused conquering narratives. We might wonder why films like *Bulletproof Monk*, *Kill Bill*, *The Last Samurai* and others like *Hidalgo* resonate with a White audience. Why must White transcultural superiority be constantly rein-scribed? Why doesn't the White audience accept or support films in which the White character is the defeated antagonist, even when it is the logical or historically accurate outcome? Why doesn't the White audience accept or support films in which White people figure minimally or not at all? Why must the White audience see itself reflected and/or represented on-screen in a dominant, victorious way? What is the effect of these films on their global and/or non-White audience? Whereas these questions are be-

yond the scope of the present study, they are nonetheless ripe for further examination. (622-3)

Such questions for further research are certainly valid. But there are problems with the manner in which they are posed. As we will explore in more depth in Chapter Four, there are problems to do with the preconception of 'the' audience as if it is *one* – as if it is a homogeneous mass. There are also problems to do with the apparent conception of 'the' audience as a 'monkey see, monkey do' knee-jerk/stimulus-response mass. We will return to such problems more fully in subsequent chapters. But perhaps most problematic of all is the move in Tierney's argument from close textual analysis and demonstrations of a *structurally-produced* ethnocentric bias in these Hollywood productions, to shifting the burden of responsibility – indeed, blame – onto the audience.

This is a peculiar argumentative move, one which does not sit comfortably next to the close readings of the textual features of the films. For, if the problem is basically *in* the narrative, semiotic and rhetorical structure of the texts, then how is *the audience* to blame for them? One likely answer is to evoke public opinion or 'demand', taste or consumer choice – as if cultural production is entirely driven by 'demand-side economics'. Such an idea is deeply problematic, even untenable (and even within the terms of an economic or economistic paradigm). But, there are also overwhelming reasons (to be found permeating the discourses of critical, cultural, textual, theoretical and discourse analytical scholarship) to doubt the validity of attributing 'responsibility' to 'the audience' who 'choose' to 'consume' such products. Although many of the approaches, theories and methodologies available to the study of media, culture, discourse and society may explicitly claim to disagree with the full ramifications of the apocalyptic moment in Frankfurt School cultural analysis, perhaps Adorno and Horkheimer summed up the problematic character of blaming 'the audience' when they argued in *Dialectic of Enlightenment* that 'The attitude of the public, which ostensibly and actually favours the system of the culture industry, is a part of the system and not an excuse for it' (1972).

Another way to specify this problem would be to observe that Tierney's approach, whilst organised and orientated by *textual* analysis, lacks the kind of *discourse* analysis that could offer a vocabulary and a critical paradigm for making sense of audience tastes and moves in rela-

tion to commodities and texts. Indeed, it seems likely that Tierney's concluding 'audience focused' questions come as a response to a tacit disciplinary injunction: the perceived requirement current within film, media
and cultural studies, to ensure that every analysis be able to demonstrate
that it 'connects' with the 'real world'. In this sense, Tierney's inconsistent concluding moves might be regarded as pre-emptive gestures seeking
to sidestep any possible accusation that the work is 'too textual', 'too
theoretical' or 'too disengaged from the real world'. Nevertheless, as
Tierney has shown rather well (through textual analysis, and *not* audience
research) in the preceding article, '*the audience*' *has in a strong sense got
very little to do with it*. That is to say: texts are produced; hegemonies
have their biases; 'mainstream' texts will reiterate those biases; audiences
will not simply 'revolt'. Or rather, they might, but only if they are not
given the desired currently hegemonic version of a (probably hetero)normative phallic hero with whom they can identify and take pleasure.

But there is a wider point here. For the inscription of national and
ethnic ambivalence in the narrative and semiotic structures of films is not
unique to Hollywood. Nor does it necessarily make all that much difference to the viewer invested in (the sheer *jouissance* of) the action anyway. Indeed, although since 1966 Hong Kong films were designed for
and aimed at 'a heterogeneous audience, both "local" and "global"', and
although 'kung fu's corporeal exhilaration seems to act on a "universal"
body, moving it to ecstasy through Bordwell's "Motion Emotion", the
genre sometimes seems ambivalent about its non-Chinese audience'
(Hunt 2003: 3). There is, for instance, 'an insistent strain of nationalism
in the Hong Kong martial arts film, observable in a range of films from
Fist of Fury/Jingwu Mun (1972) to *Once Upon a Time in China/Huang
Feihong* (1991)' (3). Therefore, Hunt suggests:

> Watching kung fu films as a white, Western fan (like myself) may involve
> a degree of identification with Bruce Lee or Jet Li, but it may also lead, at
> some point, to finding one's counterpart in the *gwailo* ('white devil'), ei-
> ther associated with imperialist oppression or the American karate experts
> that Bruce Lee was fond of humiliating. I may not want to (and, simply,
> don't) identify with Chuck Norris in *Way of the Dragon* – hairy back, not
> as cool or glamorous as Bruce – and yet part of me knows that the
> Lee/Norris coliseum fight embodies a patriotic structure of feeling that is
> supposed to at least partly exclude me. However, it is my left liberal 'post-
> colonial' self that recognises this exclusion; significantly, as a teenage
> Bruce Lee fan, I didn't feel remotely excluded by his films. In any case,

the kung fu film offers a third way in, allowing the 'outsider' to feel like
an 'insider'; that of the cult aficionado, the hard core fan... (2003: 3)

It also offers a fourth way in: that of the martial arts practitioner. In any
case, the point here is that the inscription of ambivalence toward the other
is mirrored in both the Hollywood *and* the Hong Kong films, at least insofar as they putatively deal with others and stage intercultural encounters. The question is therefore perhaps whether – or the way in which –
one takes these films to be 'public pedagogies' (Giroux 2002; See also
Chapter Two). Is one learning entirely fluid prejudices (as it were, *indis-
criminate discriminations* about any old 'other') organised by heteronormative phallic fantasies, or is one learning to fetishize and belittle a *specific* other? Or is there more – or something else going on? We will return
to these and other such questions of pedagogy, ethics and alterity more
fully in Chapter Four. But at this stage it seems most pressing to acknowledge, as do Tierney, Hunt and very many other cultural thinkers,
that such texts are widely construed as irreducibly pedagogical. As Hunt
puts it: 'these films don't just tell stories about learning and transmission;
they are, themselves, a form of learning, an ongoing "education" of the
audience' (4). As such, one question is: *what* is being learned? Moreover,
what causes what to be learned, or what factors determine what will be
learned? We will return to these questions in Chapter Two.

Tierney is fairly militant in his objection to the structural ethnocentric bias in the Hollywood films, arguing:

> The intercultural incongruities engendered by the whiteness themes are
> never directly addressed in the films; we are apparently expected to simply
> overlook or accept them. *The Last Samurai* makes Algren a martial arts
> prodigy who finds redemption among the Other. Yet, this culture is in
> immediate danger of eradication by Westernization, of which Algren is in-
> delibly a part. Much like the protagonist of *Dances With Wolves* (1990),
> Algren finds healing and acceptance among a people unlike himself, a
> people threatened by those whom the White protagonist is not unlike. In
> both films, the White protagonist becomes sympathetic to his putative en-
> emy's orientation. Because the White audience see themselves reflected in
> the White protagonist, such narratives can allow for the audience's writing
> out of complicity not only the protagonist (whose enemies come to accept
> him as a 'good' White person) but even, by extension, themselves (...).
> This ideological whitewash facilitates the audience's wilful ignorance of
> (and relationship to) history in favour of a sanitized filmic fiction that rein-
> forces historic circumstances while appearing to subvert them. *The Last
> Samurai* is a work of fiction that seeks believability while proffering the
> inversion of historic realities. (Tierney 2007: 619)

However, although this perspective claims to provide insights into the articulation between text and context, or between film and cultural ethics and politics, and although it certainly pinpoints a hegemonic representational tendency, I think that this approach falls down when it comes to discussing the wider cultural context within which this representational tendency arises and into which it feeds back. For, as well as the skewing effect of the proposed move into 'audience studies', it seems that what limits this approach is precisely its close focus on these films. For, the close textual focus is not supplemented by a clear or explicit account of *articulation* such as might be established through a cultural or discourse analysis component. Arguably, without such a component, this type of scholarship will remain constitutively unable to cast light on the very thing it deems to be centrally important – namely, the 'consequences that reach far beyond the movie theatre' (Tierney 2007: 622).

To address this imbalance, we might contrast this filmic textual analysis with Krug's discourse analysis. Of course, these two approaches are not *opposed* in a strong sense. Indeed, they may rather be distinguished according to a mere difference in focus, or scale: the microscopy of textual analysis might be contrasted to the macroscopy of discourse analysis. Both optics might in principle be regarded as operating within the same sort of paradigm, or way of looking. Thus, one might say, microscopic textual analysis is a constitutive supplement to, and source providing the materials for macroscopic studies of discourses, and vice versa. So let us return to Krug's exemplary macroscopic assessment of the historical contexts within which Bruce Lee's intervention might be appraised. Krug's (2001) essay, as we have already seen, takes an approach that is more obviously organised by discourse analysis, rather than textual or audience analysis. In it, Krug situates filmic and other representations of martial arts within a very broad historical and cultural sweep. Specifically, Krug examines the manner and mechanisms by which karate came to be appropriated – almost fully integrated into and normalised – by American culture. This history is rendered in such a way by Krug's reading that it might be called a dialectic of martial enlightenment.

Dialectic of Martial Enlightenment

A dialectic in a basic Hegelian sense entails precisely three stages (thesis, antithesis, synthesis), and this is effectively how Krug represents the history of the Anglo-American engagement with Okinawan Karate: 'The first stage of representation' is what Krug calls 'discovery and mythologizing', which as we have seen he proposes takes place broadly between the 1920s and 1970s (2001: 398). The second is the birth of martial arts as 'practices in the West', which he places broadly in the period between 1946 and 1980 (401). The third is what he calls a period of 'appropriation and de-mythologizing', from the 1980s to the present (403). In the first stage, the stage of discovery, 'karate' exists as a particular catch-all type of signifier, a mythological signifier of almost pure connotation. Observing the ways that 'the use of the idea of "Asia" among Anglo-Americans has tended to conflate the numerous peoples and cultures of a broad region of the world into a uniform ethnic and cultural mass', Krug argues that 'the cultural blending of diverse peoples and practices has also occurred in representations of the martial arts' (398). Thus '*wushu* (Chinese martial arts), karate, judo, and other forms [were] collapsed into a homogenous, imaginary block' in which martial arts here function simply 'as signifiers of all that Asia was in the imagination of the beholders' (398). As a mythological signifier in Roland Barthes' sense, 'frozen as a cultural moment ... in the instance of their discovery': 'The complexity of the thing becomes lost in its representation that exists in ready-made relationships within systems of signification and discourses' (Krug 2001: 398-399). (We might recall the way this initial conflation was lampooned in the comic occurrence of the 'judo chop' and the 'judo trip' in *Austin Powers* (1997). The eponymous hero would call 'judo chop!' or 'judo trip!' when delivering a much telegraphed and obviously ineffectual yet supposedly devastating strike or throw on an opponent, thereby sending up the early Western spy genre's use of 'exotic' techniques by conflating two clichés: the 'judo throw' and the 'karate chop'.)[4] These connotations

---

[4] According to Krug: 'The martial arts that first appeared in American cinema were in films of the 1930s, although they became much more common after the 1960s. *The Hatchet Man* (1932) depicted parts of Chinese Tong wars in San Francisco, whereas other films might occasionally show judo techniques. In general, martial arts in mainstream American, English, and Australian cinema showed only parodies of the practices, lifted out of all cultural and historical contexts. Throws from judo appeared now and then, but wushu, *jujitsu* (unarmed combat techniques from

could be said to be culturally or discursively *overdetermined*, and at this stage, the signifier 'karate was removed from the cultural systems that created and defined it and was transplanted into new meaning systems' (399).

In other words, because of the inevitable drifts and displacements that occur in acts of cultural translation, 'karate' in the West was and is always-already something different than 'karate' in Japan and Okinawa. Krug argues that 'as an object of knowledge in Japan and Okinawa, karate wove together aspects of a complex history, but as a signifier in the West, karate became a marker of difference that was already filled with meaning' (399). Doubtless this overdetermination was compounded by the fact that 'few Westerners had direct experience of martial arts, and the common knowledge of it derived from mass media representations in film and books and later in television'. These representations themselves relied on the broadly orientalist fantasies and stereotypes, so that the 'early, simplistic view of martial arts in general ensured that their appearance as cultural markers in Anglo-American cinema would perpetuate commonly held beliefs' (399).

In this sense, the signifier (or simulation) clearly precedes and constitutes the real – although quite how 'reality' could be constituted *without* signifiers and signification is unclear, of course; but the point here relates to the primacy of the signifier over the signified, and the role played by the intrusion of fantasy in this process. Such (dis)orientating fantasy intervenes through the influence of residual discourses. But for the signifier to translate into practice it cannot remain in this form. It must, in other words, be translated into intelligible terms, and articulated with extant practices. Thus, 'martial arts and other Asian films could appear in mass media only as translations into more familiar genres, such as westerns'. For, the discourses 'that operated within Asian cultures had no place in the subject positioning of Western audiences'. Accordingly, says Krug: 'Lacking these supporting discourses, representations of Asian cultures could be read only thinly, and Western ideas would be introduced to provide the depth of discursive texture necessary to give audiences subjective points of entry into the filmic stories' (2001: 400). Such is one predominant mechanism of meaning-making: articulation of the new with

---

the samurai tradition), karate, and other traditional martial arts were largely unknown as coherent sets of practices outside of their geographical areas and cultural traditions' (399).

(if not necessarily *reduction to*) the known or familiar. Thus, martial arts were a metonymic vehicle for the representation/transportation of the Asian exotic into the western mainstream. But, of course, as Tierney puts it, such 'films are not benign instances of intercultural exchange; they are quite significantly one-sided in nature' (2006: 609). So, says Krug, even though the 1970s 'saw the beginnings of attempts to represent some parts of Asia in sympathetic ways', the 'early popular representations were followed by a flurry of films that moved martial arts from the domain of Eastern, exotic, and somewhat mystical practices to a more mainstream position as action/adventure vehicles generally featuring Anglo-American protagonists' (400).

Of course, the first flurry of Western popular representations were initiated and dominated by Bruce Lee – 'the first Asian to regularly perform martial arts on Anglo-American screens', initially as 'a regular' on the TV show *Longstreet*, playing the 'personal trainer of the blind detective protagonist', and then 'with his first major picture outside of Hong Kong, *Enter the Dragon* (1973), [in which] Lee brought something of wushu to the awareness of many' (Krug 400). However, the TV series that Lee devised (*The Warrior*) and which materialised as the TV show *Kung Fu*, 'although featuring some Asian actors to portray major characters, still used an American actor as the central character' (400). Much could be said about casting the white non-martial artist David Carradine as the (putatively half-Chinese) lead role in *Kung Fu*. Yet at the time such casting was not particularly unusual. As Krug points out, 'although the use of blackface to represent African Americans had disappeared with vaudeville, Asians were still fair game through the 1960s'.

Ultimately, argues Krug, in the realms of TV and film, at least, this oriental encounter was basically driven by its commodifiable *novelty*. As he puts it:

> The 1970s marked as well a proliferation of martial arts representations onto Western television and movie screens as the fancy fighting techniques achieved a new level of commodification. The dreadful film of Mr. Peace Through Violence, *Billy Jack*, appeared in 1971; the television movie *Kung Fu* with David Carradine appeared in 1972, with the series following soon after. Transparent morality tales in most respects, these and other films were vehicles for the protagonists to display martial arts prowess on the screen and capitalize in lucrative ways on otherwise largely unremunerative activities. Chuck Norris and Bill 'Superfoot' Wallace were two Westerners who cashed in their abilities in the competition

circuit, becoming minor stars within this subgenre of film. (Krug 2001: 400)

Thus, according to Krug, the transition from a fully Asian to a preliminar-ily Westernised sense of martial art 'ownership' can be seen to have been substantially *played out in cinema*. The larger scenes and logics of the movement are not limited to cinema, however, yet can be discerned as condensed within it:

> Almost all these action martial arts feature films featured 'Asian' martial artists as well, but, reflecting the uncertain cultural and moral position of Asia, their roles were often ambiguous. Asians personified both the an-cient moral order that was believed to underpin the martial arts and that served as the source of the Anglo hero's moral superiority, and they repre-sented evil as profound training perverted by greed, ambition, or anger at a childhood defeat from the hero. The ambiguity of the representation of Asians in these films grants us a key insight. Relationships between the Western hero and the Eastern characters show in miniature the lines of power in the ideology of these films. Thus, in showing the Westerner who has acquired the secret knowledge from the master and who then surpasses either the master or other students or both, these films maintain the ideo-logical belief in the physical, social, and moral superiority of Westerners over Asians. (400-401)

This cinematic transition – the birth of the American martial arts film (still characterised by a strong link to Asia but with the martial prowess now in the hands of a 'special' American hero) – marks what Krug calls 'a transition into the second stage of appropriation: the acquisition of the Asian practices while still using Asia as the moral and historical under-pinning of that practice' (401). As he observes:

> Cain, in *Kung Fu*, suffers a dizzying number of flashbacks to his training at the Shao-Lin monastery. Chuck Norris in *The Octagon* recalls his train-ing under a Japanese master. In *The Mechanic*, with Charles Bronson, the karate master is shown defeating his Western student, revealing again the dominance of the Asian secret of martial arts. The implied premise in many of these representations is that there is some secret possessed by the masters in Asia. The idea of a secret knowledge draws on a set of signifi-ers of Asia that operate as binary oppositions to signifiers of Euro-American culture. These films suggest that the secret knowledge of Asia is knowable but only by a handful of carefully selected Westerners: those positioned through the narrative as having been selected early in life for the receipt of this special boon. The origins of these Western associations of magic with 'the Orient' are ancient and obscure. No doubt the mythical construction of the 'mysterious East' was fostered considerably through the translations of esoteric texts of Tibetan Buddhism and other sources in the 19th century. The history of the Western mapping of the world vacil-

lates between the doubtful search for Prester John's Kingdom and the ma-
cabre certainty of finding beasts, cannibals, and other horrors. (401)

This cinematic movement marks the advent of martial arts becoming, in
their own right, a new 'grounded form of knowledge', as the martial arts
moved 'into the domain of lived experience and personal history for
many living in the Anglo-American cultures'. This can be regarded as
developing in 'parallel with the mass media construction of martial arts',
and Krug proposes that a key sign of the 'second stage of appropriation
appears in the American culture when the first-known karate dojo in the
United States was opened in 1946 by Robert Trias'. (In fact, karate was
being taught in Hawaii as early as 1933.) Furthermore, 'within a few
years, numerous soldiers, particularly from the United States, who com-
prised the bulk of the Allied Forces occupying Japan and Okinawa, were
returning home and starting dojos'. So, 'by the 1970s, many schools as
well as national and international organizations promoting karate appeared' (401). However, 'what was promoted was by and large "sport"
karate, the karate that was taught in high schools in Okinawa'. That is to
say:

> Changes to the art, first developed by the Okinawan, 'Professor' Funako-
> shi Gichin, such as standardized uniforms and grading systems as well as
> the introduction of rule-bound combat (*jyu-kumite*), created a set of prac-
> tices that were sufficiently close to boxing and to Euro-American hierar-
> chies of knowledge and skill to allow the art to be widely accepted and
> practiced. These gave the art a fit with mainstream Western discourses
> sufficient to allow its acceptance and growth. (401-402)

Thus, Krug concludes, 'what grew in the United States, the United Kingdom, Australia, and in other Western cultures was arguably not karate, at
least not in the Okinawan sense, but the idea of karate as Westerners
imagined it' (402). For, the 'Asian discourses of history, culture, and
practice that created martial arts and defined its practice had not yet
gained widespread recognition in the West' (402). This abyss between
what it had been and what it could become arose because, during this
time, 'the cultural texture of karate was supplied by its practitioners' ability to draw on Western discourses, such as boxing and the military', as
well as spy fiction, of course. So, at one and the same time 'karate could
be recognized as a fighting art, similar to boxing, while being deconstructive of boxing as something abnormal to the traditional mythologies of
Western martial arts'. Overall, of course, this 'abnormality was encoded

in its use of kicks (considered unethical in boxing, although allowed in the French fighting system, *Savate*), its highly structured training systems, the philosophy it embodied, and the occultism that it intimated'. Indeed, the 'philosophic and esoteric practices of martial arts were generally not learned in the short time that Westerners spent among Asian cultures' (402). But this did not stop such ideas – the belief in profound secret enigmas – from functioning connotatively to make the practices all the more intriguing in the first instance.

The form of the integration of karate and other martial practices into Anglo-American culture was always going to be conditioned by what Krug calls 'cultural texture'. This is why, during the 1960s, 1970s and thereafter:

> Often, training articles focus on, or borrow from, body-building practices, and magazines focused on body building are often advertised in karate magazines and are sometimes sold together as sets. This blurring of boundaries between karate and other physical activities as well as the blurring of the boundaries between lived experience and mass media forms suggest that the cultural texture of karate that was present in the Eastern Pacific countries and that made karate as a set of practices does not exist in the West or has been supplanted by another set of practices, that is, sport. (402)

As such, 'the culture of sport as a dominant and traditional Anglo-American cultural practice supplies the texture into which karate is commonly woven' (402). For Krug, this subtle but profound transformation/translation is best demonstrated in a consideration of 'magazine articles with titles such as "Karate or Kung Fu: Who Has the Fastest Kick?"' – a question that is often alien, irrelevant and indeed asinine outside of a sport-orientated manner of thinking and evaluating. Krug also proposes that another significant 'manifestation of these changes may be observed in the rise of "ultimate" or no-holds-barred tournament competitions that regularly pack stadiums and appear on video or subscription television' (402) – a development, it should be noted, whose televisual dissemination has substantially deconstructed the very idea of adhering to a martial art '*style*' at all. As Royce Gracie, the winner of many of the first televised Ultimate Fighting Competitions puts it: 'At first it was style versus style, now it's athlete versus athlete, because everyone cross-trains… And now with time limits built into the fights, not always the best wins, sometimes it's just the most aggressive' (quoted in Preston 2007: 64). This transformation, from martial bouts being style against style to athlete against athlete, 'because everyone cross-trains', has an irreducible connection to the imposition of sportive and televisual conventions: rules, time-limits, and the banning of potentially lethal techniques, etc. Indeed, adds Krug:

> The acceptance of karate in America, Europe, and Australia was manifested in the development of large tournaments and competitions and the growth in the number and size of karate schools. Empires and corporations of karate schools spread rapidly and largely took the place of the *ryu* structures that framed the traditional martial arts lineages in Japan and Okinawa. In addition, a large number of new styles and schools appeared, much more in the sport tradition than following the passing on of a lineage of teaching. (402)

Sporting Mysticism

This initial transformation-translation from something other into sport was only an early stage of the dialectic. For, at this stage or in this form, traces or residues of karate's putative 'essential alterity' had yet to be fully engaged – namely, the mythic, mystical and secret powers that were a fundamental part of the initial and initialising Western fantasy of karate. What of 'esoteric philosophy', the 'underlying sciences of ch'i, meridian striking, healing, and the health enhancing aspects of improving the flow of intrinsic body energy'? According to Krug, in its migration west, 'the original *bunkai* (explanations) of kata and much of the esoteric philosophy of karate had been long removed from the arts'. Yet 'these knowledges remained a part of the mythic fabric of the arts, hinted at but rarely discussed'. So, 'from a Western perspective, they remained either untrue or a part of the Eastern tradition to which the West in general had not yet been given access' (403).

But because such enigmas were a large part of what had initiated or initially marked the characteristics of the Western interest in these activities in the first place, these enigmas remained as it were outstanding and still calling out for attention. Hence, along with the growing popularity of martial arts (and for 'popularity' one might also of course read 'market potential'), translations and studies of the original bunkai began to appear in English and other European languages. These translations mark a crucial threshold. For it is precisely the 'secret knowledge' contained therein that came to enable Westerners to claim 'complete' mastery or appropriation. However, Krug reiterates, the introduction of such alien concepts as pressure points, ch'i and meridians still could not acquire anything like widespread discursive legitimacy or even intelligibility on their own. Rather, cultural intelligibility and discursive legitimacy require an attending discourse or depth of texture as its condition of possibility – some interpretive context within which it can make sense. Krug locates this discursive context in the growth of Western discourse on Traditional Chinese Medicine (TCM), a discourse whose growing familiarity in the west (via debates and disputes about the status of TCM vis-à-vis western medicine) paves the way for the intelligibility of the outstanding esoteric ('Oriental') aspects that remain to be comprehended by Western discourse:

> The publication of many texts and the spread of the knowledge of ch'i meridians and TCM have contributed greatly to changes in understanding of the techniques of martial arts. In particular, the spread of knowledge about these practices and their establishment into institutional forms created another aspect of the depth of texture needed for martial arts to be understood in a new context. They contributed the explanations that allowed martial arts in general and karate in particular to become accepted as 'normal' practices. Rorty (…) defined normality as 'accepting without question the stage-setting in the language which gives demonstration (scientific or ostensive) its legitimacy' (…). In other words, the deep or occult philosophy of martial arts required a degree of explanation and elaboration that was not forthcoming within the field itself. Rather, other, more literate, areas in Anglo-European culture, such as medicine, first had to make the revolutionary statements that could underpin and support other sets of practices, such as karate. Only when acupuncture exists as a recognized practice can books such as *Dim Mak: Death Point Striking* (Montague, 1993) appear almost mainstream. (405)

Nevertheless, despite the appearance of having mastered the 'original' or 'true' art, this 'knowledge' is still a transformation, an alteration of something prior: 'the context of the original object of knowledge is lost', Krug reiterates:

> Knowledge of ch'i was embedded in a holistic understanding of health and TCM. Application of this knowledge to attacking was derived from an understanding of how to apply it to healing. An understanding of healing through these techniques derived from a view of the universe grounded in the interplay of esoteric forces. Outside of the context of this philosophy, the striking of key meridian points becomes a technical exercise rather like the pushing of buttons. The claim to these knowledges again serves to legitimate the practitioner as one possessing the authentic or true knowledge. These claims then become signifiers capable of adding value to the commodity of the martial art. (406)

This returns us to Tierney's observations about the entirely 'technical' entry of Neo to martial arts in *The Matrix*. In other words, we return ineluctably to the issue of abstraction, standardisation and commodification. But the story does not simply end there. Westernisation is not simply coterminous with commodification. Westernisation and commodification are not somehow synonyms. For, although in certain times and places martial arts may not *simply* or *directly* have been part of a cash relation – payment for a service rendered – it has always been integral to kinship systems and relations of debt and obligation (including financial). Rather, according to Krug, the current state of the discursive development of martial arts in Western countries is currently involved in a massive process of what we might term *re-institutionalisation*.

Institutionalisation and re-institutionalisation are not quite the same as commodification, nor the fashionable post-Deleuzean notions of territorialisation, de- and re-territorialisation. We will engage extensively with this in Chapter Four. Rather, as Krug clarifies, the issue is instead that the 'the contemporary understanding of karate is undergoing [another] fundamental change among many Anglo-Americans'. This is because there are now 'second and third generation instructors living in the West who have the benefits both of having studied in the countries of origin and of living and practicing a great distance away'. Also, 'with the deaths of legendary founding fathers of karate, the styles and organizations tend to disintegrate as senior students vie for the position of grand patriarch of the style'. For, 'The master served as a sign of genuineness and legitimacy, so long as he lived, but with his death, an endless series of simulations [arises], each masquerading as the authentic and real' (403):

> The signifier of the master, and hence of a link to the Asian tradition, could be broken either by the master's death and the absence of a successor or by the creation of a rival structure, such as a corporation or organization to replace the original school with another social structure. When this severing of the practice from its origins takes place, the sign of legitimacy changes. Martial arts then becomes reduced to those key representations that are granted legitimacy by the organization. The organization establishes ranking, certification, and the allocation of all forms of deference.
>
> Once the sign of legitimacy is acquired, karate itself can be transformed into a commodity and its method of diffusion sold through franchises, complete with door-knocking proselytes and incentive programs

for recruitment. The new sign of legitimacy, commonly underpinned by a
claim to direct lineage to one or another master or school, is reinforced
with displays of trophies won in competitions, with the McDonaldesque
reference to the number of schools or students in the organization, or by
any of the other methods used to sell hamburgers, cars, or deodorant (Krug
2001: 403-404)

Is this, then, the start and end-point of the matter in the West? Is
the 'Western' 'encounter' with 'Eastern' martial arts, as exemplified or
amplified by Bruce Lee's intervention and popularity, reducible to a
process of 'appropriation', commodification and westernised institution?
There would seem to be so much more going on, both textually and discursively. But in order to do justice to this 'so much more', a cultural
study of Bruce Lee is required to do and be something different, itself:
more rigorously analytical than most novelistic, biographical approaches
to the subject; less disciplinarily hidebound than either 'straight' film
studies or 'sober' discourse analysis; but also an approach that is different
to either the purely filmic textual analysis or the broad historical brush-
strokes of a macro-perspective discourse analysis. Such an approach cannot therefore be straightforwardly disciplinary, but must necessarily be
'interdisciplinary' in a way that problematizes the very possibility of a
straightforward synthesis of knowledge; that is to say, an approach organised by a self-aware and principled refusal to satisfy that once popular TV
melodrama demand for 'closure'. Such an approach will therefore be
what John Mowitt has called 'antidisciplinary' (Mowitt 1992), at least to
the extent that such a multimedia object as Bruce Lee requires an interdisciplinary approach. And, as any interdisciplinary effort worth the name
will inevitably pose questions about the limitations of the hermeneutic
borders of a disciplinary field, so interdisciplinary approaches will antagonise disciplinary boundaries, values and protocols. As Mowitt explains, this is because 'no one, especially those authorized to do so, can
really do interdisciplinary work the way we think it *ought* to be done'
(2003: 184). This, of course, is inextricably linked to the question of
style. As is the question of Bruce Lee. So, the question of style is what we
should broach next. But how? What style of approach will be most appropriate to broaching the question of style? And with what effects?

'What's your Style?'
The Problem of Disciplinarity

In a famous exchange in *Enter the Dragon*, a belligerent martial artist has been bullying the crew and staff of a boat transporting a group of martial artists to a competition. The bully asks Mr Lee (Bruce Lee) 'What's your style?' He is clearly out for a fight. Lee replies: 'My style? I suppose you could call it the art of fighting without fighting'. This unusual and unexpected response baffles his questioner, who demands to be shown some of it. Unable to avoid a confrontation, Lee's response takes the form of a completely banal and pragmatic demonstration of 'fighting without fighting'; by proposing that they would have more room to fight if they were to row to a nearby island, he tricks the aggressor into climbing aboard a small rowing boat in a perilously rough sea. Lee then untethers the boat and hands the rope to those who had been bullied. They proceed to toy with their now-helpless erstwhile persecutor: the perfect comeuppance for one who had so mercilessly bullied them earlier on. With this, Lee shows what 'fighting without fighting' might most literally be taken to mean. Nevertheless, despite the banality of this demonstration, every viewer *already* '*knows*' that the phrase 'the art of fighting without fighting' *really* encapsulates something *more*, something enigmatic, 'deep' and profound. We sense with heady anticipation that there is going to be a lot more to this mysterious oriental art than tricks.

We know this because in *Enter the Dragon* the sense of the enigmatic profundity of Lee's Shaolin art is omnipresent. From the very first scene of the film, the presentation of Lee and his Shaolin art insistently urges the viewer to believe that there really is more to martial arts than fighting. The opening scene of *Enter the Dragon* is a ritualistic 'rite of passage' combat sequence in a Shaolin Temple. This is immediately followed by a koan-like question-and-answer session – the first dialogue of the film – between Lee and his master, which runs as follows:

[*Scene opens: Lee approaches an elderly monk on a wooded hilltop path*]

Lee: [*bowing*]	Teacher?
Teacher:	Hmm. I see your talents have gone beyond the mere physical level. Your skills are now at the point of spiritual insight. I have several questions. What is the highest technique you hope to achieve?
Lee:	To have no technique.

Teacher:	Very good. What are your thoughts when facing an opponent?
Lee:	There is no opponent.
Teacher:	And why is that?
Lee:	Because the word 'I' does not exist.
Teacher:	So. Continue.
Lee:	A good fight should be like a small play, *but* played seriously. A good martial artist does not become tense, but ready. Not thinking, yet not dreaming: ready for whatever may come. When the opponent expands, I contract; when he contracts, I expand; and when there is an opportunity, I do not hit: [*he raises his fist, but does not look at it*] it hits all by itself.

The mysticism of this exchange is further consolidated by the very next scene in which Lee tutors a young monk, Lau, and explains that a correctly executed kick (or any combative exchange) 'is like a finger pointing away to the moon'. The full scene (actually, a scene within a scene, as Lee has had to break off his conversation with the British Agent Mr Braithwaite), runs like this:

Lee:	It's Lau's time.
Braithwaite:	Yes, of course…
Lee:	Kick me. [*Lau seems puzzled*] Kick me. [*Lau throws a side-kick*] What was that? An exhibition? We need [*pointing to his head*] emotional content. Try again! [*Lau kicks again*] I said emotional content. Not anger! Now try again! With *me*! [*Lau throws two more kicks, causing Lee to respond*] That's it! How did it feel to you?
Lau:	Let me think.
Lee:	[*Slaps Lau's head*] Don't think! *Feel*! It is like a finger pointing away to the moon. [*Slaps Lau's head*] *Don't* concentrate on the finger or you will miss all that heavenly glory. Do you understand?
Lau:	[*smiles, nods, bows*]
Lee:	[*Slaps the back of Lau's head*] *Never* take your eyes off your opponent, even when you bow…. That's it.

We will have many causes to return to these two exchanges in some considerable depth and with many different foci in the ensuing chapters. But first of all, it is most important to note that in its attribution of some enigmatic depth to martial arts, *Enter the Dragon* is an exemplary instance of the most popular kind of discourse about them. For, many of the myths, texts and discourses about martial arts often insist that there is indeed more to these fighting practices than fighting. But what 'more' is there? What more is there to martial arts than fighting? Or indeed, a more appropriate question perhaps: given that martial arts practice often consists entirely in endless training sessions without any actual fighting on the horizon, what more is there to 'martial' arts than fighting without fighting?

But perhaps we have already moved too fast. For, if martial arts can so easily be more *and* less *and* 'other' than 'fighting' (and all at the same time), then surely the *first* question to be asked is what actually *are* martial arts? This may seem obvious: an unnecessary question. But, as Hegel cautioned, 'What is "familiarly known" is not properly known, just for the reason that it is "familiar".... [For, familiarity itself] is the commonest form of self-deception' (1977: 35).

For instance, Stephen Chan gives a clear account of the crisis that even scratching the surface of the apparent obviousness of the term 'martial arts' can precipitate when he explains that 'a UNESCO survey of the world's martial arts' that he was involved with had to be abandoned 'because the various authors could not agree on the nature of the project' (2000: 69). They could not agree on a workable definition or delimitation of their shared object of study, 'the martial arts'. In other words, this putatively obvious and stable referent immediately turned out to be a rather deceptive signifier, something that can be construed drastically differently depending on one's standpoint. The UNESCO group was unable to agree on *how* to conceive of the martial arts: how to contextualise them, how to establish and assess their limits, their 'essence', and indeed how to ascertain what constitutes their 'reality'. They were especially unable to agree on whether the 'reality' of martial arts should include or exclude the myths, fictions, fantasies, and fabrications that constantly blur the edges and muddy the waters of this subject.

'My Style?' The Disciplined Production of Difference

Chan's subject area in the UNESCO study was to have been Japanese martial arts. On this topic, he offered the view that 'mythology plays a large role in the internationalization of Japanese martial arts' (2000: 69). However, this proposition, he observes, 'seemed particularly contentious' to the other authors who, holding different notions of what constitutes the reality of a martial art (and implicitly therefore a different notion of what constitutes reality as such), wanted to downplay or ignore myth. According to Chan, however, 'little progress seem[s] possible in separating histories from mythologies' when it comes to martial arts (69). This is because in their formation, dissemination and proliferation, myth demonstrably often trumps history. We might merely consider the explosive impact that a film like *Enter the Dragon* had on the fantasy life and martial arts practice the world over to see Chan's point: when it comes to the martial arts, myths and fictions can be far more influential and orientating than truth.

Brian Kennedy and Elizabeth Guo have recently gone further than this, focusing on the myths associated with the romanticised 'Shaolin Temple'. They argue that the myths about Shaolin were 'largely created in two books' (Guo and Kennedy 2005: 70). Firstly, as Stanley Henning points out: 'The origins of this myth cannot be traced back earlier than its appearance in the popular novel, *Travels of Lao Can*, written between 1904 and 1907, and there is no indication that it was ever part of an earlier oral tradition' (Henning quoted in Guo and Kennedy 2005: 70). Then, 'the second myth that popularized the Bodhidharma-Shaolin temple myth was *Secrets of Shaolin Temple Boxing*, written in 1915 by an unknown author' (70). They quote Henning approvingly, in his observation in 'The Chinese Martial Arts in Historical Perspective', that 'both Tang Hao and Xu Je Dong', the leading Chinese martial arts historians of the day, immediately 'exposed this book's lack of historicity but, unfortunately, it became popularly accepted as a key source for Chinese martial arts history enthusiasts, and its pernicious influence has permeated literature on the subject to this day' (Henning in Guo and Kennedy 2005: 71).

It is widely acknowledged that the choreography seen in *Enter the Dragon* has little direct relation with the 'real' Shaolin kung fu that the character of Lee in *Enter the Dragon* 'would really' have practised; just as the 'celluloid' cinematic choreography in Bruce Lee films had little in common with the interdisciplinary bricolage of different approaches to combat actually developed and taught by Bruce Lee himself (of which more will be said in due course). But it was not just Hollywood and Hong Kong cinema that unleashed 'myth' by manipulating fantasies worldwide, conjuring up spurious yet putatively ancient arts (now called 'wushu' and sometimes even 'wire-fu': namely, the dramatic athletic kung fu of film choreography). Chan himself lists a whole host of Japanese martial arts that are often deliberately represented, exported and consumed as if they are authentically ancient warrior arts, but which are in fact relatively recent, often twentieth-century inventions.

His point is simple: what Chan calls 'mythologising' more than muddies the waters of reality – it actually constitutes it. As he points out, there are millions 'worldwide who practise ... martial arts and believe that these arts have antique and spiritual values beyond what passes for history and cultural value in the constructions of their own cultures' (Chan 2000: 71). Indeed, he suggests that those who have bought into many of the myths of Japanese martial arts have been duped, in a sense, by the cynical ministrations of what he calls 'the Japanese cultural authorities'. These, he argues, have deliberately worked as the 'editor of mythologies' in order to make Japanese culture into a commodified artefact. This mythology is commodified in myriad ways: both 'in fact' (through the production of new 'ancient' martial arts) and 'in fiction' (through film, literature and other such productions). These artefacts are produced and consumed as if authentically ancient culture, when in fact they have been deliberately produced: conjured up, exported, (re)imported and consumed.

Given this complexity, the question of how to define, delimit and make sense of the 'martial arts' inevitably encounters the problem that 'martial arts' exceed simple categorisation. Indeed, in order to try adequately or exhaustively to approach and to attempt to understand fully what martial arts 'are', one must seemingly cover a vast interdisciplinary breadth. To grasp the 'whole truth' would seem to demand mastery of realms as diverse as archival research, history and historiography, translation, comparative philosophy, culture and religion, psychology, sociology, political economy, marketing, aesthetics, politics, cinematography, and popular culture, to say the least. Given the multiple dimensions of 'martial arts', the question is: what sort of paradigm could possibly hope to be adequate to the task? The problem here is that any approach will privilege certain dimensions and subordinate, be ignorant of, blind to or otherwise exclusive of others. Every version of 'interdisciplinarity' cannot but be led by a *particular* disciplinary preference, and so will differ from other possible versions of interdisciplinarity, therefore producing different (often utterly contradictory forms of) knowledge. Omniscience is not possible. Every account or manner of 'understanding' will be enabled and limited by a particular partial bias.

Given Chan's argument about the ensnarement of Japanese martial arts within a commodifying process, then, from a Marxian perspective, such as that recently (re)developed by the influential cultural critic, Slavoj Žižek, Chan's observations might immediately be taken to be the start and end-point – the *culmination* – of an argument. That is, from the perspective of Marxian economism (the view that the dictates of the economy determine in the last instance the beliefs and practices of culture and society), then the point about commodification may be regarded as the last word on the matter – as if proving that culture has been decisively colonised by capitalism, that all beliefs and practices are ideological (because they are commodified myths that we have bought into), and that cultural practices like martial arts are simply a kind of modern 'opium of the masses'.

However, Chan himself is evidently neither a Žižekian nor any other kind of economic reductionist, as he does not propound such a view. On the contrary, he contends that whilst, on the one hand, one cannot simply or uncritically believe all of their 'history' – 'Much of what seems to be antique is not' (Chan 2000: 69) – on the other hand, martial arts cannot just be viewed as commodity pure and simple. In this respect, he gives examples of martial arts in African shanty townships where karate has become 'an alternative source of values and cultural shelter to those shut outside the wealth of the Western economy, and who have been divorced by location and the exigencies of poverty from a deep indigenous sense of culture' (70). Here, there is something strongly 'cultural', indeed even immanently *political* about martial arts. They become bound up in identity, in identification, in organic community, and can be construed as taking on a place and significance that is far from simply consumerist.

So, an over-economistic or reductively Marxian take on culture as capitalist-colonised seems limited. What alternative paradigms are available that we might bring to bear on martial arts? Any answer will already be biased and therefore in every way 'partial'. But, from the point of view of the contemporary interdisciplinary arts and humanities, there is 'obviously' much that is psychoanalysable in martial arts (given the palpable presence of masculine desire, fantasy and fear, as well as cultural projections about 'the other', for instance). There is also much that seems to cry out for Foucauldian styles of analysis of the body in discourses and relations of power – not forgetting post-Foucauldian and post-colonial considerations of 'orientalist discourse'. Martial arts phenomena demand historicisation, too, of course. But even if something 'universal' is discerned in the impetus to begin martial arts training – perhaps the sense of 'lack' that might crystallise in the subjective desire to become powerful or invincible – such a 'symptom' can of course be treated in many manners: reiterated or recurring 'symptoms' need not necessarily be approached through Freudian or Lacanian optics. There are vastly differing ways to interpret even a 'universal' or 'general' feature, from the most positivist, behaviourist or essentialist paradigms to the most relativist, postmodern or deconstructive. In terms of the latter, for instance, Jacques Derrida's ruminations on death and its relation to questions of responsibility in *The Gift of Death* (Derrida 1995) almost call out to be applied to a consideration of the martial arts. Or, to put this another way: surely consideration of the martial arts should be accorded the dignity and seriousness of philosophy, especially insofar as they seem so closely related to questions of death, desire, responsibility, discipline, mortality and purpose. As Derrida argues at one point:

> a concept of *discipline* covers a number of senses…: that of training, first of all, or exercise, the idea of the work necessary to maintain control over orgiastic mystery…. Secondly, this discipline is also philosophy, or the dialectic, to the extent that it can be taught, precisely as a discipline, at the same time exoteric and esoteric; as well as that of the exercise that consists in learning to die in order to attain the new immortality, … the care taken with death, the exercise of death, the 'practicing (for) death' that Socrates speaks of in the *Phaedo*. (1995: 12)

To regard Derrida or even Socrates as Samurai/martial theorists may not turn out to be as preposterous as it might at first sound. For, many things come in response to the inevitability of death and the problem of responsibility: philosophy and discipline are but two. There are even uncanny affinities and connections between the samurai manual, the *Hagakure* (Yamamoto 1979) and Hegel's master-slave dialectic (Hegel 1977). This can be seen played out in exemplary fashion in the film *Ghost Dog: The Way of The Samurai* (1999), which we will discuss in a later chapter.

Yet nor can martial arts unequivocally be said to be 'purely' 'philosophical'. For they are also sites of sheer pleasure, thrill-seeking, competition, engagement, escapism, and fantasy; martial arts are as available to the ideology of individualism as to that of community. Sociologically-aware claims have been made about some of the contexts in which they proliferate: the immediate and enduring popularity of martial arts films and practices in American black ghetto communities has been widely noted and theorised, for instance (Brown 1997; Hunt 2003; Marchetti 2001). But 'martial arts' arise and function in these contexts very differently from when martial arts tropes and themes are appropriated in management self-help discourses, wherein Japanese swordsmanship texts like *The Book of Five Rings* or books like *The Art of War* are made to play the part of business manuals. We might consider, for instance, the significance of the fact that the first testimonial on the cover of one edition of *The Book of Five Rings* reads:

> Today's business people will find ... [this] 350-year-old martial arts classic ... compelling and tantalizingly relevant. Perseverance, insight, self-understanding, inward calm even in the midst of chaos, the importance of swift but unhurried action: Musashi's teachings read like lessons from the latest business management gurus. Who couldn't succeed in business by applying Musashi's insights on conflict and strategy! (Musashi 1994: Cover blurb)

Furthermore, martial arts again take on a very different function, form and status in New Age and hippy ideologies and lifestyles in the West, where hippy fetishism about mystical 'universal harmony' replaces capitalistic, macho or militaristic fetishism about 'conflict'. And what may be just playful, hobbyist, hippy or hip hop ideology in the West is something quite different in East Asia, where many 'martial' practices (such as *chigung/qigong* and *Falun gong*) have been variously repressed *and* recruited in nationalist political discourses (Xu 1999).

'The art of fighting *without* fighting?'

So, there is no simple or univocal answer to the question even of what is being 'done' when martial arts are said to be 'done' – or indeed, what 'is there' when martial arts are said 'to be'. In a study that is germane to this discussion, Greg Downey broaches some of the ramifications of this, in a discussion of *capoeira* (Downey 2002), a Brazilian phenomenon that hovers undecidably somewhere between combat, dance, ritual, sport, subculture, quasi-religion and aimless game, all at the same time. He relates this to its complex history: *capoeira* was a fighting art developed by slaves in Brazil that, like arts devised by colonised peoples in the Philippines and elsewhere, was from the start disguised as a dance and passed off as a harmless ritual. Accordingly, this carnivalesque aspect became inscribed into its practice, at the same time as it served as the primary fighting resource, first of slaves and thereafter of the Brazilian underclass. Viewed as a scourge by the authorities (like Karate in Okinawa [Funakoshi 1975], and indeed many other underclass martial practices worldwide—including those of Europe and the UK [Brown 1997]), *capoeira* in Brazil was actually illegal until the 1920s, until the force of various militaristic and nationalist discourses led to its incorporation into military, police, and educational syllabi.

Although Downey does not use such language in his study of the complexity and uncertainty of *capoeira*'s ontological status and its ensnarement in always politically motivated contexts, what his study nevertheless points to is the *undecidability* of *capoeira*. What is it? What is being done, and why? What does it *mean*, what does it *do* – in *any* register? Downey convincingly argues that *capoeira* does not fit into any of the dominant categories for classifying and dealing with physical activities, and that because of this difference (or divergence, or excess), regular 'efforts by the state (and other nationalist institutions) to co-opt, control and recast [it] as a sport have failed repeatedly' (2). However, despite its demonstrably politically-charged status – first a slave activity, then an illegal underclass practice, then subjected to various politically motivated efforts of institutional appropriation and domestication – Downey wants to criticise the academic tendency to leap to the conclusion that therefore there must be something fundamentally political about such activities. Against this impulse he contends: 'these projects failed not because of politically-motivated "resistance", but because of growing boredom, dissatisfaction and disinterest in sporting projects' among *capoeira* practitioners. Thus, he suggests, 'the case of capoeira may point to a more widespread pitfall in macrosocial interpretations of historical events as political processes' (2-3).

So, in this schema, martial arts both are and are not 'political'. They *are* political insofar as they exist within an irreducibly political context (for what context is not in some sense contingent, structured by bias and therefore political?) and may be appropriated by various discourses, ideologies, agencies or interests. But on the other hand, they are *not* political, if by political we are referring to some conscious political *intention* or even just a clear kind of politicised *impetus*. Downey's criticism of the implicit 'Cartesian' conception of politics operative within too much scholarship is admirable (even if this is unintentional on his part). So is the sense in which it emphasises that just because something is problematic or uncontrollable, that does not necessarily make it politically subversive. Yet his conclusion nevertheless leaves something to be desired, for it proceeds problematically, both acknowledging the unavoidable intrusion of the political context into any activity or identity and yet writing that off as if it is an insignificant supplement, and choosing instead to construe the practice in terms of what Lacanian psychoanalysis would call pure '*jouissance*' – pure pleasure, enjoyment: as if it's all simply a bit of fun.

Of course, what psychoanalysis calls '*jouissance*' – not to mention fantasy, fear, projection, identification, and a whole host of other psychoanalytically specifiable factors – is in play in the largely unconscious constitution of desire. But the point to be emphasised is that any such unconscious formation will come in response to a contingent situation, and hence it will be a *political* or *contextual unconscious*. The factors bearing on the formation of desire and orientation will be in some sense 'political'. This suggests that practices might be diagnosed in terms of their historical, political context. Jian Xu (1999) gives an account, for instance, of the repression of esoteric and occasionally martial practices, such as Falun Gong and Qigong, in Maoist China. This repression was followed by a veritable explosion of interest in the post-Maoist context. The repression and the interest continue. How does one make sense of this? As Xu puts it, all of the recent key studies of martial arts 'place the body-in-cultivation in a specific historical context; they maintain that the individual, physical body both registers and reveals the national sociopolitical landscape [and that] the body can express the emotional self repressed by the state' (1999: 961). The logic of this is based on the claim that, as Derrida explains, 'Repression doesn't destroy, it displaces something from one place to another within the system' (1995: 8).

However, Xu is discussing China during a certain period, where the state could be regarded as indubitably hegemonic. But, one might ask, what about the formation of desire and practice *elsewhere*? The nation state is not necessarily that which dominates the political context or constitutes the form and content of the political unconscious everywhere else. In the postmodern context and condition, analyses are perhaps to be weighted differently. What could be said to be 'behind' or 'at the root' (or roots) of the proliferation of the martial arts in the contemporary West? In what way might this relate to a political unconscious? And what significance might this have for anything?

'Fighting without Fighting': Interdisciplinarity, Bruce Lee and Multiculturalism

To broach this, let us first recap and reiterate the argument that myths supplement reality, and hence are not simply untrue or imaginary. If this is so, it deserves to be asked in what way reality might supplement myth. We began with the cinematic emergence of Bruce Lee, which certainly blazed an influential trail that fired up the imaginations, fantasies and practices of untold numbers of people the world over. This cinematic moment might be regarded as a 'real mythic' event. But in what way might this origin relate to other origins – as it were, the historical and cultural conditions of possibility for such a 'mythic' emergence?

Bruce Lee's senior student, the Filipino eskrimador, Dan Inosanto, gives this account of the formation, birth, and baptism of 'jeet kune do', the martial art that Bruce Lee 'invented':

> It all began in the early part of 1968 while Bruce and I were driving along in the car. We were talking about fencing, Western fencing. Bruce said [that] the most efficient means of countering in fencing was the *stop-hit*. A stop-hit is when you do not parry and then counter, it's all done in one step. When the opponent attacks, you intercept his move with a thrust or hit of your own. It is designed to score a hit in the midst of the attacker's action, and is the highest and most economical of all the counters.
> Then Bruce said, 'We should call our method of fighting the "stop-hitting fist style", or the "intercepting fist style"'.
> 'What would that be in Chinese?' I asked.
> 'That would be Jeet Kune Do', he said.
> Jeet Kune Do means the way of the stopping fist, or the way of the intercepting fist. So, instead of blocking and then hitting, our main concept is to dispense with blocking completely, and instead to intercept and hit. We realize that this cannot be done all the time, but this is the main theme.

> Up until 1967 our method was called 'Jun Fan' Gung Fu, which was a
> modification of various techniques from Northern Praying Mantis, South-
> ern Praying Mantis, Choy Li Fut, Eagle Claw, Western Boxing, Hung Gar,
> Thai Boxing, wrestling, Judo, Jiu Jitsu, and several Northern Gung-Fu
> styles. [But] It is obvious that Wing Chun was the main nucleus and [that]
> all the other methods evolved around it.
> [....]
> In later years he became sorry that he ever coined the term Jeet Kune
> Do because he felt that it, too, was limiting, and according to Bruce,
> 'There is no such thing as a style if you totally understand the roots of
> combat'. (Inosanto 1980: 66-7)

There is far more to be mined from this remarkably rich passage than we
will do in this introductory foray. We will however be able to return to it
in later chapters. In terms of the consideration of the place of myth or
fantasy in martial arts discourse, what is perhaps most remarkable in Dan
Inosanto's account of the formation of jeet kune do, is the *absence* – indeed, the strict *exclusion* – of classical (orientalist or oriental-esque) martial arts mythology.

Is this an absence of myth as such? Inosanto's account (like most
of Bruce Lee's own similar accounts) might be classed as one that is cen-
tred on efficiency and economy, on the one hand, and on the other organised by a multiculturally promiscuous interdisciplinarity. In other words,
in place of the mythology of 'ancientness' and 'mysticism', what is present in Lee and Inosanto are the themes of efficiency and economy, and
the – at the time definitively radical and controversial – advocation of
interdisciplinarity and *hybridity*. Inosanto tells us that jeet kune do was
conceptualised, baptised and inaugurated in California, given a Chinese
name but inspired equally by the Western art of fencing, derived from an
interdisciplinary approach to any and every fighting style available, selected and dissected with a view to efficiency. Viewed in this way, this
may be very telling. For, what we have here is interdisciplinary *bricolage*,
multiculturalism, and efficiency. And surely one need not belabour the
point that the 1960s saw more than one inventive, interdisciplinary 'revolution'. Perhaps merely mentioning '1968' may be enough to conjure up a
certain *zeitgeist* (or a certain dread!).

What else was going on in the sixties? Apart from the wars and
famous student revolts, let me also point to the following. In 1962, *Doc-
tor No* was released. Also in 1962, the same year Jacques Derrida's first
book, his translation and introduction to Edmund Husserl's *Origin of Ge-*

ometry (Derrida 1962/1978) was published, Bruce Lee gave a spectacular demonstration of kung fu at Ed Parker's International Karate Championships, an event that, according to Inosanto, 'proved to be the major turning point in his career' (1980: 36). The following year, Lee published *Chinese Gung-fu: The Philosophical Art of Self-Defense* (Lee 1963/1987). America met Lee's kung fu as France met Derrida's deconstruction. In 1964, the Centre for Contemporary Cultural Studies was established in Birmingham, the same year that the tape of Lee's demonstration secured him a screen test that would lead to the role of Kato in the TV series *The Green Hornet* (produced by the makers of *Batman*). Only in 1968, the year Stuart Hall became director of the Birmingham Centre, did Lee – slightly after Derrida – baptise his own 'method-that-wasn't-really-a-method'. However, he would come to regret the name 'jeet kune do' slightly before Derrida would come to regret calling deconstruction 'deconstruction'. (Stuart Hall, incidentally, has always defended the name 'cultural studies': he never seems to have had problems with the name 'cultural studies', apparently because unlike names like 'deconstruction' or 'jeet kune do', the name 'cultural studies' effectively works in an opposite direction; denoting the multiple, the partial, the incomplete and the amorphous, in its very plural vagueness, as opposed to denoting some putatively singular and definite identity.)

Now, readers might be concerned about the legitimacy of the implicit but telegraphed presupposition that one might possibly even begin to generalise anything at all from such conspicuously select, heterogeneous and unrelated things as these moments in the institution and dissemination of 'cultural studies', 'deconstruction', and 'Bruce Lee'. You might protest, as Fleiss protested to Freud about psychoanalysis, that making such preposterous connections is simply 'wit gone wild, overingenious analogizing lacking the necessary discrimination' (Fleiss quoted in Weber 1982: 106). And you would, of course, be wise to do so. Nevertheless, there is a theoretical proposition that might be inferred here; namely, that something that might be called (following Jameson) a 'political unconscious' exerts an influence in a historical context, which acts upon *formation*. In this sense, the *formation* of Bruce Lee's approach to martial arts seems to be comparable to the *formation* of cultural studies. Both, I am suggesting, may be further compared with the *formation* of Derridean deconstruction. The question is: what enables and what is the status and significance of this apparent similarity or 'structural' (or, indeed, *post*-structural) affinity? And what might be the importance, legitimacy, verifiability and status of such a claim?

Let us turn, first, to the formation of cultural studies. Stuart Hall describes cultural studies as 'a discursive formation, in Foucault's sense' (Hall, Morley and Chen 1996: 263), within the 'milieu' of the open and radical New Left (Rojek 2003: 23): open (as they say) to alterity, ethico-politically motivated, pushing limits, borders, conventions, boundaries, hierarchies, exclusions. Second: deconstruction. Derrida captures the same sense (if not exactly the 'same' scene)[5] when he says of deconstruction and the many, *many* detractors of it:

> If it were only a question of 'my' work, of the particular or isolated re-search of one individual, [these scandalised denunciations of deconstruction] wouldn't happen. Indeed, the violence of these denunciations derives from the fact that the work accused is part of a whole ongoing process. What is unfolding here, like the resistance it necessarily arouses, can't be limited to a personal 'oeuvre', nor to a discipline, nor even to the academic institution.... If this work seems so threatening to [some], this is because it isn't eccentric or strange, incomprehensible or exotic (which would allow them to dispose of it easily), but as I myself hope, and as they believe more than they admit, competent, rigorously argued, and carrying conviction in its re-examination of the fundamental norms and premises of a number of dominant discourses, the principles underlying many of their evaluations, the structures of academic institutions, and the research that goes on within them. What this kind of questioning does is to modify the rules of the dominant discourse, it tries to politicize and democratize the university scene... (Derrida 1995a: 409-10)

Uncannily similar to the declared ethos of Hallian cultural studies and Derridean deconstruction, and indeed 'a whole ongoing process', Bruce Lee too deliberately and self-consciously 'inter-disciplined', 'democratised', and 'anti-essentialised' kung fu. Lee insisted that there is no substantial essence to it and that one need not be Chinese to do it. Moreover, perhaps because of his experience of racism at the hands both of Chinese and American institutions, Lee was allegedly obdurately colour-blind. As a youth in Hong Kong, the discovery that Lee had some German ancestry reputedly led to his exclusion from Grand Master Yip Man's Wing Chun School's tutelage for some time; whilst, later, in America, Lee consis-

---

[5] However, the similarities between Derrida's statements about the problems and problematics of 'Greph' (Groupe de Recherches sur l'Enseignement Philosophique) and 'Ciph' (Collège International de Philosophie) and Hall's statements about cultural studies and 'the Centre' are striking. See Jacques Derrida (2002).

tently interpreted his failure to secure a lead acting role as a matter of Hollywood's racism. For instance, Lee's ideas for a show called *The Warrior* only became the TV series *Kung Fu* when the starring role was given to a ridiculously orientalised white American actor, David Carradine – and Carradine would later also star in another unmade Lee project, *The Silent Flute* (a.k.a. *Circle of Iron* [1978]). Similarly, Lee's egalitarian approach to teaching met with quite a lot of 'institutional' resistance in the form of the racially inflected anger of the American Chinese martial arts community.

This kind of multiculturalism would seem to be the bread and butter of cultural studies – a formation that arose in response to or in tandem with (and as part of) 'a whole ongoing process' of deconstruction and reconstruction. But with this observation comes a serious question: does the very claim that this is all part of the same interrelated ensemble undermine cultural studies' own ability to construct a reliable knowledge of it? Given that cultural studies is directly implicated in the *same* 'discursive formation', what is the nature of this formation, or movement or conjuncture, this 'whole ongoing process' in which Bruce Lee, cultural studies, deconstruction, and – crucially, perhaps – the more widespread or generalised 'democratisation' of multiculturalism, interdisciplinarity, and 'openness to alterity' are all active players?

'The First American-Produced Martial Arts Spectacular!' Bruce Lee as Ideology

In order to broach these questions and to enter into some of the wider issues and problematics that arise here, let us consider further the cultural relations and effects of the factual and fictional (*factional*?) 'event' of Bruce Lee. One biography of Bruce Lee puts it particularly well. Bruce Thomas' *Bruce Lee: Fighting Spirit* begins by inviting us to ponder the significance of the ostensibly banal fact that the influence of Bruce Lee was such that the biographer, as he puts it, 'an Englishman ... was able to begin learning a Chinese martial art from a Welshman' (Thomas 1994/2002: xii). This otherwise quite mundane observation – that Bruce Lee, thanks to the Hollywood cinematic apparatus, could popularise the main art he studied, Wing Chun kung fu, all over the world – is not insignificant. In fact, as Lee's biographer goes on to suggest, Bruce Lee could in this and many other respects actually be said to have 'bridged cultures [and] revolutionized the martial arts'. At the same time, he explicitly 'taught a fierce philosophy of individualism, became a film icon and re-made the image of the Asian man in the West' (Thomas 1994/2002: xi).

Such an achievement is no mean feat. Just because *now – after* Bruce Lee – 'kung fu' and 'Bruce Lee' *seem* ordinary, usual, trivial, very little, almost nothing, this does not mean that they *are*. In fact, it is surely right here that we most need to remember Hegel's caution that 'what is "familiarly known" is not properly known, just for the reason that it is "familiar"... [and that familiarity itself] is the commonest form of self-deception' (1977: 35). For, it may be significant that, on the subject of this remarkable transformation, Bruce Lee's biographer actually ex-presses an approbation that is in fact a fairly typical view: Bruce Lee, he says, both revolutionised and popularised the martial arts. Moreover, he both 'bridged cultures' and 'remade the image of the Asian man in the West' (xi). He certainly did the latter. But were cultures *really* bridged? For, when facing the facts of Bruce Lee's emergence, the interpretive options available remain contradictory. For instance, either Bruce Lee the icon worked to *counter* racial stereotypes and orientalist prejudices, and to 'bridge cultures'; or Bruce Lee the icon actually *relied upon, exploited* and *deepened* racial stereotypes and orientalist prejudices – simply chang-ing the western stereotype of the oriental from negative contempt or ha-tred to putatively 'positive' yet nevertheless fetishistic fascination with a now eroticized other. Moreover, do films really 'bridge cultures'? Or do they divide a culture from itself, replacing a possibly traditional self-perception with a Eurocentric celluloid simulacrum?

Of course, the remaking of the image of the Asian man in the West may prove ethically and politically positive, insofar as certain representa-tional boundaries and conventions are modified, with monolithic white-ness whittled-away, Eurocentrism decentred, multiculturalism multiplied, and so on. But is this a cultural *encounter*, or a *bridge*, as such; part of a widespread or generalised 'democratisation' and 'openness to alterity'? This can be rephrased: Has there really been a multicultural encounter or transformation, when (1) Hollywood makes a martial arts movie, or (2) when a white Westerner watches this kung fu film, or, as a consequence, practises a nominally oriental martial art? If we answer 'yes' (with Bruce

Lee's biographer), then we also confirm an implicit proposition of cultural studies: that *all* culture (from 'physical' activity to filmic fantasy) *is effectively political*. (And one might be said to hold a version of this view if, for instance, one ever gets really bothered by a racist, sexist, or otherwise unjust or inaccurate representation on television. For, if we *didn't* think such things as cinematic or media representations 'really' made any difference, then we would not be bothered.) What would it be to answer, 'no, there is no real cultural or political transformation with the entrance of the dragon (except possibly the further fetishistic commodification of that 'dragon')'? What position could say 'no'?

Slavoj Žižek takes just such a position. Žižek is unequivocal in the claim that the putatively 'radical' ethical and political insights of what he calls deconstructionism, postmodernism, multiculturalism or 'politically correct' cultural studies are completely ideological: i.e., in the service of the inexhaustible commodification processes of capitalism. Any 'celebration' of such 'multicultural encounters' is, for Žižek, straightforwardly misguided. This is precisely why Žižek disavows what he calls 'politically correct cultural studies' approaches and adopts instead a stalwart Marxist perspective: he regards all anti-essentialism and multiculturalism as mere indices, symptoms and signs of the success of capitalism's neo-liberal ideology. The supposedly 'radical' insights of cultural studies are, he argues, merely the forefront of neoliberal commonsense and are as such necessarily false.

In this paradigm, all the multicultural hybrid, East-meets-West identity-performativity of Welsh Wing Chun masters and spectacular Asian-American pseudo-Shaolin celluloid stars 'inspiring' countless imaginary and actual, factual and phantasmatic encounters, interventions and events across the world, *actually* indicates nothing more than the deceptive deconstructive simulacrum of global capitalism. Indeed, for Žižek, just as Protestantism was the necessary ideology of 'industrial stage' capitalism (life is hard, then you die, but if you've been good and sedulous, you go to heaven), so the western appropriation of Taoism and Buddhism equals the necessary ideology of postmodern 'late capitalism' (don't cling – go with the restructuring flow). This is because the belief systems that Žižek interchangeably calls 'Western Buddhism' or 'Taoism' are belief systems that, he claims, 'perfectly fit' the *'fetishist* mode of ideology of our allegedly "post-ideological" era' (2001: 12-13). These,

he claims, enable 'you to participate fully in the frantic pace of the capitalist game while sustaining the perception that you are not really in it'
(15) – that, for instance, you may work in finance in the city, but you hold
the belief that the 'real you' is you when you are doing yoga. So, for
Žižek, what he calls contemporary Taoism, Western Buddhism, 'New
Ageism', the neoliberal ideology of 'tolerance', and so on, are all best
seen as equivalent reaction formations to, and in the service of, a relent-
less capitalism. The job of such practices and belief systems is to keep us
shopping and 'tolerating' and 'respecting difference' – as long as that
difference is merely the difference of different types of shopping, and not
the rejection of consumerism. Hence: Feng Shui good; Islamic fundamen-
talism bad. The one amounts to 'out with the old, in with the new – constantly'; the other to 'out with the new, in with the old – once and for all'.
For Žižek, we have all become accommodated to the permanent, relent-
less revolution of capitalism. As he argues, 'To put it in Hegel's terms,
the 'truth' of [the 1968] transgressive revolt against the Establishment is
the emergence of a new establishment in which transgression is part of
the game' (2001: 31). It may *seem* 'radical', but, he counters, 'in the generalized perversion of late capitalism, transgression itself is solicited'
(20); 'transgression itself is appropriated – even encouraged – by the
dominant institutions, the predominant doxa as a rule presents itself as a
subversive transgression' (2001a: 141). Needless to say, to Žižek's mind,
this rings true even for such supposedly radical, emancipatory or otherwise transformative intellectual efforts like the 'progressive' cultural
studies impulse towards inter-, post- and anti-disciplinarity that developed
'to overthrow the Eurocentrist curriculum' (2001: 215). To him, it is
merely another facet of the 'deconstructive' or 'deterritorialising' logic of
capital.

In this picture, then, the essential 'truth' of Bruce Lee and 'western' martial arts ideology and practice, along with cultural studies, Derridean deconstruction, and multiculturalism *tout court*, could basically be
characterised as exemplary – indeed, sublime – objects of ideology. In
this picture, too, therefore, despite all appearances to the contrary, and
despite any apparent ethico-political improvement of reduced racism,
cultural hybridity, apparent meetings of East and West, or anything else,
all that we meet in Bruce Lee (and 'multiculturalism') would be the ideological effects of commodification and ideological fetishisation (Žižek

2001: 12-15). This, for Žižek, is the effect and power of capitalism's 'real abstraction'. And this is why he lumps together and disdains so much multiculturalism, deconstructionism, new ageism, cultural-studies-ism and postmodernism as expressions of capitalist neoliberalist ideology. In this paradigm, Jacques Derrida, Stuart Hall and Bruce Lee – or at least their progeny – have a certain uncanny 'homology'. Thus, a problematic political implication arises. Deconstruction, cultural studies, and Bruce Lee may well be equivalent lapdogs of neoliberalism. Moreover, perhaps both culture and academia are 'political' or have 'implications' only inso-far as they are indices or symptoms of capitalism's unfettered reign. The popularity of martial arts is fetishistic, phantasmatic, and an unfortunate displacement away from authentic political acts or practices.

'Show me some of it!' The Way of Authenticity

The Žižekian position is, then, not only crudely Marxian (not dissimilar to the most pessimistic reading of Adorno and Horkheimer's 'Culture Indus-try' argument) but – surprisingly, perhaps – also philosophically Heideg-gerian. The relevance and significance of this claim will hopefully be-come clear, for Heidegger, as is well known, was deeply interested in the texts of oriental philosophy, in particular the *Tao Te Ching*. Specifically, Heidegger was very interested in the question of whether there could be an authentic *philosophical* 'bridging' across cultures – and, hence, whether there could be a 'genuine' or 'authentic' multiculturalism ungov-erned by a capitalist logic of commodification.

We see this interest most clearly in Heidegger's 'Dialogue on Lan-guage: Between a Japanese and an Inquirer' (1971). In this Socratic Dia-logue-style essay, the 'Inquirer' character (Heidegger) argues that 'a true encounter [between East Asian and] European existence is still not taking place, in spite of all assimilations and intermixtures' (1971: 3). Translated into the terms of this discussion, such a claim would be as much as to argue that Bruce Lee did not 'bridge' anything. To this assertion, Heideg-ger's obsequious 'Japanese' guest suggests: 'Perhaps ['a true encounter'] cannot take place' (3). The reason given for this impossibility is what the 'Dialogue' calls the problem of 'Europeanization'/Americanization – namely, the 'modern technicalization and industrialization of every continent, [from which] there would seem to be no escape any longer' (3). As such, this is *like* Žižek's point about capitalism. But Heidegger takes it elsewhere. Indeed, the Žižekian position is actually contained within and 'sublated' (i.e., completed and superseded) by the Heideggerian argument. For Žižek's argument is that capitalism is the condition of possibility and therefore of *impossibility*, and the motive force, of cultural (non)encounters today. However, for Heidegger, the fundamental problem – more fundamental than Žižek's capitalism – is what the 'Dialogue' calls 'European conceptual systems' (3). In the 'Dialogue' these are claimed to be essentially different from East Asian conceptual systems. But the difference is also material, as well as aesthetic. In fact, for Heidegger, here, the 'European conceptual systems' are said to be most pointedly present in that synthesis of 'Western' aesthetics and 'Western' technics: the film camera.

Accordingly, in Heidegger's text – or, at least according to his imaginary visitor – *all* film (even Kurosawa's film, *Rashomon* [1950], which the two characters discuss) is an index of an unavoidable Europeanization. This is because as soon as something – *anything* – is captured on camera, it is committed to a fully Western 'objectness' (Heidegger 1971: 17). This 'objectness', we are told, is apparently alien to all things essentially East Asian, because cinematic 'objectness' demands conventions of representation and conventions of *reading* representations that are irreducibly European. Thus, as Stella Sandford points out, Heidegger's 'Dialogue' is in fact fundamentally 'preoccupied with the issue of the possibility or impossibility of an East-West dialogue' (2003: 14). Scholars like Reinhard May have read this text 'as proof both of Heidegger's indebtedness to East Asian sources and his attempts to cover this over' (14). But, argues Sandford, 'it is equally plausibly read as a statement of Heidegger's belief in the fundamental and incommensurable *differences* between philosophical traditions, and of the extraordinary difficulty, if not the outright impossibility, of a true dialogue, despite the best intentions of the interlocutors' (14).

So, where does this leave us? It suggests that the fundamental problem with Žižek's position, despite the obvious moment of truth it contains, remains its economic reductionism – the reduction of *everything* to the pseudo-profound 'fact' (or objectness) that there *is* an economy and that things can and will be bought and sold. Yet, despite Žižek's *ad hominem* insinuations, it is important to note that it is certainly *not* actually the economy that cuts off the possibility of 'authenticity' or that compromises any 'encounter'. Rather, the problem is with the very concept itself, what Derrida would once have called its 'logocentrism', plus its essentialism. Authenticity, conventionally construed, is impossible. Similarly, the problem with this Heideggerian position is, as Sandford clearly points out, that in fact there *is* no 'essential East' or 'essential West' that are somehow two coherent identities as if tragically cut off from each other. There is only a coherent and distinct 'East' and 'West' in the fantasy productions of reductive, essentialist, Eurocentric and orientalist or occidentalist paradigms. Indeed, Sandford reminds us, *any* interest that Heidegger might have had in '*the*' East is purely an index of his investment in fantasies about '*the*' West.

'These styles become institutes':
The (Political) Institution of Culture

Why does this matter? Its significance relates to the political status of events of institution: it is the question of what passes for knowledge and what sociopolitical effects that may have. If this seems too grandiose a claim, at the very least it means that a different theoretical paradigm is required for the cultural studies of martial arts than a Žižekian non-approach to culture. A straightforwardly *psychoanalytic* approach might tend to universalise and depoliticise, independent of context. A straightforwardly economistic approach is insufficient, to the extent that it descends into equally universalistic mantras about the delusions and simulacra of capital. Both of these mutually incompatible and ultimately incoherent failings are arguably present – indeed, perhaps as the key ingredients – in Žižek's approach. As such, Žižek's approach to culture and politics may actually be said to be fundamentally anathema to cultural studies (and political studies), even if on first glance his writings sometimes appear to be a kind of political or cultural studies. This is not to say that the insights of psychoanalysis or Marxism are to be rejected. On the contrary, they are necessary – 'necessary but insufficient', as deconstructionists used to say – at least as long as they overlook the institutional problematic, the broadly Gramscian post-Marxist matter of the contingency and power of institution. Žižek simply dismisses this when he claims 'the "truth" of [1968's] transgressive revolt against the Establishment is the emergence of a new establishment in which transgression is part of the game' (2001a: 31). For Žižek, the fundamental backdrop to this constant change is the supposedly unified entity called capitalism. With this, he renounces not only the political propensities of culture and institutions but also the propensities of both politics and study themselves.

What is the alternative to such renunciation? Appropriately enough, it is actually very enlightening to turn from Žižek to one of Bruce Lee's own tantalising formulations. Discussing the martial arts of his day, Lee argued that:

> Each man belongs to a style which claims to possess truth to the ex-clusion of all other styles. These styles become institutes with their expla nations of the 'Way', dissecting and isolating the harmony of firmness and gentleness, establishing rhythmic forms as the particular state of their techniques.
>
> Instead of facing combat in its suchness, then, most systems of martial art accumulate a 'fancy mess' that distorts and cramps their practitioners and distracts them from the actual reality of combat, which is simple and direct. Instead of going immediately to the heart of things, flowery forms (organized despair) and artificial techniques are ritualistically practised to simulate actual combat. Thus, instead of 'being' in combat these practitio-ners are 'doing' something 'about' combat. (Lee 1975: 14)

This insight can surely be taken seriously. However, the mistake that Bruce Lee made was to believe that what he constructed actually succeeded in going 'directly' and 'immediately to the heart of things'. That is, Lee too (like Žižek) falls into the trap of believing that his own constructions are 'objective', free from 'institution', free from belief, from theory, from myth and fiction – as if simply 'true'. But there is no getting away from the contingency of institution, the contingency of cul-ture. Everything is instituted. And institutions are consequential. As we have clearly seen, Bruce Lee was from the origin a postmodern, interdis-ciplinary, multicultural and – despite Žižekian dismissiveness of such things – *consequential founder of many forms of institution*. The 'event' of Bruce Lee was clearly not *simple*. Perhaps not 'deep' or 'enigmatic' in any romantic sense, it was nevertheless multiple and complex, simultane-ously mythic and real, both theoretical and practical, equally imaginary and institutional. So, *vis-à-vis* the martial arts and questions of cultural knowledge more widely, what is clear is that the approach must always be supplemented with the awareness that 'an institution... is not merely a few walls or some outer structures surrounding, protecting, guaranteeing or restricting the freedom of our work; it is also and already the structure of our interpretation' (Derrida 1992: 22-3). So the question will always remain: what's your style?

Chapter 2
Film—Fantasy:
The Communication of
Screen Violence

Each man belongs to a style which claims to possess truth to the exclu-
sion of all other styles. These styles become institutes with their explanations
of the 'Way', dissecting and isolating the harmony of firmness and gentle-
ness, establishing rhythmic forms as the particular state of their techniques.
Instead of facing combat in its suchness, then, most systems of martial art
accumulate a 'fancy mess' that distorts and cramps their practitioners and
distracts them from the actual reality of combat, which is simple and direct.
Instead of going immediately to the heart of things, flowery forms (organized
despair) and artificial techniques are ritualistically practiced to simulate
actual combat. Thus, instead of 'being' in combat these practitioners are
'doing' something 'about' combat.
- Bruce Lee (Lee 1975: 14)

Keeping it Real

The first (and enduring) discourse that sprung up about Bruce Lee in the
1970s was overwhelmingly dominated by one word. This word was ut-
tered in reverential, awestruck tones, and printed in emphatic italics. That
word was *real*. Bruce Lee was *real* (Hunt 2003; Inosanto 1980; Miller
2000; Thomas 1994/2000). This did not, of course, refer to his acting in
general; but rather to his screen *action* – or what was believed to be 'behind' it or 'beyond' it. His fighting was received *as real*. Or, at least, as
realistic. But more than this, the sense was (and widely remains) that

what was taken to be realistic choreography in the films reflected or re-lied on the real ability of the real man. And, what is more – of more value than a singular demonstration of a singular talent – Bruce Lee appeared to speak a truth about reality that offered lessons to everyone: 'a positive pedagogy, something more than Orientalist mumbo-jumbo', says Meaghan Morris (2001: 175); something more than mere spectacle or image; actually, rather, 'lessons in using aesthetics understood as a prac-tical discipline', a way 'to gain access to aesthetic power in bad existen-tial conditions'; not just an impossible fantasy but a promise of a way to 'act them out in the world' (176). According to film critics from Ackbar Abbas (1997) to Leon Hunt (2003) and beyond, the initial and initializing consensus was that 'Bruce Lee placed a new emphasis on individual, au-thentic virtuosity, displacing trampoline-aided stars … and embodying the "stuntman as hero"' (Hunt 2003: 23). But, it is crucial to add, it was the belief that his choreography appeared to speak something like the truth about actual physical fighting that enabled Bruce Lee to forge a par-ticular relation between film spectatorship and cultural fantasy. This is not fantasy in the sense of a daydream or a pipe-dream, but fantasy in the (initially psychoanalytic) sense of a belief that is lived, a belief that in-forms, sustains and even guides real-life practices.

For, even though it was cinematically mediated, the entrance of the dragon was widely taken to be the entrance of something *real* – and 'real' in many or even all of the senses given to this word by *The Oxford Eng-lish Dictionary*. Thus: 'Having an objective existence; actually existing as a thing'; or 'having an existence in fact and not merely in appearance, thought, or language', or even, more philosophically-speaking, 'as having an absolute and necessary, in contrast to a merely contingent, existence'; that which is 'opposed to imaginary, or impossible' (such as *'real time'*, which is of course 'the actual time during which a process or event oc-curs'); an 'actually existing or present as a state or quality of things; hav-ing a foundation in fact; actually occurring or happening'. Furthermore, this real also carried a strong sense of real as 'natural, as opposed to arti-ficial or depicted'. It is 'that [which] is actually present or involved, as opposed to *apparent, ostensible*, etc.' It is 'the actual (thing or person); that properly bears the name'. The *'real thing'* is 'the thing itself, as con-trasted with imitations or counterfeits; […] the "genuine article"'. Fur-thermore, this real also has the sense of 'sincere, straightforward, [or] honest'; possibly even 'true or loyal to another'; and certainly – so the consensus runs – 'Free from nonsense, affectation, or pretence'; something 'genuine'; and 'aware of, or in touch with, real life'; 'Consisting of actual things'; 'Corresponding to actuality; true'. 'A real thing; a thing having (or conceived as having) a real existence, either in the ordinary or in a metaphysical sense'. 'That which actually exists, contrasted (*a*) with a copy, counterfeit, etc., (*b*) with what is abstract or notional'. 'Really, truly, actually; in reality'.

Bruce Thomas's account of Lee expresses a lot of this clearly. As he puts it, 'to see Bruce Lee on film is to see a human body brought to a level of supreme ability through a combination of almost supernatural talent and a lifetime of hard work' (1994/2000: 258). Stephen Teo agrees (whilst adding an essentially ethnic dimension to the discussion): 'Chinese audiences take pride in the image Lee projects as a superb fighting specimen of manhood who derives his status from "traditional" skills' (1997: 114). Of course, although Teo emphasizes the nationalistic implications of Lee's films – and quite aside from the rather less than 'traditional' or less than 'Chinese' characteristics of Lee's martial arts, which we will return to in subsequent chapters – what surely becomes apparent to *all* audiences in watching Bruce Lee is 'that his kung fu skills are not the results of supernatural strength or special effects'; rather, audiences are *shown* that 'this skill is achievable, a result of fitness and rigorous training':

> A scene in *The Way of the Dragon* illustrates the first principle of discipline and training in kung fu: before his gladiatorial bout with Chuck Norris in the Roman Coliseum, Lee warms up physically, stretches his muscles, cracks all his joints, reaches for his feet. Lee shows himself to be a specimen of thorough training, a true-to-life fighter and not the imaginary creation of an action movie director. (Teo 1997: 114)

Thus, such a perspective, whether coming out of the mouth of someone such as Thomas (who Teo would regard as offering a 'Western' perception) or Teo (who presumably therefore is offering an 'Eastern' perspective, or rather, a perspective which putatively 'comprehends' both), is nevertheless a perspective which 'sees Bruce Lee as someone who was both impressive onscreen and "real"' (Hunt 2003: 28). But what is meant by 'real' in this context? In the context of most debates about film and the representation of martial arts, the word is closely related to the notion of 'authenticity'. This word, too, carries many and varied possible connotations, of course; and its analysis often reveals that 'authenticity' – unless very highly circumscribed and qualified – may actually be something of an impossible notion, strictly speaking, at least in the cultural or representational field.

For how does one decide what is an authentic 'thing' and then represent it 'authentically'? All things are complex, hybrid and never simply quite what one might want them to be (Lee's 'traditional' 'Chinese' martial arts, of course, were at least equally as informed by boxing, fencing, and taekwondo as by wing chun or Shaolin – which Lee allegedly had remarkably little formal training in, 'traditional' or otherwise), in any case. Moreover, all representations *add* something, *emphasize* something, *omit* something, *alter* something. But, as there is no getting away from representation in the first (and last) place, this leads to a problem. How does one represent the real 'authentically'? Moreover, if all thought, language, writing, sound and visual marks are themselves types of representation, then can we ever be said to have authentic and real access to the authentic and real? Isn't it already a representation? In this case, isn't it already therefore 'inauthentic'?

Jacques Derrida called this 'the problematic of the sign and of writing' in relation to 'the thing itself, the present thing', where 'thing' might mean either 'meaning or referent' (1982: 9). Thus, says Derrida, 'When we cannot grasp or show the thing, state the present, the being-present, when the present cannot be presented, we signify, we go through the detour of the sign' (9). But, as he famously goes on to demonstrate, this 'detour' is necessary and inevitable. Signification may *seem* secondary. But it is in fact primary, inevitable and constitutive. Of course, this interminable situation, wherein representation never quite *gets* 'it' and never quite 'measures up' to some sense of the 'truth' of things, can lead to a sense of frustration – everything seems 'not quite this' and 'not quite that' but always also more and 'other'. It can also lead to a kind of 'negative theology' in many contexts: a belief that no representation can adequately do justice to the truth, the whole truth, and nothing but the truth. Thus, as Rey Chow notes in a related discussion of representations of 'China', for instance:

> The dismissal of things that are 'packaged' here is part of a deeply in-
> grained belief in the absolute originality and difference of 'China'. If Chi-

nese intellectuals often say that 'China' is beyond what 'foreigners' can understand, this saying is, I think, already a figure of speech that simply makes use of the convenient presence of 'foreigners' to gesture toward something else. What is really meant is not that foreigners cannot understand 'China' but that 'China' is that ultimate something – that ultimate essence beyond representation. (Chow 1995: 50)

At the very least, concepts of reality and authenticity are always going to have to be quite strenuously defined and circumscribed by caveats and qualifications, and it is unlikely that a fully satisfying sense of having 'captured' that certain 'it' anything like 'fully' will ever be attained. As such, a consideration of *representation per se* is both appropriate and even called for within any discussion of reality or authenticity. It is also why, according to Hunt, 'debates about "authenticity" have recurred both in Chinese critiques of kung fu films and in English-speaking subcultures surrounding Hong Kong cinema, although with different emphases' (2003: 21). For, whilst on the one hand, notions of realism and authenticity might be approached simply in terms of 'editing, undercranking and wirework' (22), on the other hand, Hong Kong cinema itself 'has largely been theorised in terms of the hybrid, the transnational, the postmodern and the postcolonial', and 'none of these are authenticity-friendly concepts' (21-2). So, particularly in cultural-theory-infested waters, any discussion of 'authenticity' will be very likely to feel a pressure to respond in ways that are more complex than those easy forms of perfunctory evaluation which proceed in terms of making claims about 'real' martial arts practice versus cinematic 'tricks' (like editing, undercranking and wirework).

Rather, the cultural complexity of the question of authenticity keeps coming back to haunt us. It can be said to infuse and permeate even supposedly 'mere' technical considerations. For instance, as Hunt observes, all popular and academic debates about authenticity in martial arts film have 'been intensified by the increasing visibility of technology and special effects in fight choreography and its implications for a genre with a particular investment in the "real"' (21). Therefore, as a key claim about Bruce Lee relates to his putative realism and the realistic character of his choreography, then 'cultural' questions return in the range of interpretations about Bruce Lee's very realism: on the one hand, critics like Abbas regard Lee's 'authenticity' and 'realism' as testifying to his 'authentic and heroic Chinese identity' (Abbas 1997: 29; Hunt 2003: 22). On the other hand, critics such as Chiao Hsiung-ping propose that Lee's 'avoidance of special effects and fondness for long shot/long take shooting testifies to his cross-cultural credentials, [and demonstrate therefore] a triumph of Western "realism" over "Oriental fantasies"' (Hunt 2003: 22). This latter argument may recall the Heideggerian argument about the cultural effects of the domination of Western technicity as manifested in the film camera which we met in the previous chapter and to which we will return again below, or to 'absolute difference' arguments. Indeed, the evocation of a 'Western realism' to be opposed to 'Oriental fantasy' may simply refer us to orientalism. But, we must bear in mind Chow's argument that the familiar 'dismissal of things that are "packaged" … is part of a deeply ingrained belief in the absolute originality and difference of "China"': a belief in an 'ultimate essence beyond representation' (Chow 1995: 50)) Thus, wherever we enter this discussion, we are always going to be drawn back to the fundamental problematics of 'representation', of 'communication', and indeed even of 'culture' per se. This chapter will accordingly enter into this fray in due course, but in a way that is appropriate to and organised by our object of interest here.

Hunt does likewise, firstly by relating the changing inflections and emphases of authenticity debates to the complex relationship between external political factors and the cultural imaginary. Thus, he proposes, 'while readings focused on Hong Kong's 1997 reunification with China can be simplistic and overdetermined, it seems significant that "authenticity" has diminished as Hong Kong has embraced a more hybridised, postcolonial identity, both "Chinese" and not' (2003: 22). Indeed, writing just before the 1997 reunification with China, Abbas suggested that in 'kung fu films of the nineties, two realizations have sunk in'. The first is that 'it is no longer possible to appeal with any conviction to some vague notion of Chineseness, as China itself may turn out to be the future colonizer, in fact if not in name, once the present one has departed'. The second is that 'it is no longer possible to see local developments as separable or proceeding in isolation from global developments' (Abbas 1997: 31). Abbas may have a valid point that during 'undoubtedly the most important years in Hong Kong's short history' (29), the period from 1970 to 1995, 'we see all the more clearly the unstable shape of coloniality inscribed in these films' (29). Nevertheless, changing interpretations of authenticity may well reflect ongoing dialectics and discursive reactions not only organised by 'external' global politics but also by 'internal' developments in the global cinematic intertext – developments, that is, in cinema in general, and perhaps representational techniques and styles in particular.

As Meaghan Morris argues, in a provocative response to critics who regard film as some kind of 'mirror', arguably 'films reflect on looking, not reality at large' (2001: 172). To clarify her claims, Morris makes use of Sam Rohdie's argument in 'Sixth Form Film Teaching in Hong Kong' that the cinema, primarily, is 'not a commentary on life, but a commentary on cinema' (qtd. in Morris 2001: 172). As such, Rohdie and Morris invert and displace many facile understandings of the nature of cinematic representations as 'reflections'. This is of course extremely useful. But, as Morris goes on to reiterate, it remains necessary to proceed to invert and displace this exclusively cinematic focus once more, and to plug it back into the wider cultural relations and effects that it has been Morris' aim first to complicate, by provisionally refusing to rush into discussions about 'reality'. Morris returns us to the question of the 'articulation' (connections, relations, reticulations) within which films work and play by way of a consideration of culture as pedagogy (to which we will return at the end of this chapter). Similarly, we will commence our own consideration of cultural relations and effects by way of a detour through considerations of representation, fantasy, interpellation, and indeed what might be called processes of 'cultural translation' (Chow 1995: 182-4).

Seeing the Violence

In order to broach all of this, first let us consider some cinematic representational techniques and styles which, at the very least, have influenced cinematic representational techniques and styles, but which may also have wider cultural ramifications. When it comes to film fighting, Hunt proposes that there have been 'three rough phases in the development of martial arts choreography since kung fu's global impact in the 1970s' (2003: 23). The first movement was Bruce Lee's new 'individual, authentic virtuosity, displacing trampoline-aided stars' (23). The second was a 'shift towards the choreographer as hero' (23). And the third, 'initiated by Producer-Director Tsui Hark and choreographer-director Ching Siu-tung', devolved on a 'mastery of technology'. This can be seen when 'special effects became much more ubiquitous in 1990s "new wave" films like *Once Upon a Time in China,* which offered a fast-cut, hi-tech spectacle'. This genre change involved 'the prevalence of wires to make fighters defy gravity [which] led some fans to re-dub the genre "wire-fu"' (24), and meant that it became possible to 'choreograph non-martial artists [as if they were martial artists] through a combination of special effects and doubles' (24).

Throughout all phases, it is possible to regard martial arts and action fight choreography, as well as the psychic structure of its fandom, as entailing what Hunt calls 'a seemingly impossible investment in both documentary realism and fantasy' (28). In the case of Bruce Lee's choreography, this takes the form of 'a desire for transparent mediation, championing long takes and wide framing as a guarantee of the "real"' (2003: 35). The effect is often one in which (apparently) 'the camera acted as a reporter, recording reality not altering it' (Davidson as qtd. in Hunt 2003: 35). This, we might say is why, for instance, Bruce Lee's fight with Chuck Norris in the Roman Coliseum is regarded reverently as 'real' – or as a real to be revered. Lee's 'corporeal authenticity' is demonstrated through what Hunt calls a 'no-tricks aesthetic' (37) which achieves an effect of documentary realism, even though the representation is far from 'innocent':

> Cheng Yu contrasts it with Lo Wei's fight scenes, which, he argues, made greater use of editing and close-ups to 'convey the impact of the fight' (1984: 25). The Coliseum fight favours long and medium shots, so that 'the style is closer to capturing the *fight-performance* or representing a reportage of a fight from the ring-side' (25). But Lee's shooting style is not quite as 'dispassionate' as Cheng makes it sound. He uses slow motion. Like Lo Wei, he uses subjective camera techniques – Lee kicks into the camera and stares 'us' out. He uses constructive editing, so that we get to see kicks delivered in long shot but actually *land* in close-up. Sections of the fight do conform to Cheng's description – a sequence of low kicks used to deflect Norris' attacks, a slow motion 'dance' that consists of a long take showing Lee gliding and prancing, constantly out of his hirsute foe's reach. The preceding fight against Bob Wall and Wong In-Sik uses the shooting style popular at Seasonal studios from the mid-1970s – zoom shots used to conceal cuts, the action predominantly framed in long shot. No scene captures Lee's speed more impressively – at a National Film Theatre Screening in 1999, audiences still gasped and applauded. On two occasions, Lee and his opponent initiate kicks simultaneously – his land before the other's have risen above waist-height. The scene averages three to four moves per shot, but their speed and accuracy are breathtaking. (37)

Of course, documentary realism is only half the story. To perceive something of the simultaneous and contrary investment in fantasy, a comparison is helpful. We might consider, for instance, the fight scene between Daniel Cleaver (Hugh Grant) and Mark Darcy (Daniel Firth) in *Bridget Jones' Diary* (2001). Although this scene uses many of the same techniques as those Hunt describes above, quite unlike Lee's or other martial arts fights, the *Bridget Jones* action scene here is constructed as comic. This is so even though one might reasonably propose that the latter has moments of much more verisimilitude or vraisemblance than any Bruce Lee or *Bourne Identity* (2002) fight sequence: there are, for instance, mistakes, misses and clumsiness. But here, this 'realism' (conveyed through their apparently *realistic incompetence*) is what helps to make Grant and Firth's fight comic. Of course, this comedy is amplified by their obsessive politeness, or what may be called their 'typically English' manners, plus the witty commentary of the assembled Chorus-like witnesses. Thus, the start of the fight is presented as comical because of the presumably preposterous spectacle of an upper-class English 'gent' formally throwing down the working class pub gauntlet ('Alright Cleaver, outside!') in a posh dinner party in an extremely well-heeled area of London. Cleaver responds with incredulity: 'I'm sorry? "Outside"? Should I bring my duelling pistols or my sword?' As the fight starts in the street, one of the dinner guests immediately runs across the street to a nearby restaurant, opens the door and cries out with delight to rally all of the diners there: 'Fight!' he shouts breathlessly. Many in the restaurant are evidently immediately interested. 'Well quick!', he implores them, 'It's a *real* fight!', throwing his head back and rolling his eyes in joy as he emphasizes the word 'real'. Like schoolchildren, many of the staff and some of the diners in the restaurant pour out into the street to watch what is presented as a preposterous and highly rare treat.

We rejoin the fight to hear Cleaver asking for a break, for a rest. In one of the many moments of ridiculously hyperbolic English gentility, Darcy allows him this. Ever the cad, Cleaver abuses this good grace by hitting him over the back of the head with a metal dustbin lid, about which the assembled audience cry 'Cheat! Cheat!' Everyone here, therefore, is caricaturally, stereotypically English, as fantasized by the mind of the most Jane Austin-, Shakespeare-, Dickens- or Sherlock Holmes-infused touristic consciousness imaginable.

The protagonists go on to throw kicks that miss their target, plus kicks that have no apparent target and are actually aborted half way through; they grapple clumsily, and fail to gain any kind of control or dominance at any stage of the fight. Neither is able to find opportunities, dominate or clinch victory other than in moments that are 'outside' the fight. Firth's character, Darcy, lands a knockout punch only after they have agreed to end the fight: they have both agreed ('Enough!') and have separated, exhausted. But as Darcy turns to leave, Cleaver mutters an insult, which causes Darcy to turn around and hit him one last, decisive time. The fight itself is interrupted at several points in order for the characters to display 'typically English' manners, such as apologizing for the disruption and offering to pay for the damage and mess caused in the restaurant, as well as waiting while a birthday cake is ceremoniously presented to a diner along with a public round of 'Happy Birthday'. All of which seeks to construct the fight as ridiculous, both technically and in terms of the punctilious manners and mannerisms of the protagonists. The fight is deliberately anti-action-choreography (except perhaps for the very final punch, whose knockout consequences are dramatized in slow motion), and is made farcical through the combatants' incongruous efforts to preserve decorum and politesse even during their highly untoward transgression of polite behaviour. The entire event is mock heroic farce.

The event of Bruce Lee's fight to the death against Chuck Norris in *Way of the Dragon*, on the other hand, is regarded reverently by many martial arts fans. This is surely because it offers extended voyeuristic and fetishistic focus on Lee's body and also because it presents us with one of Lee's performative 'lessons' 'about' martial arts. At first, Lee is very rigid, structured, 'formal', and hence, for his opponent, he is predictable. But then he changes to a much more 'fluid' style – first bouncing lightly on his toes like a boxer, then nimbly evading and parrying Norris' attacks for quite a while, until Norris punches and kicks himself to a state of fatigue. At this point Lee turns from defense to attack by 'interrupting' or 'breaking into' Norris' own formal and plodding rhythm with unconventional and anarchic moves. When Norris realizes *why* he is being beaten, he tries to emulate Lee's 'free' (Muhammad Ali-like) bouncing. But in doing so, he has effectively fallen into a trap. For he has not trained like this, having been stultified by formal karate training: hence Lee is now even more able to break through Norris' first attempts to improvise a free rhythm and structure. The effects are devastating: Lee breaks Norris's arm and then his leg, entirely incapacitating him. But Norris insists on trying to fight on. As if acknowledging that this futile effort to continue constitutes some kind of point of great honour (he'd rather die than give up), Lee is apparently obliged to kill Norris. Thereafter, he covers Norris' corpse with the top of his karate gi, lays his black belt 'respectfully' upon it, and, as if genuflecting down on one knee, places his right fist within his left palm and stares into the distance – a gesture which condenses allusions to both Christian prayer and to the standard Chinese martial arts bow (one fist in the other palm represents yin and yang, and is a formal gesture of respect in Chinese martial arts. It is also, of course, the greeting prominently given by Lee and Lau in the early pedagogical scene in *Enter the Dragon*.)

In terms of these fights, then, *Way of the Dragon* and *Bridget Jones' Diary* may seem very different. Upon closer inspection, however, they are actually rather interesting mirror images. For, the main things that make the *Bridget Jones* fight comical are the situationally-incongruous formality of the fight's initiation (an upper class gent throwing down a bar-room gauntlet), the incompetence of the protagonists, their ridiculous adherence to manners, and the dialogue of the 'Chorus' (Bridget and her friends). *Way of the Dragon* is constructed as if to be profoundly serious and moving. Yet it is constructed by way of a remarkably similar structure: the fight (it must be recalled, a fight about ownership of a restaurant), in the 20th Century, is located in the ruins of the Coliseum in Rome, of all places; the protagonists arrive wearing full martial arts uniforms (in public), engage in ritualistic and yet distinctly camp warm-ups (several times, Norris shakes his blonde hair almost coquettishly); they adhere to manners that are, arguably, ridiculous; and the attention given to the fight by the camera is supplemented by shots of a kitten, running around, meowing, and playing with a toy. To say the least, one has to have a very particular investment in a very particular fantasy *not* to find the Bruce Lee scene at least equally as preposterous and comical as the *Bridget Jones* scene.

Furthermore, whilst the point of this comparison is not simply to adjudicate or make strong claims about verisimilitude or authenticity by way of supposed reference to some 'real yardstick' or invocation of 'the truth' of fighting, it seems pertinent to tarry awhile with the fact that

Cleaver and Darcy's flailing, stumbling, missing and grappling represents an element of fighting that, as it were, is *unspoken* or excluded, if not actively repressed from much martial arts fight choreography.[6] For, martial arts choreography is overwhelmingly represented in accordance with the dictates of a certain fantasy about fighting, which is precisely not sullied by the ugly possibility of throwing techniques that miss, struggling unglamorously, tripping over, rolling around on the ground, or being hit and involuntarily crying out 'Ouch! That *really* hurt!' Thus, Hunt directs us to Brooks Landon's (1992) notion of 'the aesthetics of ambivalence' (Hunt 2003: 28) that permeates martial arts films' choreographies. This, through the complex interplay of physicality, the desire for the real, its construction through generic techniques, technical 'trickery', set-pieces, clichés, and so on, boils down to the peculiarity of 'accepting the "fake" as "real"' (28).

This acceptance of the fake as real is testimony to the 'seemingly impossible' investment in both documentary realism and fantasy that characterizes the organisation of martial arts spectatorship, subjectivity and desire. But what is its significance? Accepting the fake as real is of course something that is done rather a lot. It is done over and over again, temporarily, by viewers who are more or less deliberately playing the Wordsworthian game of suspending their disbelief. But it is also what martial arts fans and practitioners do in accepting Bruce Lee's or any other piece of martial choreography as 'real' or 'authentic'. For, this aesthetics of ambivalence, with its impossible double investments, actually infuses discourses, practices and orientations of martial artists themselves. Therefore, a simultaneous investment in realism and fantasy is not simply 'impossible'. Or rather, impossibility does not stop it from happening. Quite the contrary: it is prevalent. This 'impossible investment' is something that has to be sustained by a cinematic negotiation of these two conflicting demands which actually pull representations in two opposite directions: one pull is toward an excess of visibility (showing in great

---

[6] For a consideration of the potential significance of the 'unspoken', see Spivak's proposed use of Macherey's 'formula for the interpretation of ideology': 'What is important in a work is what it does not say. This is not the same as the careless notion 'what it refuses to say', although that would in itself be interesting: a method might be built on it, with the task of measuring silences, whether acknowledged or unacknowledged. But rather this, what the work cannot say is important, because there the elaboration of the utterance is carried out, in a journey to silence...' (qtd. in Spivak 1988: 286)

detail) while the other is to a dearth of visibility (concealment, obfuscation, hiding). For, *vis-à-vis* martial fantasy, *too much* documentary realism arguably has the same effect as not enough. This refers to what Ackbar Abbas calls the 'point of *degeneration* of the genre, the moment when the genre self-destructs' (1997: 32). Abbas, however, is only concerned with, as it were, 'one end' or one version of the dissolution of the phantasmatic. As he writes of (what is in his opinion the over-technologized) film *Ashes of Time* (1994):

> It is no longer a choreography of human bodies in motion that we see. In fact, we do not know what it is we are seeing. Things have now been speeded up to such an extent that what we find is only a composition of light and color in which all action has dissolved – a kind of abstract expressionism or action painting. It is not possible, therefore, to discern who is doing what to whom: The heroic space of Bruce Lee is now a *blind space* (one of the four heroes in fact is going blind); moreover, it is a blind space that comes from an *excess* of light and movement, that is to say, an excess of Tsui Hark-style special effects. *Ashes of Time* gives us a kind of double dystopia, where heroism loses its raison d'être and special effects lose their air of optimism and exhilaration. Wong's film marks a point of *degeneration* of the genre, the moment when the genre self-destructs. The idea of presence and authenticity implied in the ethos of heroism is subverted, and the hope of happy inscription in a technology-based global utopia implied in the optimistic use of special effects is imploded. (Abbas 1997: 32)

This sort of transformative moment, or movement, can arguably be seen in many other films, genres and even media. For instance, one might consider examples as diverse as the battle scenes in the Hollywood film *Gladiator* (2000), the supposedly tense scenes in *Sunshine* (2007), or even the scenes demonstrating the preparation of food in TV cookery programmes such as *The F Word* (Channel 4, 2008). Up until around the time of *Gladiator*, mainstream battle choreography had been dominated by a kind of sharp-focus realism. The battle scenes in the earlier *Braveheart* (1995) or *Saving Private Ryan* (1998), for example, graphically depict every event of entry and exit wounding, the details of each maiming blow and event of bodily destruction in their large-scale battle scenes. Films such as *Blade* (1998) and *The Matrix* (1999) take high fidelity visibility further, such that the fight sequences often become veritable studies of speed, anatomies of movement through ultra-slow motion and the arcing movement of the viewpoint around slowed down events such as a bullet's path or the execution of a flying kick ('bullet time', as it is called). But *Gladiator* opts instead for blurring, for the frustration of vision. Our relation to the events depicted is one in which the camera and editing behave as if we are embedded as confused, scared, and overwhelmed participants. Such blurring has been combined with intricate editing to speed up fight exchanges in *The Bourne Identity* (2002) and subsequent sequels. Indeed, the increased speed and blurring of focus, achieved through editing and excessive focus on very small details, is equally present in recent choreographies of food preparation in cookery programmes, as I mentioned above. In all cases, what is apparent, fundamentally, is that the technical supplement (so-called 'special effects') is always at work as an ineradicable and necessary supplement that is constitutive of the representation of the real.

Another end of the dissolution or collapse of the genre might be identified where ever there is an *excess* of documentary realism. This can take many possible forms, from the embarrassing spectacle of the choreography of a film like *The Silent Flute* (aka *Circle of Iron*) (1978), in which Richard Moore's direction is unable to conceal / is responsible for revealing David Carradine and Jeff Cooper's apparently 'authentic' inability to do anything other than make preposterous pseudo-oriental pseudo-martial arts 'shapes'. Another limit of the genre can be seen in *The Karate Kid II* (1986), in which Daniel Laruso is meant to have mastered an advanced/obscure 'drum' technique. In both of these films, the camera observes the action in wide and long shots until the moment of the putative delivery of nebulous techniques. In *The Silent Flute*, nonsensical 'shapes' move into arbitrary and nonsensical non-techniques and destroy the fantasy. In *The Karate Kid II*, however, the moment of delivery of the drum technique – which apparently involves yielding to the other's force and returning it multiplied by way of a deft movement of the torso – is shown only through close ups on the face and chest. The technique is not shown or seen – so completely in fact that you might say *The Karate Kid II* is all about a technique that it does not show. As such, it is surely a strong contender for film that has been most structured by an 'absent presence'.

One problem with *The Silent Flute* (and *Karate Kid II*) is the problem of representing superlative and supreme fighting in the mode of documentary realism when you do not have superlative and supreme fighters or 'special effects'. Although it might seem that the only thing that could have saved *The Silent Flute* on any level would have been the presence of its original co-writer, the deceased Bruce Lee, it remains equally the case that the 'effects' of any film always derive from the work of its representational techniques. The cinematography is in fact more important than martial techniques in the representation of violence or fight sequences. The use of jump cuts, splicing, short shots, shifting camera angles and so on can enable anyone or any scene to seem more impressive, more dramatic, and paradoxically more 'realistic'. This is shown extremely well in the rooftop training scene in *Ghost Dog: The Way of The Samurai* (1999), in which Forrest Whittaker struts, skips and slashes with knives in a quite possibly random manner, but which the rapid intercutting of the editing manages to propose is some kind of advanced, subtle and difficult martial arts form. Indeed, perhaps the prime mainstream example of the constitutive work of the technological supplement (the editing) can be seen in *The Bourne Identity*.

The first time we see Jason Bourne fight is a scene in which he disarms and incapacitates two Russian police officers with startling rapidity. It is extremely impressive. However, we actually see very little of the fight scene, as the camera is not a simple passive observer of the scene, but is actually embedded within it: the camera shifts and blurs as the angles jump rapidly from one technique to the next. The scene was evidently shot in several extremely short bursts. It is the editing that reconstitutes the disparate parts as a rapid and skilful fight scene. But it is also the involved point of view deployment of the camera itself as-if being a part of the action. If you were there, would you catch all the details? Or would you actually see more of a blur than clean and crisp events? This acceleration and blurring of the choreography characterizes all of the *Bourne* films. In the third *Bourne* film, Jason's fight with the 'Asset' in an apartment is so blurred as to make distinguishing any particular exchange or technique virtually impossible. This has become one of the standard forms of representing hand-to-hand combat in Hollywood films at least since *Gladiator*. If we compare *Gladiator* with *Braveheart*, this paradigm shift is very apparent. In the battles in *Braveheart* one sees every sword stab, knife slash, arrow pierce and club thump land on every pugilist's bursting body. In *Gladiator*, however, one sees virtually none. This boils down to the status of the camera on and/or within the action. In the former, the camera sees. In the latter, the camera endows us with all the characteristics of the role played by a panicking extra in a disaster movie.

What this technological and generic technique does is conjure up the violence *in lieu* of any choreography. Had *The Silent Flute* been able to employ this device, perhaps the end result would not have been so awful. Similarly, perhaps we might have been spared the embarrassment of such films as *The Karate Kid II*, in which the lack of any comparably catchy move to the first *Karate Kid*'s 'crane technique' was glossed over simply by filming all of the fights in head and torso close-up. Thus, instead of *seeing any techniques*, what was shown were the supposed *effects* of the unseen technique on protagonists' facial expressions and bodily shocks, twists and convulsions caused by techniques we have not actually seen.

Perhaps the problem with such films is the attempt to represent a *principle*. In *Dragon: The Bruce Lee Story* (1993), Bruce Lee's famous guest-spot at Ed Parker's karate competition is depicted as a peculiar event in which a belligerent Bruce Lee taunts and goads his audience by telling them that he has come up with a new martial art that is not encumbered by any of the constraints of *their* martial arts. The pantomime-like audience boo and hiss. Lee throws down the gauntlet: he'll beat anyone in 60 seconds. When the time comes for the film to demonstrate Lee's radical new innovations, what is shown is nothing new at all: freedom from constraint is represented through the form of moving around between exchanges in a 'fluid' or 'skippy' manner – a pale imitation of the way Lee actually moves when he changes style in the Coliseum fight in *Way of the Dragon*.

'Although there's little doubt [Lee] understood the necessity of coordinated offensive and defensive movement, preached it and wanted to move beautifully,' as Miller implacably points out, 'compared to boxers he was not a consummate mover' (2000: 162). What this meant was that although 'he was pretty good at in and out, forward and backward movements', the problem was that 'he pranced instead of gliding ... which sacrifices power while magnifying the effects of blows with which your opponent(s) catch(es) you'. Moreover, 'he had little idea how effectively to accomplish more subtle side-to-side movements' (162) – a technical limitation which means that, 'as has been shown when martial-arts trained fighters attempt to box professionally, their lack of lateral mobility and a general upper body stiffness often helps to sit them down hard on the seat of their jammies' (162). The fact that Bruce Lee reportedly wanted to rectify *precisely* such weaknesses makes it deeply ironic that these very same weaknesses are *precisely* what Miller says remain – or are even amplified – by Bruce Lee's 'emancipated' style. The problem of representing a principle is perhaps the problem of representing something that cannot literally be 'seen' or indicated as simply 'present'. For, rather than presenting, principles have to be *demonstrated*, and this often relies on the supplementary work of an argument: a problem that extends in many directions.

For Ackbar Abbas, the absent presence (or present absence) – the spectre, or indeed 'the real' – that haunts and thereby silently and invisibly structures many Hong Kong martial arts films is related to what he calls 'technocolonialism'. Messages about colonialism (post and techno) are what Abbas finds to be ultimately 'communicated' or *demonstrated* (although not simply *shown*) in many such films. Thus, his discussion of the blurring, blinding cinematography in many fight scenes concludes with a claim that, in an 'indirect way' – i.e., *through this choreography –* 'the film speaks to some of the problems and anxieties of *technocolonialism* which shows itself only abstractly and negatively as something that cannot be directly represented, particularly not by means of sophisticated technological equipment' (Abbas 1997: 32). However much one may either accept or question Abbas' argument here, what is incontestable is the fact that *the form* of his argument may be related to an overwhelming tendency. This takes the form of the scholarly act of diagnosing of what is 'communicated' by or 'through' the texts of (post)modernity – the claim that this or that absent presence is to be regarded as silently structuring, orientating or haunting this or that work. In other words, that is, although one may question Abbas' conclusions, he is certainly not alone in arguing that absent and not-directly-presentable/representable 'presences' such as modernity or postmodernity, coloniality or postcoloniality, are 'communicated' through cultural texts such as this. This is not an isolated event. Indeed, as Rey Chow points out:

> Both Heidegger and Benjamin would associate modernity with the changing conceptualizations of art. In the essay 'The Origin of the Work of Art', Heidegger would compare the effect of a work of art on the observer to a thrust or a blow; Benjamin, specifically discussing film in his essay 'The Work of Art in the Age of Mechanical Reproduction', would describe it in

terms of shock. According to Gianni Vattimo, who alerts us to the fact that
these two otherwise very different essays were both published in 1936,
Heidegger's and Benjamin's conceptions have at least one feature in
common – 'their insistence on disorientation'. Vattimo goes on to define
this disorientation, which, for many European intellectuals is characteristic
of the creativity of art in the age of generalized communication. (Chow
1995: 5-6)

Broad brush strokes or sweeping statements about historical epochs like
modernity or regimes like coloniality and their posts have been and continue to be made, as have assertions about masculinity in general, globalisation in general, and so on; and these might all be seen to be 'communicated' by Bruce Lee – or at least intuited, inferred, or induced by the
viewpoint equipped and inclined to try to demonstrate the haunting, structuring work or effects of such themes. I do not seek to contest such arguments here. But I do want to bracket them off and begin again, from a
consideration of what can be 'seen in' Bruce Lee films – by looking at
what happens and what Bruce Lee *does* – in order to return to the question of the range of 'things' that are 'communicated' in/by/through Bruce
Lee. Rey Chow argues that many of the key historical episodes of intellectual and cultural encounters with the forces of 'modernity' are 'specifically grounded in visuality' (1995: 5). Thus, I would like to undertake
a reading that is both *literal* and 'specifically grounded in visuality' here.
Of course, such a foothold in literality and visuality cannot proceed without argumentative construction, and cannot but move away from that
which can literally be seen present. Such a construction can only avoid
repetitive predictability by deliberately seizing on the productive inevitability of disorientation and reorientation. For, if such construction is inevitable, and indeed even characteristic of the creativity of art in the age
of generalized communication, then such disorientation and reorientation
should not be resisted here, and should instead be engaged rather deliberately. For there may well be more than one 'lesson' communicated here,
through more than one mode of communication. In this context, then, we
might ask, what *other* lessons are communicated by Bruce Lee?

The 'communication' of Bruce Lee

One lesson is clearly reiterated throughout Lee's oeuvre: it takes the form of the reiteration of the movement from superlative physical violence to supreme calm. In particular, one can clearly see it enacted and re-enacted regularly throughout *Enter the Dragon* (1973). Repeatedly, Bruce Lee fights, wins, stops, is utterly calm. He bests hordes of opponents, then sits down in the lotus position. He kills a man, waits, walks away. Amidst the mayhem of a mass battle, he sees his enemy, stops, ignores all else, walks towards him.

Leon Hunt notes:

> In *Hong Kong Action Cinema* Bey Logan recalls the scene in *Enter the Dragon* where Lee, standing stock still but surrounded by movement, fixes his piercing gaze on (the off-screen) Han – 'if that shot doesn't raise the hairs on the back of your neck, then you've probably bought the wrong book', he suggests (1995: 23). Lee's 'aura' is often denned in terms of charisma, and charisma is evidently guaranteed by stasis as much his movement – 'Many later martial arts heroes failed because the camera finds them uninteresting when they are *not* jumping or kicking or punching' (23). Lee's 'presence' is attention-getting and sexually magnetic – the curled lip, smouldering stare or mocking smirk, his trademark gestures (thumbing the nose, his cocky 'bring it on' hand gesture to opponents). (Hunt 2003: 43)

My basic argument will be that this reiterated rhythmic cycle from stillness to explosive movement back to stillness encapsulates the fundamentals of the *event* and the *communication* of Bruce Lee. Accordingly, my proposal is that Bruce Lee was indeed a *cultural event*, and not merely a moment in the realms of cinema. Rather, this rhythmic motif, reiterated by Bruce Lee, actually enabled (or completed) a profound transformation *both* in Western *discourses* of the body and in Western *bodies*. It signals a displacement, a transformation, in many registers and realms: public, private, discursive, psychological, and corporeal. My aim here is to show that, in the words of Jacques Derrida, 'what happens in this case, what is transmitted or communicated, are not just phenomena of meaning or signification', for 'we are dealing neither with a semantic or conceptual content, nor with a semiotic operation, and even less with a linguistic exchange' (1982: 309).

This is so even though the entrance of the dragon was primarily of the order of what postmodernists called the simulacrum, or what psychoanalytical cultural theory calls fantasy (phantasy). For, fantasy and physical reality cannot be divorced, given that even 'in what makes reality seem original to us, fantasy is at work' (Mowitt 2002: 143). That is, fantasies are both social and psychic, in a way that frustrates the possibility of a simple or sharp distinction between objective and subjective, and indeed between the inside and the outside of the subject. Fantasies *supplement* the subject: they are an element from *outside* that is also at the heart of the *inside* (Derrida 1981; 1998). According to Judith Butler, fantasies are dynamically linked with what she calls 'social norms', values and practices that 'are variously lived as psychic reality' (2000: 154). Crucial here is the word 'variously'. For, identity is always *performative*: one is not born a subject, one becomes one, and there is no essential 'being' behind this doing, effecting, and becoming. In Butler's words: 'Norms are not only embodied'; rather, 'embodiment is itself a mode of interpretation, not always conscious, which subjects normativity itself to an iterable temporality' (152). Reciprocally, therefore: 'Norms are not static entities, but [are] incorporated and interpreted features of existence that are sustained by the idealizations furnished by fantasy' (152).

In one respect, the fantasy offered by Bruce Lee may be regarded as *perfectly normal*: as a point of identification, the heroic (phallic) subjectivity that Lee offers is straightforwardly patriarchal or heteronormative. Yet, in another respect this particular fantasy is a *reinterpretation* of such norms, a very particular *reiteration*: a reiteration that did not simply *repeat*, but at a particular historical moment actually *transformed* norms, fantasies and discourses (Derrida 1982: 318; Butler 2000: 152). In other words, Bruce Lee intervened into the fantasy life, discourses and lived practices of international culture in a particularly remarkable way. This perspective not only enables us to grasp the sense in which it is possible to 'place the body-in-cultivation in a specific historical context' and see how 'the individual, physical body both registers and reveals the [...] sociopolitical landscape' (Xu 1999: 961). It also helps to clarify the connections and complexity of 'communications' between signification, semiosis, identification, desire, bodily practice, and the discursive shifts of the movements of history.

Indeed, the historical moment of the 'entrance' of Bruce Lee might perhaps best be regarded as the tail end of the first generation of a counterculture whose seeds had been sewn in World War Two; a counterculture which had emerged in the 1950s and proliferated in the 1960s (Brown 1997; Heath and Potter 2005). However, the 'mechanics' of this entrance – or rather of the transformations that it precipitated – can be approached most concisely in terms of a psychoanalytically inflected reading of the notion of 'interpellation' (Althusser 1971; Mowitt 2002). Of course, this Althusserian notion has acquired a rather a bad name; first because it apparently remains bound to an unfashionable Marxism, but mainly because it apparently simplistically implies that *what* interpellates individuals as subjects must always be determinate 'Ideological State Apparatuses' (Althusser 1971). The problem here would be that subjects must be 'entirely the effects of the state apparatus' (Mowitt 2002: 49), and this would suggest that agency, never mind 'resistance [...] is all but foreclosed' (49). However, according to Mowitt, the 'Marxist' dimension of interpellation is not at all certain. For, interpellation has also played a 'constitutive role in the emergence of what is now, somewhat reluctantly, referred to as post-Marxism. To this extent, interpellation participates in a "properly" dialectical elaboration of the very theoretical tradition which it might otherwise be said to have sublated' (43). Thus, given the plurality and complexity of addresses, hails, commands, suggestions, sources of identification, and the contingency of response, interpretation and performance, a 'conflict of interpellations' easily and often arises (49). Consequently, the subject is not merely a passive reflection of structure. Rather, subjectivity is an ongoing performative process amidst conflicting interpellations. In the postmodern, polyvocal and media saturated world, the interpellations which tend to prevail are, one might say, *those calls that answer a call*. And what the Bruce Lee simulation of physical prowess 'did' was simply to call out to viewers: *'Hey, you! This could be you! All you need to do is train in kung fu, and you too can become (closer to) invincible!'*

    Interpellation through a simulation becomes significant because, in Žižek's words:

> fantasy is a hallucinatory realization of desire. ... [However,] It is not the case that the subject knows in advance what he wants and then, when he cannot get it in reality, proceeds to obtain a hallucinatory satisfaction in reality. Rather, the subject originally doesn't know what he wants, and it is the role of fantasy to tell him that, to 'teach' him to desire. (Žižek 2005: 304)

Or, as Kaja Silverman puts it: 'the subject not only learns to desire within the symbolic order; it learns "what" to desire' (1983: 177-8). Significantly, this 'suggests that even desire is culturally instigated, and hence collective' (130). Therefore, this arguably takes us into the realms of the constitution of subjectivity itself. For, as Silverman asserts:

> Identity and desire are so complexly imbricated that neither can be explained without recourse to the other. Furthermore, although those constitutive features of subjectivity are never entirely fixed', neither are they in a state of absolute flux of 'free-play'; on the contrary, they are synonymous with the compulsion to repeat certain images and positionalities, which are relinquished only with difficulty... (Silverman 1983: 6)

Elsewhere, Silverman adds:

> Part of what it means to pursue the relation of fantasy to the ego is to grasp that the subject's own bodily image is the first and most important of all the objects through which it attempts to compensate for symbolic castration – to understand that the [Lacanian] *moi* is most profoundly that through which it attempts to recover 'being'. The self, in other words, fills the void at the center of subjectivity with an illusory plenitude. (Silverman 1992: 4-5)

Thus, the event of Bruce Lee is first that of a simulacrum conjuring up a fantasy. But the matter certainly does not end there. For what it explicitly called out for was a very physical encounter with the bizarre new/ancient Oriental thing called kung fu. In itself, this new 'lifestyle option' can be viewed as culturally significant. To reiterate Bruce Thomas' point about Bruce Lee, it was entirely down to his *films* that he, 'an Englishman [...] was able to begin learning a Chinese martial art from a Welshman' (Thomas, 1994/2002: xii). Such a quotidian practice may seem very little – almost nothing – but it is both subjectively and socio-culturally significant. For, in the subject, such training leads to what Greg Downey calls the 'transformation of the novice, the change of his or her muscles, attention patterns, motor control, neurological systems, emotional reactions, interaction patterns, top-down self-management techniques, and other anatomical changes' (2006, unpublished manuscript). Moreover, socio-culturally, as Lee's biographer claims, Bruce Lee's intervention was one which apparently 'bridged cultures, revolutionized the martial arts, taught a fierce philosophy of individualism, [...] and remade the image of the Asian man in the West' (Thomas 2002: xi).

We will consider further these claims about 'culture bridging' in due course. But first, we should note the link between *the simulation*, the *subjective fantasy* and *bodily practice*. As many writers have argued with a variety of approaches, bodily practices are what literally make us, and they are what can remake and change us. To grasp what this means, and to consider the way that subjects appropriate and live 'social' and 'publicly available' fantasies, as well as to consider the ways that fantasy intervenes into and influences psychic life, subjectivity and bodily practices, we may indeed perhaps find no better publicly available example than the case of Bruce Lee. For the fantasy offered by Bruce Lee touched hundreds of millions, across the globe. Of course, it is not a *physical* touch. Rather, to borrow a poetic expression from Heidegger, it is a touch 'in which there is concentrated a contact that remains infinitely remote from any touch [...] suffused and borne by a call calling from afar and calling still farther onward' (1971: 16). And although not physical, this is nevertheless a call to the body. Of course, there is a huge gulf between call and response, between *fantasizing* and *becoming*. What the fantasy proposed by Bruce Lee demands is physical training: kung fu.

In addition to the well-documented significance of Bruce Lee's place in the cultural discourses of America's renegotiation of its post-war relationship to its Eastern Others, what the event of Bruce Lee overwhelmingly precipitated was a virtually global popular encounter with kung fu. Or, more specifically: *with the fantasy of kung fu*. For, as is well known, the 'Shaolin kung fu' of *Enter the Dragon* bears little if any relation to the actual 'kung fu' that may have been practised in any of the Shaolin monasteries or elsewhere. Indeed, even the term 'kung fu' itself is acknowledged to be a misnomer, and moreover a *Western imposition*, the synecdochic transformation of a general term for 'effort' or 'discipline' into the name for 'all Chinese martial practices'. In response to the accusation of the lack of 'reality' of Lee's cinematic kung fu, students, friends and disciples of Bruce Lee have themselves always made plain that what is seen in Bruce Lee films is *knowingly* spectacular and *deliberately* hyperbolic choreography. What Bruce Lee 'really practiced', they continue, was *his own brand* of innovative and trailblazing fighting: *jeet kune do* (Inosanto 1980). It is the 'real practice' of jeet kune do that is considered by fans and disciples as offering the proof of Lee's combative genius, and as evidence of his having *sublated and surpassed* 'traditional' martial arts by inventing a superior 'interdisciplinary' hybrid. Of course, this hybrid is construed by other martial artists as merely reflecting the fact that Lee never actually *completed* any formal training syllabus in any one martial art (Smith 1999). My point here is not to adjudicate on the status or martial credentials of jeet kune do (as if such a thing were objective). Rather, it is simply to reiterate that in any and every eventuality, what Bruce Lee offered was *a fantasy* of kung fu. With the films, the fantasy is of an *ancient, mystical, mysterious* kung fu. With jeet kune do, the fantasy is of a *rational, efficient, interdisciplinary* martial 'science'. As discussed in the previous chapter, Krug's history of the American 'appropriation' of the oriental martial art of karate is salient here. This history, we can recall, involves three stages: 'discovery and mythologization', 'demystification', and 'appropriation'. Krug places Bruce Lee films on the cusp of the first and second stages. However, he deals only with Bruce Lee's cinematic kung fu. Considered together with Lee's 'real' jeet kune do practice, it is arguably the case that we see each of these 'historical' periodizations played out in the case of Bruce Lee. Thus, in the films we see discovery and mythologization; in the writings and certain interviews and TV roles we see demystification; and in his hybridisation or 'bricolage' construction of jeet kune do, we see deterritorialisation, deracination and appropriation. Freud proposed that phylogeny recapitulates ontogeny. Arguably, we see this here.

But, Bruce Lee is certainly not responsible for *the* fantasies of kung fu. Indeed, the Shaolin warrior monk that he plays in *Enter the Dragon* is already a mythical figure of a dubious historical status, which antedates Bruce Lee. Historians have always cast doubt both on the origin myth of Shaolin Kung Fu, in which wandering monk Bodhidharma introduced Zen meditation to the unfit monks of the Shaolin Temple and, as a result of the physical discipline required for Zen meditation, also inadvertently invented kung fu. Historians also consistently challenge the subsequent myths of the improbable physical abilities of Shaolin monks. As we saw in the previous chapter, Kennedy and Guo suggest that the myths of Shaolin were 'largely created in two books': a popular turn of the century novel, *Travels of Lao Can* (Lui 2005), and an apparently totally fabricated and instantly debunked 1915 training manual entitled the *Secrets of Shaolin Boxing* (Unknown 1971; Kennedy and Guo 2005: 70-71). Similarly, it is relevant to reiterate that, as Henning points out, the origins of the Shaolin myth 'cannot be traced back earlier than its appearance in the popular novel, *Travels of Lao Can*, written between 1904 and 1907, and there is no indication that it was ever part of an earlier oral tradition' (qtd. in Kennedy and Guo 2005: 70). *Secrets of Shaolin Boxing* contained accounts of improbable/impossible processes and end results of Shaolin training. It was instantly debunked by the leading contemporary martial arts historians of the time (Tang Hao and Xu Je Dong), yet this book in particular had a significant impact. For, even though quickly exposed, 'unfortunately [it] became popularly accepted as a key source for Chinese martial arts history enthusiasts, and its pernicious influence has permeated literature on the subject to this day' (Henning as qtd. in Kennedy and Guo, 2005: 70-71).

Pernicious influence, utter fantasy, little relation to reality: but, in terms of physical practice, *nothing about this distance from 'reality' really matters*. The encounter with kung fu was (indeed, *is*) an encounter with (a) fantasy. This cinematically mediated fantasy called primarily to the *body*. According to critics like Abbas, this fantasy-construction called to Eastern and Western bodies in slightly different ways. From a 'Western' perspective, one need not distinguish, discriminate between or indeed even know about or care about the vast internal, external, political, cultural, ideological and cosmological differences between, say, (Chinese) 'kung fu' and (Japanese) 'Samurai' when what *matters* is a fantasy about physicality. The fantasy here happily connects elements, ideas and practices that hitherto have been geographically, culturally, politically and otherwise distinct, but that can be appropriated as emotionally, semiotically or affectively intimate or identical. However, for 'Eastern' subjects, Abbas suggests, the interpellation effected by Bruce Lee works within the frameworks of a nationalistic imaginary, calling, as we have seen to an identification with 'traditional' skills.

In either case, what this means might be clarified by a consideration of a perhaps unexpected example: the film *Ghost Dog: The Way of The Samurai* (1999). In this film, the life of a black youth (Forrest Whittaker) is saved by a mafia gangster who shoots two white teenagers who were beating him (apparently) to death. The youth subsequently devotes his life to the 'Samurai code' and to martial arts training. As an adult, he becomes 'Ghost Dog', an enigmatic assassin who works exclusively, invisibly and anonymously for his gangster saviour. Yet, despite this, he has attained a paradoxical and improbable status within the local ghetto community: Ghost Dog is both *well-known* (well-respected) in the community (moreover, by gangs and rappers of all colours – a surely impossible fantasy), and yet he remains secretive, *unknown* and often effectively invisible. Throughout the film, Ghost Dog regularly refers to the book *Hagakure: The Way of the Samurai* (Tsunetomo 1979), and quotations from this book intersperse the film and the soundtrack. These enlighten viewers and listeners as to precisely what the 'Samurai code' may be or entail. Thus, the film directly proposes that through an encounter with a translated Japanese text, and through *fantasy* (identification with a fantasy social position – for one *cannot be* a Samurai outside of feudal Japanese social relations), and the *discipline* of martial arts, a black youth from violent ghetto streets can 'become', to all intents and purposes, a ninja. The ninja were of course a legendary/mythological clan of Samurai forced into hiding and turned assassin. This is precisely what Ghost Dog has become.

Now, this does not seem to be simply a manifestation of the individualist ideology of self-invention. Rather, the premise of the film is best illustrated in a scene in which Ghost Dog encounters two red-neck hunters who have illegally killed a black bear and seem more than prepared to do exactly the same thing to the very palpably black man who is questioning them about their actions:

> *Hunter*:   You see, there aren't too many of these big black fuckers left around here, so when you get a good, clear shot at it, you sure as hell take it.
> *Ghost Dog*: That's why you shoot them, 'cause there's not that many left?
> *Hunter*:   There ain't all that many coloured people round here, neither.
> *Ghost Dog*: In ancient cultures, bears were considered equal with men.
> *Hunter*:   This ain't no ancient culture, mister.

> *[Hunter reaches for a gun. Ghost Dog shoots both hunters]*

> *Ghost Dog*: Sometimes it is.

This is the proposition of *Ghost Dog*: *sometimes this culture can be or could become another culture* – and, I hasten to add – *even when the only 'direct access' to or 'contact with' that other culture is 'translated', 'mediated', 'packaged' and reliant upon a (phantasmatic) identification with a fantasy*. The question to ask here is, simply: *Can it?*

Such uses of Bruce Lee and *Ghost Dog*, in different but equivalent ways, propose peculiar theses about what might be called the relation between lived bodily practices, subjectivities and historical 'reality'. Of course, as we have seen, we cannot pretend to be able to disentangle 'reality' from 'fantasy'. But there remain ontological and epistemological – as well as cultural, economic and political – questions about *what is going on* in such apparent 'encounters' and 'hybridizations' as these. For, although it is possible to construct what J. J. Clarke calls a long list of 'the West's intellectual encounters with Eastern thought', it remains equally valid and necessary to 'ask philosophical questions about the very possibility of crossing linguistic and cultural boundaries, and about the adequacy of inter-cultural communication, and [to] reflect on the nature of the hermeneutical process which [...] is at the heart of these encounters' (1997: 181). In other words, these films propose and maybe even constitute peculiar sorts of cross-cultural 'encounters'. But, what is at the heart of such putative 'East-West encounters', so many of which are initiated or organised by (fantasies about) martial arts?

It Hits all by Itself

Before the contemporary proliferation of popular cultural encounters with 'Oriental' martial arts, there were some earlier, retrospectively rather less popular encounters, of a rather different order (Krug 2001). For instance, writing in the 1950s, at the cutting edge of the emerging counterculture, the first words of the Preface of Alan Watts' enormously influential book, *The Way of Zen* (1957), remark on the 'extraordinary growth of interest in Zen Buddhism' and in East Asian culture and thought in the West: 'this interest has increased so much that it seems to be becoming a considerable force in the intellectual and artistic world of the West', he proposes, and suggests that it 'is concerned, no doubt, with the prevalent enthusiasm for Japanese culture which is one of the constructive results of the late war' (Watts 1957: 9). In other words, because what the counterculture (of beatniks, peaceniks, hippies and New Agers) was *counter to* was the culture which went to war with the East, the counterculture therefore chose to adore the East. The post-Second World War and subsequent Vietnam War countercultural turns away from faith in Western institutions (and away from *institutions* and *the West* per se) and towards the 'mystical' and the Oriental was doubtless bolstered by the sense that (as Watts discusses at the very beginning of chapter one of *The Way of Zen*) 'Zen Buddhism is a way and a view of life which does not belong to any of the formal categories of modern Western thought'. Indeed, Watts proposes, it 'is not a religion or philosophy; it is not a psychology or a type of science', but rather 'an example of what is known in India and China as a "way of liberation", and is similar in this respect to Taoism, Vedanta, and Yoga' (1957: 23).

In other words, Watts is optimistic about the cultural implications of the Western interest in changing the 'formal categories of modern Western thought', and hence the forms and institutions of modern Western culture, through an encounter with Eastern thought. But, as we saw in the previous chapter, writing at roughly the same time as Watts – and arguably almost as interested in Buddhism, Taoism and 'Eastasian thought' – another (rather less 'popular') philosopher was rather less optimistic. In the Socratic-style text, 'A Dialogue on Language: Between a Japanese and an Inquirer' (1971), first published in 1958, Martin Heidegger fictionalises himself as the inestimable Inquirer, host to a rather obsequious Japanese guest, who suggests that perhaps 'a true encounter [between East Asian and] European existence is still not taking place, in spite of all assimilations and intermixtures' (1971: 3). Indeed, 'Perhaps [a true encounter] cannot take place' (1971: 3), suggests the Japanese guest. The 'Dialogue on Language' proposes that this is because the modern world is dominated by what it calls American-led 'Europeanization'. This has resulted in the 'modern technicalization and industrialization of every continent', from which 'there would seem to be no escape any longer' (3). The fundamental problem with this process is said to be that 'technicalization and industrialization' brings with it what the 'Dialogue' calls the dominance of 'European conceptual systems' (3). In other words, the technologically determined dominance of 'European' ways of thinking that threaten to extinguish all true cultural alterity.

Interestingly, the 'Dialogue' proposes that these problematic 'European conceptual systems' are most pointedly present in that synthesis of 'Western' aesthetics and 'Western' technics, *the film camera*. 'Perhaps you have seen' Kurosawa's film, *Rashomon* (1950), says Heidegger's Japanese quest. 'Fortunately, yes; unfortunately, only once' responds the Inquirer: 'I believed that I was experiencing the enchantment of the Japanese world, the enchantment that carries us away into the mysterious. And so I do not understand why you offer just this film as an example of an all-consuming Europeanization' (16). But, for Heidegger's imaginary visitor, *Rashomon is* an index of Europeanization because as soon as something – *anything* – is captured on camera, it is committed to what Heidegger's 'Dialogue' calls a fully western 'objectness' (17), an 'objectness' that is apparently alien to all things essentially East Asian. This 'objectness' indicates conventions of representation and conventions of *reading* representations that are irreducibly European. Hence, says Heidegger's Japanese guest, this means that 'seen from the point of view of our Eastasian existence, the technical world which sweeps us along must confine itself to surface matters, and... that...'. He tails off, unable to complete his thought. The Inquirer finds the right words for him and suggests: '... that for this reason alone a true encounter with European existence is still not taking place, in spite of all assimilations and intermixtures'. Indeed: 'Perhaps cannot take place', concludes the Japanese, perhaps glumly (Heidegger 1971: 3). So, here's the rub: the 'Dialogue on Language' suggests that even for the Japanese *to be able to conceptualise* any of this 'I need precisely your [European] language' (16).

Thus, under the Western gaze, 'the Japanese world is captured and imprisoned [...] in the objectness of photography, and is in fact especially framed for photography' (16). Furthermore, 'photographic objectification is already a consequence of the ever wider outreach of Europeanization' (17). Therefore, proposes the 'Dialogue', 'the Eastasian world, and the technical-aesthetic product of the film industry, are incompatible' (16). Thus, suggests Stella Sandford, Heidegger's 'Dialogue on Language' is fundamentally 'preoccupied with the issue of the possibility or impossibility of an East-West dialogue', and that while scholars like Reinhard May (1996) have read it 'as proof both of Heidegger's indebtedness to East Asian sources and his attempts to cover this over', she concludes that the 'Dialogue' is just as plausibly to be understood 'as a statement of Heidegger's belief in the fundamental and incommensurable *differences* between philosophical traditions, and of the extraordinary difficulty, if not the outright impossibility, of a true dialogue, despite the best intentions of the interlocutors' (Sandford 2003: 14).

Yet there is a paradoxical element to Heidegger's text. This can be observed in the ambivalence of the speaking position attributed to the Japanese guest, when it comes to the possibility of an authentic encounter of any kind. Speaking of *Rashomon*, the dialogue runs:

> *J*:   We Japanese consider the presentation frequently too realistic, for example in the duelling scenes.
> *I*:   But are there not also subdued gestures?
> *J*:   Inconspicuities of this kind flow abundantly and hardly noticeable to a European observer. I recall a hand resting on another person, in which there is concentrated a contact that remains infinitely remote from any touch, something that may not even be called gesture any longer in the sense in which I understand your usage. For this hand is suffused and borne by a call calling from afar and calling still farther onward, because stillness has brought it. (Heidegger, 1971: 16)

The claim here and elsewhere throughout the 'Dialogue', is that this trace of an authenticity which allegedly *escapes* Western technics, aesthetics, and Western forms of reading (ways of seeing) *nevertheless escapes from the film*. We know this because we have just been informed that it *remains perceptible* to this Japanese viewer. Much could be made of this paradoxical claim, which boils down to the tautology: the imperceptible, untranslatable, ungraspable thing is nevertheless there, perceptible and graspable, albeit only to those who are able to perceive it thanks to their enculturation. For, in fact, one could say this about *anything 'in' any text at all*. So, rather than the Heideggerian conclusion (of *you can't see what I can because you're essentially different*), J. J. Clarke proposes that 'arguments which apply to [the impossibility of] communication between Europe and China apply with equal force, not only between modern and mediaeval Europe, but also between any two individuals attempting to communicate with one another' (1997: 182).

Thus, before celebrating or denying the possibility of cross-cultural 'encounters', what needs to be established is the *nature of* the 'possibility of crossing linguistic and cultural boundaries' and the *nature* of 'intercultural communication' (Clarke 1997: 181). As Clarke sagely reminds us, it is important to 'reflect on the nature of the hermeneutical process which […] is at the heart of these encounters' (181). Yet, it is equally important to ask: *is* 'the hermeneutical process' necessarily always 'at the heart' of intercultural (or any other) encounters? Or rather: is that *all* there is? For, mightn't *Enter the Dragon* (and even *Ghost Dog*) be added to the list of East-West 'encounters', even though such encounters are obviously not simply 'authentic' (in a naïve or nostalgic sense)? Such films are certainly 'American produced'. The first movie poster for *Enter the Dragon* proudly declared that it was 'the first American produced martial arts spectacular'. So, such productions beg the Heideggerian question of how they could possibly be said to have 'bridged cultures' or to have constituted any kind of authentic encounter. But, let us return to our opening motif: Bruce Lee fights; Bruce Lee is still. What is there here? This encounter is not an 'authentic' encounter, of course. But nor is it 'hermeneutic' in the dry intellectual (logocentric) sense. Rather, the encounter is with a body, its power, an aesthetic, with desire, with eros, and involving all manner of fantasies. At its heart is not an intellectual 'hermeneutical process'. And even though all that is 'there' is obviously a semiotic simulacrum which may be deemed anything from patriarchal to orientalist to fetishistic to commodifying, the *spectacle* of Bruce Lee *calls to the body 'directly'*, in precisely the same way music calls to the body directly (Gilbert and Pearson 1999: 44-47; Mowitt 2002). When music starts playing, it is not a 'hermeneutical process' that makes your feet start tapping and your body start moving. In exactly the same way, Bruce Lee is *music to the eyes*.[7]

The key iteration of our motif occurs at the end of the most spectacular fight sequence of *Enter the Dragon*: Bruce Lee's prolonged battle with hordes of the evil Han's guards. During this frenetic and protracted fight, Lee systematically and artfully bests wave after wave of assailants with bare hands and a range of traditional martial arts weapons. The fight ends abruptly when Lee runs into a vault and thick steel doors slam down all around him, preventing his exit. Instantly realising there is nowhere to go, the sweating and bleeding Bruce Lee simply sits straight down,

---

[7] Gilbert and Pearson (1999) enquire into the nature of music's effects and note that the 'nonverbal aspect of music's effectivity which has given rise to its strange status in western thought' (1999: 39). The dangerous hedonistic bodily effects of music led Socrates to want only simply, functional, militaristic music (in Plato's *Republic*); many others still try to tie music down to 'meanings' (40); Kant hated '*Tafelmusik*' – table music, music that is not designed for *contemplation* (41), etc. They argue: 'this tradition tends to demand of music that it – as far as possible – *be meaningful*, that even where it does not have words, it should offer itself up as an object of intellectual contemplation' (42). However, music is felt by the body. They propose, 'music – like all sound – is registered on a fundamentally different level to language or modes of visual communication' (44); and 'music can be said to, as Robert Walser suggests, "hail the body directly"' (46). I am simply saying, so does Bruce Lee.

crosses his legs, hangs his nunchakus around his neck, and pulls his heels onto his thighs, adopting the classic meditative lotus position. Now, *this* is what 'enters' with *Enter the Dragon*. In the instant switch from amazing fighting to meditative calm sitting, a clear and unequivocal connection is made between 'mystical', 'spiritual' alterity and the disciplined body. And *this* is a *rearticulation* – a *rewiring*, a *rearrangement* – of the usual connections made in Western discourses,[8] in which the spiritual is (or was) *opposed* to the physical, or the body. In *Enter the Dragon*, audiences are repeatedly shown an entirely novel transformation of this traditional relation.

Of course, this rearticulation is not at first entirely intelligible. This is perhaps why the film needs to (re)introduce it several times, in different ways: to reiterate it rapidly in the first three scenes, and intermittently throughout the film. Thus, before introducing plot, before any characterisation, and in fact, before anything else, the beginning of *Enter the Dragon* aims at delivering the lesson of this new equation. Perhaps most clearly, scene three is entirely pedagogical: the young Shaolin monk kung fu master, Lee (Bruce Lee) gives a lesson to a student, a young boy called Lau. This scene actually begins with Lee meeting the British agent, Mr Braithwaite, in a garden. They are served tea. 'This is very pleasant', observes Mr Braithwaite. But before they can get down to the business of discussing the mission that Braithwaite has for Lee (the mission that will drive the plot), they are interrupted. A boy turns up. Seeing him, Lee says:

Lee:	It's Lau's time.
Braithwaite:	Yes, of course…
Lee:	Kick me. [*Lau seems puzzled*] Kick me. [*Lau throws a side-kick*] What was that? An exhibition? We need [*pointing to his head*] emotional content. Try again! [*Lau kicks again*] I said emotional content. Not anger! Now try again! With *me*! [*Lau throws two more kicks, causing Lee to respond*] That's it! How did it feel to you?
Lau:	Let me think.
Lee:	[*Slaps Lau's head*] Don't think! Feel! It is like a finger pointing away to the moon. [*Slaps Lau's*

---

[8] For a full account of the theoretical concept of 'articulation' (and rearticulation), see Laclau and Mouffe (1985). For a recent study of the significance of 'articulation' as the key term of contemporary cultural theory, see Bowman (2007).

	head] *Don't* concentrate on the finger or you will miss all that heavenly glory. Do you understand?
Lau:	[*smiles, nods, bows*]
Lee:	[*Slaps the back of Lau's head*] *Never* take your eyes off your opponent, even when you bow.... That's it.

The camera cuts back to Braithwaite, who is smiling and nodding (*our*) approval. For, even though this lesson has delayed his delivery of the plot, all is forgiven: this peculiar lesson feels much more important. But what has been learned? Certainly nothing *logocentric*, to do with words, statements or meanings. So what is 'it'? In fact, in the preceding scenes, we have already been shown what Lee 'knows'. Immediately before this pedagogical scene, for instance, we have seen Lee with his own Teacher. This is the second scene of the film. The first scene saw Lee winning a ceremonial – apparently graduation-like – fight in the Shaolin Temple. After passing that physical test, Lee goes to his own teacher (as if for the *viva voce*):

[*Scene opens: Lee approaches an elderly monk on a wooded hilltop path*]

Lee: [*bowing*]	Teacher?
Teacher:	Hmm. I see your talents have gone beyond the mere physical level. Your skills are now at the point of spiritual insight. I have several questions. What is the highest technique you hope to achieve?
Lee:	To have no technique.
Teacher:	Very good. What are your thoughts when facing an opponent?
Lee:	There is no opponent.
Teacher:	And why is that?
Lee:	Because the word 'I' does not exist.
Teacher:	So. Continue.
Lee:	A good fight should be like a small play, *but* played seriously. A good martial artist does not become tense, but ready. Not thinking, yet not dreaming: ready for whatever may come. When the opponent expands, I contract; when he contracts, I expand; and when there is an opportunity, I do not hit: [*he raises his fist, but does not look at it*] *it* hits all by itself.

So, in the first few minutes of *Enter the Dragon* we have seen: a rite-of-passage ceremonial fight, Lee with his teacher, and Lee with his student. The second and third scenes are lessons, *showing* (but not *explaining*) what Lee 'knows'/is. Now, it may be clear to post-Foucauldian academic eyes that what subtends all of this going 'beyond the mere physical level' is *not* disembodied 'spirituality' but physical *discipline* (with Lee amounting to the highest production of Shaolin discipline – indeed, the most perfect example of a Foucauldian 'docile body'). Nevertheless, what this strange pedagogy is actually at pains to emphasise is an entirely un-equivocal yet still unusual equation between subject, body and 'spiritual-ity'. And this is a difficult lesson to 'show' (let alone to 'explain'). For, as Smith and Novak point out:

> Because meditation is commonly linked to the vague term 'spirituality', it is sometimes tarred with that term's negative connotations toward the body. Those who have not undertaken Buddhist meditative training, there-fore, can hardly be expected to guess how intimately connected it is to an awareness of one's own body. The body may be the site of our bondage, but it is also the means of our extrication. ... Indeed, it barely exaggerates the matter to regard Buddhist meditation as a lifelong training in right body awareness. (Smith and Novak, 2003: 80)

Enter the Dragon constructs and conveys this particular connection and introduces the key indices of this 'new mystical eastern' discursive con-stellation extremely efficiently. Indeed, what it proposes, through the model of Lee, is an inversion and displacement of Freud's Enlightenment motto *'Wo Es war, soll Ich werden'* ('where the id was, there ego shall be'): in other words, let the light of conscious knowledge replace the darkness of ignorance. Instead, in Lee's physical spirituality, the path to insight that is proposed follows almost the opposite maxim: *where ego was, let 'it' be*. But *'it'* is no longer the barbaric primary impulses of an id that must be repressed. Rather it is a fundamental harmony and enlight-enment achieved through a non-egotistical but disciplined mastery of the mind and body. In other words, whilst meditation *per se* may not be much of a spectator sport, nor make for very exciting viewing, Hollywood nev-ertheless managed to represent a strong trait of the '60s countercultural interest in oriental alterity through the mystical and spiritual 'way of lib-eration' and 'enlightenment' produced by the 'training in right body awareness' embodied in the spectacular character of Lee's mythical Shaolin Temple warrior monk. *There is thus the potential of a 'communi-cation' between physical bodies induced by an interpellation that is me-diated – disseminated – by the cinematic apparatus.* In other words, this is a *simulation* which engages *fantasy* which precipitates in *practice* that leads to subjective, physical and discursive *transformation*. For, such practice may well be or become Zen or Buddhist meditation, Taoist chi gung, or any number of other bodily technologies. Thus, the simulacrum may well offer an 'entrée into Chinese philosophy, medicine, meditation, and even language' (Wile 1996: xv). *Or* it may of course produce chimeras, fictions, fantasies, and absurdities, such as the wonderfully ridiculous invented 'martial art' of 'Rex Kwon Do' in *Napoleon Dynamite* (2004).[9]

Don't Concentrate on the Finger!

What is there to be learned from this? This is just another way of asking: What is there? To think about the lesson, let's rewind to the touching pedagogical scene in which Lee points Lau to the physically graspable, metaphorically evocable but linguistically unsayable 'it'. As you will recall, Lee tests Lau by gesturing and saying 'It is like a finger pointing away to the moon'. Then he slaps Lau and says: 'Don't concentrate on the finger or you will miss all that heavenly glory'. Lesson learned. But, what is it? As we are not simply Lee's obedient disciples, let's allow ourselves the luxury of one last quick furtive look at Lau looking at the pointing finger, for which he was so sternly reprimanded.

In an essay entitled 'What is there?', Maurizio Ferraris proposes that *any* response to the ontological question of 'what is there?' always boils down to the work of 'A finger, generally the index, [which] gives a sign towards something, and indicates it as *this*'. And this, he points out, 'is *presence*, ontology in the simple and hyperbolic sense' (2001: 96). Ferraris then goes on to consider what he calls that 'obstinate superstition that holds [that children are] incapable of abstraction [because they] look at the finger ... instead of what the index is pointing to' (100). He notes that the conventional interpretation of the classic child's mistake is that it shows children are *incapable* of abstraction. (Similar statements have been made about the so-called 'Chinese Mind', of course.) But Ferraris suggests that surely children who look at the finger and not at what it points to 'are if anything *more* abstract [than adults], since they produce an inflation of presences' (100). For what they are staring at (if not 'see-

---

[9] The magnificent 'Rex Kwon Do' scene from *Napoleon Dynamite* can be seen on www.youtube.com at http://www.youtube.com/watch?v=5nfr4-J3fio

ing') is *the agency which designates – the act of designation* – rather than that which is intended. Thus the over-attention of the naïve, captive and attentive disciple inadvertently and unintentionally points to the fact that we are always guided, led, directed, pointed to something, by some guide or guiding act of designation. Designation is determined by a designator. Disciples are taught what to look at and what to see and what not to see. What disciples *see* is what they are in a sense *shown* (or trained) *how to see*. Thus, as Ferraris puts it: 'the presence of the index is no less problematic than everything it points to' (2001: 98).

Of course, Lee's character is seeking to dissolve the 'Western' problematic in which, behind the index (the finger pointing us to what *is*), 'there is first of all a *cogito* with respect to which [things] are present' (Ferraris 2001: 98). As Lee has already told us, 'the word "I" does not exist'. Similarly, perhaps, Alan Watts once asked: 'What happens to my fist (noun-object) when I open my hand?' (1957: 25) The question seeks to suggest that ways of thinking determine what can be seen, understood, or communicated. Thus, what may seem like an *object* may perhaps be better construed as an *event* or a *process*. In a similar sense, the concept-metaphors used to think about 'culture' have themselves shifted from conceiving of it as a fixed or essential *thing* towards thinking of it as an *event*, a *process*, or – overwhelmingly nowadays – as *communication*. But, what is communication? And how is 'it' communicated? As Jacques Derrida once asked: what does the word *communication* communicate? We tend to 'anticipate the meaning of the word *communication*' and to 'predetermine communication as the vehicle, transport, or site of passage of a meaning, and of a meaning that is *one*' (1982: 309). But, he observes:

> To the semantic field of the word *communication* belongs the fact that it also designates nonsemantic movements... [O]ne may, for example, *communicate a movement*, or [...] a tremor, a shock, a displacement of *force* can be communicated – that is, propagated, transmitted. [...] What happens in this case, what is transmitted or communicated, are not just phenomena of meaning or signification. In these cases we are dealing neither with a semantic or conceptual content, nor with a semiotic operation, and even less with a linguistic exchange. (1982: 309)

Such is the communication of the fantasy corpus of martial arts: it cannot be reduced to a hermeneutical or logocentric communication of meaning, nor even the direct transmission of a 'real' tradition. It is always the performative reiteration of 'material' from heterogeneous realms or registers:

myths, spectres, symbols and simulacra being as operative in – and as organising of – bodily practice as any positive or empirically specifiable 'real'. Of course, such communications, events, exchanges or encounters can be placed in historical contexts, and can be historicized. But they should not be regarded as 'therefore' being simple epiphenomenal 'expressions' of larger (or 'more real') historical processes. Rather, such events as 'Bruce Lee' are equally *productive* of their historical contexts. Such events are rearticulations which 'rewire' and transform discourses, ideologies, fantasies and bodies. But what is the nature of this rewiring?

Bruce Lee and the (re)wiring of Masculinity

Henry Giroux's cultural study of film, *Breaking into the Movies* (2002), has a large final section dedicated to the question(s) of the cultural significance of violent films. The final chapter of this section, the final chapter of the book, and hence perhaps something akin to Giroux's deliberately chosen final word on the matter(s), is a reading of *Fight Club* (1996). His argument about this film is that:

> Unlike a number of Hollywood films in which violence is largely formulaic and superficially visceral, designed primarily to shock, titillate, and celebrate the sensational, *Fight Club* uses violence as both a form of voyeuristic identification and a pedagogical tool. Although *Fight Club* offers up a gruesome and relentless spectacle of bare-knuckled brutality, bloodcurdling and stylistic gore, violence becomes more than ritualistic kitsch: it also provides audiences with an ideologically loaded context and mode of articulation for legitimating a particular understanding of masculinity and its relationship to important issues regarding moral and civic agency, gender, and politics. (Giroux 2002: 272)

Obviously, such a study seems immediately relevant to any consideration of the significance of Bruce Lee. Indeed it is. But what to my mind is most significant about Giroux's analysis is that one thing he completely fails to notice is the way that Bruce Lee's absent presence structures certain key aspects of the film, particularly in terms of male fantasy in its relationship to the performance of masculinity. Lee's presence is felt in the form of Brad Pitt's character – the schizophrenically hallucinated alter-ego, Tyler Durden. For, Durden struts like Lee when he fights; squares off like Lee, flicking his nose and settling into his stances (as does Neo in *The Matrix*, of course, along with many other parodies and pastiches of Lee); he even plays with nunchakus and makes Lee's cinematic catcalls in the background to one scene. But Giroux fails to take any of this into account, even though surely it will be significant if, as Giroux regards it, *Fight Club* is all about being a man. For the 'alpha male' in the film is, of course, Brad Pitt's (so to speak) *impossibly masculine* Tyler Durden – a character who often plays at being Bruce Lee.

For Giroux, the problem with *Fight Club* is that in it 'masculinity is defined in opposition to both femininity and consumerism, while simultaneously refusing to take up either in a dialectical and critical way' (271). So, despite what many may have argued about the film, as Giroux sees it, '*Fight Club* functions less as a critique of capitalism than as a defense of a highly stereotypical and limited sense of masculinity that is seen as wedded to the immediacy of pleasure sustained through violence and abuse' (271). The masculinity proposed by Tyler Durden presents itself as 'natural' or 'original', but as Giroux reminds us, *exactly* because of this version of 'nature', *Fight Club* should therefore be regarded as 'complicitous with the very system of commodification it denounces since both rely upon a notion of agency largely constructed within the immediacy of pleasure, the cult of hypercompetitiveness, and the market-driven desire of winning and exercising power over others' (271). Moreover, 'the ideology of the "survival of the fittest" becomes literalized in the form of a clarion call for the legitimation of dehumanizing forms of violence as a source of pleasure and sociality' (271). And herein lies Giroux's problem.

If we put aside Giroux's immensely problematic – arguably untenable – insinuation that elsewhere, outside of films like *Fight Club*, 'pleasure' somehow relates to 'justice, equality, and freedom' – 'Pleasure in this context has less to do with justice, equality, and freedom than with hypermodes of competition mediated through the fantasy of violence' (271-272) – the issue he takes with *Fight Club* nevertheless remains clear:

> this particular rendering of pleasure is predicated on legitimating the relationship between oppression and misogyny, and masculinity gains its force through a celebration of both brutality and the denigration of the feminine. Hence, *Fight Club* appears to have no understanding of its own articulation with the very forces of capitalism it appears to be attacking and this is most evident in its linking of violence, masculinity, and gender. In other words, *Fight Club*'s vision of liberation and politics relies on gendered and sexist hierarchies that flow directly from the consumer culture it claims to be criticizing. (272)

This is, of course, because the 'feminization' most critiqued within the film is that of the making of men into consumers. Thus, in Giroux's reading, although the film appears to have a problem with consumerism, it takes it out on women, through an 'its intensely misogynist representation of women, and its intimation that violence is the only means through which men can be cleansed of the dire affect women have on the shaping of their identities' (275):

> From the first scene of *Fight Club* to the last, women are cast as the binary opposite of masculinity. Women are both the other and a form of pathology. Jack begins his narrative by claiming that Marla is the cause of all of his problems. Tyler consistently tells Jack that men have lost their manhood because they have been feminized; they are a generation raised by women. And the critical commentary on consumerism presented throughout the film is really not a serious critique of capitalism as much as it is a criticism of the feminization and domestication of men in a society driven by relations of buying and selling. Consumerism is criticized because it is womanish stuff. Moreover, the only primary female character, Marla, appears to exist to simultaneously make men unhappy and to service their sexual needs. Marla has no identity outside of the needs of the warrior mentality, the chest-beating impulses of men who revel in patriarchy and enact all of the violence associated with such traditional, hyper masculine stereotypes. (275)

If this is indeed the state of affairs depicted within *Fight Club*, then to Giroux's mind this is a matter of *wider cultural* and not just *filmic* significance. This is because, on his reading (and despite the protestations of many directors and film critics), films are not hermetically sealed pieces of innocent fun. Films *connect*. Films *impact*. Films intervene and inform, in various ways. Using his favourite vocabulary, Giroux argues:

> Films such as *Fight Club* become important as public pedagogies because they play a powerful role in mobilizing meaning, pleasures, and identifications. They produce and reflect important considerations of how human beings should live, engage with others, define themselves, and address how a society should take up questions fundamental to its survival. At the same time, if we are to read films such as *Fight Club* as social and political allegories articulating deeply rooted fears, desires, and visions, they have to be understood within a broader network of cultural spheres and institutional formations rather than as isolated texts. The pedagogical and political character of such films resides in the ways in which they align with broader social, sexual, economic, class, and institutional configurations. (282)

Thus, says Giroux, 'praise of the fun completely ignores how it might be taken up as a form of public pedagogy or public transcript'. Praise of the film does not consider the social and political implications of the fact that the film 'resonates and functions through its refusal to rupture dominant codes within a much larger discursive arena in which violence, masculinity, and sexism are being presented by the right-wing and dominant media'. In other words, it is a mistake to regard this or any film text 'as if it were merely hermetic', or an isolated island. For doing so would make us 'unable to engage it through a language of articulation that addresses *Fight Club* in the context of contemporary representations and politics, particularly around the inter-relationship among gender, violence, and masculinity' (277-278).

This is doubtless very important stuff. In many ways I agree completely with Giroux's broadly 'discursive approach': films articulate, films supplement, etc. However, I also agree very much with Meaghan Morris's complaint about what she calls 'a strictly armchair way of seeing or not-seeing films which first views them as evidence of some social or political mess, then treats them as guilty stand-ins for that mess – and wages a war of attitude on other viewers' (2001: 171). Giroux's relation to the text is certainly 'politically correct', in the sense given to it by Morris – a discussion that we will return to in some depth in Chapter Four. Indeed, his reading is very moralistic. This is so much so that it is arguably not really a 'reading' of the film at all – at least not in the 'dialectical' sense that he claims to champion. Indeed, one might even say that it is perhaps *primarily only Giroux* for whom 'masculinity is defined in opposition to both femininity and consumerism' in the film, insofar as it is Giroux who is also guilty of 'refusing to take up either in a dialectical and critical way' (271). This is first because Giroux does not seem interested in taking the narrative and dramatic *movement* of the film into consideration. For Giroux, that is, the film is treated as a static image of a problematic masculinity: as if we all identify with and/or desire Tyler Durden. Yet the film asks us to *identify with* 'Jack', and, like Jack, to *desire* Tyler. But it also asks us – along with Jack – to realize the problematic character of the dehumanized fascist community that Tyler's reign precipitates. Thus, Tyler does not remain in the same 'position', for us, or in the same relation to us. First he is the object of desire, then he transforms into its monstrous double. Moreover, at the same time as Tyler is transforming, so the film's movement through the homoerotic Oedipal relationship is transforming the status of Marla, and Jack's relationship to Marla. This is something that Giroux does not seem to notice: Marla and Jack presumably 'live happily ever after'. In this sense, the film comes down firmly on the side of a fairly standard heteronormativity: kill your father, but not really, and marry your mother, but not really. Furthermore, and surely more significantly, *Fight Club* also makes fairly clear that the real incarnation of everything Jack has conjured up in the form of Tyler is actually Marla. Marla is the real, living version of the carefree, fearless, anarchic soul that Jack can only imagine being.

A lot more could be said about this. But what seems clear at this point is that it is possible to say both yes and no to Giroux at the same time. Mostly, he very importantly evokes a clear notion of the *articulation of film* as a significant *cultural* factor. Yet he seems unable to *read* the film. Or, rather, his reading is unconvincing in many respects. It is not dialectical – not even as dialectical as the film itself. It is moralistic – taking the film as a symptom and agent of wider social problems, and blaming the audience for liking it. Moreover, *it is way too tidy*. That is, Giroux takes what Meaghan Morris calls a 'ploddingly sociological approach': 'By plodding, I do not mean a sociology which goes out to explore the dense social contexts of film consumption today; in cinema as distinct from television studies, we've had very little of that. I mean a strictly armchair way of seeing or not-seeing films which first views them as evidence of some social or political mess, then treats them as guilty stand-ins for that mess – and wages a war of attitude on other viewers' (2001: 171). One consequence of this is that Giroux can place the film in an economy of supposed social relations and effects and judge it accordingly. But he does not allow for the complexity of viewing relations nor the multiplicity and undecidability of effects. Giroux does not show any interest in the psychoanalyzable intertextuality of the film's construction of masculinity – a psychoanalyzable intertextuality that is organized enormously by Tyler's visual references to Bruce Lee.

How might this change Giroux's reading of *Fight Club*, and 'violent film' more generally (if such a grouping could be made)? To recap, he regards it first of all as a Hollywood attempt to talk about the deleterious effects of capitalism on culture and subjectivity, but that in the end it fails and demonstrates Hollywood's inability to offer a critique of capitalism. This is because the critique of consumerism which permeates the film the film descends, he argues, into a rather thin psychologism by the end. Thus, the film collapses into an agreement with Edward Norton's character that he was just going through a very peculiar time – as he walks off into a happy ever after with his new girlfriend. In executing Tyler Durden, he has exorcised his demons and can accede to non-schizophrenic love with his woman. Thus, in a strong sense, the whole anti-consumerism and anti-capitalism that gets the film moving has been something of a subplot to the love story of the male and female leads.

But if the film is to be regarded as a kind of talking about capital-ism – and a difficulty or impasse in Hollywood's ability to critique capi-talism – it is also equally a kind of talking about Bruce Lee. If the film is 'communication', then perhaps it communicates a lot about Bruce Lee, or his relation to culture and subjectivity. In fact, *Fight Club* also offers a sustained psychoanalytic account of subjectivity. And this dimension or mode of address of the film is a lot more compelling and sustained than that of the anti-consumerist-focus that Giroux identifies. That is to say, if the denouement of the film devolves irreducibly on Norton's striking at himself – shooting himself in the throat, in fact – to rid himself of his de-mon, this is the very element that Giroux's reading does not consider and cannot apparently comprehend. Instead, Giroux simply brushes off this crucial aspect of the film, and prefers to leave it as a rather inconsequen-tial 'mystery':

> In a psychic meltdown that is long overdue, Jack realizes that he and Tyler are the same person, signaling a shift in the drama from the realm of the sociological to the psychological. Jack discovers that Tyler has planned a series of bombings around the unmentioned city and goes to the police to turn himself in. But the cops are members of Operation Mayhem and at-tempt to cut off his testicles because of his betrayal. Once more Jack res-cues his manhood by escaping and eventually confronting Tyler in a build-ing that has been targeted for demolition by Operation Mayhem. Jack fares badly in his fight with Tyler and ends up at the top of the building with a gun in his mouth. Jack finally realizes that he has the power to take control of the gun and has to shoot himself in order to kill Tyler. He puts the gun in his mouth and pulls the trigger. Tyler dies on the spot and Jack mysteri-ously survives. Marla is brought to the scene by some Operation Mayhem members. Jack orders them to leave and he and Marla hold hands and watch as office buildings explode all around them. In an apparent repudia-tion of all that he/Tyler has been about, Jack turns to Marla and tells her not to worry, 'You met me at a weird time in my life', suggesting that life will get better for the both of them in the future. (267)

Giroux is right to note that this culmination signals a shift from the socio-logical to the psychological within the film. It is true that *Fight Club* recoils from its critique of capitalism and consumerism. But it changes things somewhat when one notes that the film actually gains its consistency and coherence in an entirely symbolic and semi- or pseudo-psychoanalytic register. In a realist sense, Norton's character is indeed schizophrenic, and it is in his victory over Durden that normality is restored: Norton identifies the problem as involving a strong aspect or element of himself, so he strikes at himself, and thereby defeats that part of him that is unacceptable – his dangerous supplement, so to speak. This device is seen in lots of films: *A Beautiful Mind* (2001) for instance, or – better – *How to get Ahead in Advertising* (1989). In these narratives, the protagonists succeed by struggling with and then repressing the aberrant/abhorrent element. In both, the subversive voices are silenced, although the subversive elements remain, on the sidelines, on the margins, as a blemish. They haunt or antagonise the victor, but he remains in control. In *Fight Club*, however, the subversive element is apparently executed. But even if we remain within the realms and terms of the conservative heteronormative realism that the film champions in its denouement, the question remains: if Tyler Durden amounts to the personification of the ultimate male fantasy of masculinity – everything men want to be – then what happens to that fantasy after Tyler's execution? What other fantasy takes its place? Or is masculinity now a fantasy-free zone? That is, how can Norton's character have killed, removed, and exorcised his constitutive fantasy?

Tyler Durden has been the embodiment of a particular fantasy of masculinity: fearless, powerful, empowering, lean and muscular, blasé and yet 'rational', competent, etc.: he 'exemplifies an embodied masculinity that refuses the seductions of consumerism, while fetishizing forms of production – from soaps to explosives, the ultimate negative expression of which is chaos and destruction'. In this way, argues Giroux:

> Tyler represents the magnetism of the isolated, dauntless antihero whose public appeal is based on the attractions of the cult personality rather than on the strength of an articulated democratic notion of political reform. Politics for Tyler is about doing, not thinking. As the embodiment of aggressive masculinity and hyper-individualism, Tyler cannot imagine a politics that connects to democratic movements, and is less a symbol of vision and leadership for the next millennium than a holdover of early-twentieth century fascist ideologies that envisioned themselves as an alternative to the decadence and decay of the established order of things. (268)

What seems particularly significant through all of this is the extent to which the physical superlative that is Durden is obviously modelled on Bruce Lee. Durden's posture, his movements – especially when fighting Norton – in his techniques, and in particular his way of 'showboating' are all appropriated directly from Bruce Lee films. Just to make sure we 'get' these references, *Fight Club* also has Tyler playing with nunchakus in the background of several scenes. In these moments, we catch him mimicking the screeches and screams of Bruce Lee whilst hitting random pieces of furniture with the 'nun-chucks' – a weapon that was popularised in the West be Bruce Lee: two short lengths of wood (each about twelve inches long) linked together by a four to six inch length of chain or cord. What seems most striking in these scenes is the comical effect of Durden's evident incompetence with this weapon. The question of whether this comical incompetence is a deliberate or intentional element within the film is less important than the fact that the film puts the nunchakus in Tyler's hands in the first place, and that he parades around with them in a manner doubtless all too familiar to countless teenage boys (myself included). In fact, the nunchaku scenes in *Fight Club* are strongly reminiscent of the episode of the sitcom *Friends* in which we are introduced to Phoebe's brother. Ross sees him 'practicing' with nunchakus in silhouette on Monica's balcony and he asks Phoebe, 'What is that? Karate?' To which Phoebe replies, 'Oh no, he just makes it up'. Similarly, when Tyler is 'training' with nunchakus, he is *clearly* making it up.

The status of Bruce Lee as vehicle for a certain fantasy is not considered by Giroux, who prefers to consider the question of violence 'directly'. For Giroux, the *basic, literal* proposition of *Fight Club* is that 'senseless brutality becomes crucial to a form of male bonding, glorified for its cathartic and cleansing properties' (272-3). The problem with this is that, 'by maximizing the pleasures of bodies, pain, and violence, *Fight Club* comes dangerously close to giving violence a glamorous and fascist edge' (273). Indeed, he proposes, aesthetically *Fight Club* 'mimics fascism's militarization and masculinization of the public sphere with its exultation of violence' as a 'space in which men can know themselves better and love one another legitimately in the absence of the feminine' (273). Hence his damning conclusion that Fight Club is 'a packaged representation of masculine crisis' which simply and problematically 'reduces the body to a receptacle for pain parading as pleasure, and in doing so fails to understand how the very society it attempts to critique uses an affirmative notion of the body and its pleasures to create consuming subjects' (273). To critics who might wish to assert that such films are merely a bit of fun, Giroux retorts that any such 'comments exhibit a cavalier indifference to the ways in which films operate as public pedagogies within a broader set of articulations' (278-9). What are these pedagogies? What is 'communicated'? To Giroux's mind:

> films function as public discourses that address or at least resonate with broader issues in the historical and sociopolitical context in which they are situated. There is no sense of how *Fight Club* – or films in general – bridge the gap between public and private discourses, playing an important role in placing particular ideologies and values into public conversation while offering a pedagogical space for addressing specific views of how everyday lives are intertwined with politics, social relations, and existing institutional formations. For instance, Fincher seems completely unaware of how his portrayal of violence and hypermasculinity resonates with the reactionary mythology of warrior culture that reached its heyday during Ronald Reagan's presidency and found its cultural embodiment in figures such as John Wayne, Oliver North, and a host of Hollywood movies celebrating rogue warriors such as *Lethal Weapon, Missing in Action, Robocop,* and *Rambo.* (279)

But for whom does it resonate thus, and for what reasons? Giroux acknowledges that, like any other cultural text, *Fight Club* 'can be read differently by different audiences, and this suggests the necessity to take up such texts in the specificity of the contexts in which they are received' (282). Nevertheless, his conviction is that 'educators, social critics, and others can shed critical light on how such texts work pedagogically to legitimate some meanings, invite particular desires, and exclude others' (282). This seems reasonable enough. But, he continues with the following rather peculiar formulation: 'Acknowledging the educational role of such films requires that educators and others find ways to make the political more pedagogical' (282). With this, Giroux asserts his broadly Gramscian conception of culture as *contingent education,* and of 'culture' and 'education' as coterminous and interchangeable terms. Inevitably, of course, this places 'the educator' – i.e., Giroux himself – in a very important position. But even more inevitably, therefore, this position is constantly and always already usurped, by the pesky popular cultural productions that aren't being responsible and educated enough for his taste. The only solution is to drum the proper messages into any who will listen – to 'attempt to make students and others more attentive to visual and popular

culture as an important site of political and pedagogical struggle' (283).
Of course, despite the odds being stacked against the impact of such an
'attempt' registering on the wider cultural and political discourses that are
its object, Giroux's proposed pedagogy is very progressive and sophisticated, as we can see:

> Such a pedagogy would raise questions regarding how certain meanings
> under particular historical conditions become more legitimate as represen-
> tations of the real than others, or how certain meanings take on the force of
> commonsense assumptions and go relatively unchallenged in shaping a
> broader set of discourses and social configurations. Such a pedagogy
> would raise questions about how *Fight Club*, for instance, resonates with
> the ongoing social locations and conditions of fear, uncertainty, sexism,
> and political despair through which many people now live their lives.
> More specifically, a pedagogy of disruption would engage a film's at-
> tempts to shift the discourse of politics away from issues of justice and
> equality to a focus on violence and individual freedom as part of a broader
> neoliberal backlash against equity, social citizenship, and human rights.
> Such an approach would not only critically engage the dominant ideolo-
> gies of masculinity, violence, and sexism that give *Fight Club* so much
> power in the public imagination, but also work to expose the ideological
> contradictions and political absences that characterize the film by chal-
> lenging it as symptomatic of the growing reaction against feminism, the
> right-wing assault on the welfare state, and the increasing use of violence
> to keep in check marginalized groups such as young black males who are
> now viewed as a threat to order and stability. (283)

There is indeed a great deal to be said for Giroux's characterisation of
what *Fight Club* may register or resonate with. But it strikes me that for-
mulating the key problematic as if it relates to what people might 'learn'
from films to be slightly naïve. As Stuart Hall pointed out in the 1970s,
'We know that representations of violence on the TV screen "are not violence but messages about violence": but we have continued to research
the question of violence [...] as if we were unable to comprehend this
epistemological distinction' (1980: 131). Similarly, as Meaghan Morris
reminds us, 'film worlds are fictional, they are realms of fantasy and desire in which the process of make-believe itself is of central concern'.
Accordingly, she suggests, 'the "worthy issues" we call social themes are
often alibis for what really moves us in the cinema, "the wonderful aso-
cial wish to do whatever you please"' (2001: 172). Of course, she recog-
nizes that there is always 'a phantasmatic "connection" between films and
other realities, perhaps between spectators' (172). But the point is, despite
his valuable assertion of considering film as or within relations of *articulation*, Giroux's notion of 'communication' is perhaps both slightly too

literal and (hence) rather limited (in being logocentric) – a sort of *academic fantasy* about how cultural pedagogies *should* work. (We will return to this topic in Chapter Four.)

For, again, whether conceived as 'communication' or as 'pedagogy', cultural communication or pedagogy may well not work in anything like the dry hermeneutic and moralistic ways that many critics would prefer. Messages about violence may neither necessarily be violent nor even 'about' violence. Reciprocally, then, maybe cultural critics concerned about culture and pedagogy need not worry so much about the consequences of violent messages. They may not be rewiring us, making us into little psychopaths. Maybe 'messages' and 'communication' don't work so smoothly or predictably.

My Dad's Bruce Lee

To see what I am suggesting by this, I would propose to look neither at empirical statistics, nor at arguments about media effects. Rather, I would suggest that we might learn a lot from looking at or, rather, listening to the surprise pop hit of Christmas and New Year 2005-6 in the UK. This was a song called 'JCB Song' by the band Nizlopi (2005). Everything about it can be regarded as surprising. Released by a hitherto largely unknown band, 'JCB Song' song reached number 2 in the BBC Radio One singles chart. Commentators deemed this event particularly remarkable because it was successful apparently without very much in the way of a marketing campaign or commercial apparatus behind it. So its success seemed to relate largely to the song's inherent appeal. The question of where the source of such an appeal might lie would seem difficult to ascertain, given that musically the song is simple and unremarkable, lyrically it is child-like (it is sung by an adult but in the first person of a five year old boy, 'Luke'), and it is arguably neither particularly innovative, trailblazing, nor indeed even of its moment (nor even fashionably out of step with its moment). Indeed, it could not really be said to enact the norms or fantasies either of most popular music of the time, nor those of most typical 'Christmas' hits in particular.

Nevertheless, what the song lacked in terms of fashionableness it more than made up for in terms of what might be termed a certain recognisable fantasy structure, a fantasy structure that is played out in the mode of nostalgia. Predominantly played in melancholic minor chords, except during the final jubilant refrains, 'JCB Song' tells the story of a short journey (in the eponymous JCB digger). It is unclear whether the account is of only *one* moment within *one* journey, or whether it is a memory of regular childhood journeys merged into one emotional recollection. Either way, the song is about a momentous moment: one small step in a subjective process that is also a giant leap in terms of a relation to reality. The song begins, slowly:

> Well I'm rumbling in this JCB
> I'm five years old and my dad's a giant sitting beside me
> And the engine rattles my bum like berserk
> While we're singing 'Don't forget your shovel if you want to go to work'
> My dad's probably had a bloody hard day
> But he's being good fun and bubbling and joking away
> And the procession of cars stuck behind
> Are getting all impatient and angry but we don't mind

Then the chorus – nostalgic in the extreme for most adults, even those whose fathers didn't drive a big yellow digger:

> We're holding up the bypass, oh
> Me and my dad having a top laugh, oh-whoa
> I'm sitting on the toolbox, oh
> And I'm so glad I'm not in school boss
> I'm so glad I'm not in school, oh no

Even the literally 'so glad' and therefore putatively 'happy' lyrics of the chorus are coloured melancholy by the minor mood of the music and the timbre of the singer's voice. Again, the fact that the singer is an adult using the words of himself as (if) a five year old reinforces the nostalgia. The emphatic negative 'oh no' after the assertion of being 'glad' not to be in school introduces the likelihood that Luke is particularly happy *here* also because *here* is *not there*. The next verse explains why this might be:

> And we pull over to let the cars pass
> And pull off again, speeding by this summer green grass
> And we're like giants up here in our big yellow digger
> Like Zoids or Transformers or maybe even bigger
> And I want to transform into a Tyrannosaurus Rex
> And eat up all the bullies and the teachers and their pets
> And I'll tell all my mates 'my dad's BA Baracus
> Only with a JCB and Bruce Lee's nunchakus'

So, the problem is 'the bullies and the teachers and their pets'. One more chorus, this time lengthened by an extended reflection on being 'glad I'm not in school, boss / So glad I'm not in school'; and then the song stops. A caesura. A musical and lyrical hiatus. Key change. Tempo change – like a gear change (the gear change of a JCB climbing up a hill). And a jubilant final section, beginning with an unaccompanied, upbeat chant ('Said, I'm Luke, I'm five and my dad's Bruce Lee! / Drives me round in his JCB!'), shortly joined by upbeat and up-tempo skiffle drumming, and then the rest of the musical accompaniment (guitar plus a lively new aspect offered by a banjo). The victory chant continues, merging straight into one more upbeat rendition of the chorus, then one more series of jubilant chants, and then the song ends.

Arguably, then, the song recounts – actually, *performs* – something like a Freudian 'screen memory': a childhood event, scene, scenario or detail recalled with incredibly strong affective intensity and clarity in adulthood. For Freud, screen memories serve the function of defending against, by blotting out or covering over, pain or trauma. As we have just heard, these lyrics not only recount but actually perform, in the present tense, this child's extreme happiness at being *here*, in the JCB, with dad. But this intensely declared happiness is not just because dad is being a 'top laugh'. The lyrics also reveal that the *other* reason for the intensity of the happiness is directly related to an anxiety and an unhappiness elsewhere (another scene of interpellation). This other scene is school, with 'all the bullies and the teachers and their pets'. Thus, the scenario set out in this song is basically the working out of a psychic drama. School is where the problem lies. School is the big problem.

This is his big problem: the big bullies, the big teachers and their pets. His dad is also big. JCBs are big. Being in the JCB with his dad makes him part of the 'good big' and also equals womb-like sanctuary, safety. This is all rendered through the trope of *size*. The song is at first all about size. Largeness first stands for invulnerability. First of all, 'dad is a giant sitting beside me'. Then, next, '*we're* like giants up here in our big yellow digger'. Then a transformation into the phantasy world expressed in the lexicon of a child: to Luke, thanks to being 'up here' the digger, it feels like they are 'like Zoids or Transformers or maybe even bigger'. And this feels good. Size matters. This is because of what you can do with it: if he could only *be* a Tyrannosaurus Rex, then he really could 'eat up all the bullies and the teachers and their pets'.

This is why Luke declares that he wants to 'transform into a Tyrannosaurus Rex'. It is a fantasy solution to a practical problem. A Tyrannosaurus Rex would be able to 'eat up all the bullies and the teachers and their pets'. But even the five year old knows that such a thing is an impossible fantasy, and that there remains a harsh reality to be lived in, a real problem to be faced. Then the penny starts to drop, he starts to come to a realisation, solves a riddle, and makes a decision – and the song consists effectively in the performative moment of the making of this decision, the realisation of a solution. Seeing as he can't really do the impossible phantasmatic transformation into the ultimate 'big daddy', the Tyrant King, Tyrannosaurus Rex, he'll do the next best thing: 'I'll *tell* all my mates my dad's BA Baracus / Only with a JCB and Bruce Lee's nunchakus'. He's nearly there. The full solution appears only in the final jubilant section of the song, after the hiatus, the long pause. The jubilant, upbeat quality of this final section performs the relief and release of realising how to solve the problem, 'in reality'.

It all happens very quickly and economically in the song: competing interpellations, the journey from the relief of escape and enclosure, to fantasy, on to phantasmatic wish fulfilment, and finally to a pragmatic decision. First, imaginary fantasy: 'we're like giants up here in our big yellow digger / Like Zoids or Transformers or maybe even bigger'. Second, phantasmatic wish fulfilment: 'And I want to transform into a Tyrannosaurus Rex / And eat up all the bullies and the teachers and their pets'. Third, decision: a compromise formation, but a way to incorporate fantasy into reality in a way that modifies (an orientation within) reality: 'And I'll tell all my mates 'my dad's BA Baracus / Only with a JCB and Bruce Lee's nunchakus'. After one final reiteration of the present situation – one that is entirely Oedipally overdetermined and overcoded – 'we're holding up the bypass / Me and my dad having a top laugh... And I'm so glad I'm not in school boss', the song pauses, as if in the moment of impact, the full realisation of the solution, and then becomes triumphant, a chant, almost a mantra: the riddle is solved: to sort out the bullies and the teachers and their pets, Luke will actually go one better than telling all his mates that his dad's BA Baracus with a JCB and Bruce Lee's nunchakus – better than this, he will tell them, as he repeats, chants, jubilantly, over and over again, that his dad *is* Bruce Lee. His refrain – 'I said I'm Luke, I'm five and my dad's Bruce Lee / Drives me round in his JCB. / I'm Luke, I'm five and my dad's Bruce Lee/ Drives me round in his JCB' – equals a solution, a resolution, a dissolution of the problem, an orientation in the face of the problem, a way to defend against the pain it formerly caused. And this solution involves a profound and multi-layered identification, at once real and phantasmatic, personal and social: a victory for a hybrid of the competing interpellations. For, his dad is to him already as good as Bruce Lee, invincible, invulnerable. (Recall: 'the procession of cars stuck behind / Are getting all impatient and angry *but we don't mind*. This is important: others become angry, yet dad remains unruffled.) To tell his mates that his dad *is* Bruce Lee will serve many functions. If the gamble pays off, this will be the way that he can retain them as allies, recruiting them to his fantasy, as well as opening up a space for subsequently *handling* the bullies and teachers and teachers' pets. His mates may even be able to understand the 'real' reason why if and when he is attacked he need not even fight back or get his dad to fight for him: it is because – in the manner of all good martial arts and action hero movies – he would certainly win – he has always already won. *Obviously*. His dad's Bruce Lee: how could you *ever* beat that? Indeed, to recall Bruce Lee's famous reply to the bully in *Enter the Dragon*, Luke has just learned 'the art of fighting without fighting'.

Perhaps the many permutations and permeations of this 'lesson' could profitably be learned by more people – not just film and cultural critics, but pragmatists of all orders. For, if it is somehow 'wrong' for films like *Fight Club* (or indeed even perhaps films like *Way of The Dragon*) to propose direct face to face physical action in the present as a viable 'strategy' of either survival, reconstruction or social change, then perhaps it is equally misguided for the cultural critic to proceed according to an equally phantasmatic logic of 'direct action' or of supposedly 'keeping it real', as if culture 'works' ('communicates' or 'teaches') literally or directly.

Chapter 3
Fantasy—Fighting

Revenge Fantasies, East and West

'Almost everyone I've met who practises martial arts got hooked on it as an impressionable teenager', observes Brian Preston (2007: 70). 'They saw a Bruce Lee movie, or a Jet Li movie, or some guy on TV splitting bricks with the blade of his bare palm, or Royce Gracie kicking ass in the UFC' and they became 'hooked'. Preston proposes that this is because the 'adolescent mind easily surrenders to fantasy, and the majority of fantasies fall neatly into three categories: success, sex, and revenge':

> In life we tend to outgrow our teenage fantasies of success – at twenty you realize you'll never drive Formula One or score on a penalty at the World Cup, at thirty you admit you'll never be a rock star and open for U2, at forty you accept you'll never be president or prime minister. That leaves sex and revenge as lifelong fodder for fantasy. Sex needn't concern us here. This is about revenge. (Preston 2007: 70)

This is of course a fairly casual deployment of the notion of fantasy, a term that has a significantly different and loaded resonance in the realms of cultural and film studies. Slavoj Žižek explains the sense in which fantasy is understood in such academic contexts. First, although fantasy is certainly 'a hallucinatory realization of desire' (Žižek 2005: 304), nevertheless, in the Lacanian sense, it is not the case that 'the subject knows in advance what he wants and then, when he cannot get it in reality, proceeds to obtain a hallucinatory satisfaction in reality' (304). This would actually be rather closer to the psychoanalytic mechanism of 'wit', which Freud thought to be at work in making and 'getting' jokes. Rather, says

Žižek, 'the subject originally doesn't know what he wants, and it is the role of fantasy to tell him that, to "teach" him to desire' (2005: 304). Of course, Preston's book, *Bruce Lee and Me: A Martial Arts Adventure*, is a novelistic work of what the author himself calls 'narrative non-fiction'. As such, it is safe to assume that considerations of readability will have outweighed attention to what we might want to call theoretical rigour, or the exercising of methodological (pre)caution before using terms or making claims or conclusions.

Yet, even though it would be wise to take issue with the smooth facility of Preston's connections, statements and claims, and even though it is of course prudent to question, challenge or examine their validity and test their limits, at the same time we ought nevertheless to recognise the value of these thought-provoking observations. This is not least because, as Rey Chow has argued, 'what we need to examine ever more urgently is fantasy, a problem which is generally recognized as central to orientalist perceptions and significations' (1998: 75). This is because fantasy ought to be 'understood to be a kind of structuring and setting that is indispensable to any consideration of subjectivity' (76). Fantasy, she argues, 'is not simply a matter of distortion or wilful exploitation, but is rather an inherent part of our consciousness, our wakeful state of mind' (76). Indeed, it bears directly on matters of self-regard, of the structuring and organization of one's relation to or construction-perception of 'reality', and can therefore take us beyond questions of 'subjectivity to philosophical issues of phenomenology and ontology' (76). As Chow asks of Gallimard, the male protagonist in *M. Butterfly*, we might equally ask of those enamoured of martial arts fantasies and figures: 'what happens when a man falls in love, not with a woman or even with another man, not with a human being at all but with a thing, a reified form of his own fantasy?' (78)

Now, even if Preston's claims are anecdotal and 'casual', there is something significant in the fact that they are so readily intelligible, uncontroversial, and even plausible. That is to say, we might well be able to take issue with the rigour of the method that supports the assertions, but the very fact that they can be made so clearly and easily, without fear of causing controversy, plus the very widespread range of the anecdotal sources, perhaps testifies to a wider cultural consensus – at least to the extent that you or I might also be able to concur that, yes, almost everyone *I've* ever met who practices martial arts got hooked on it as an impressionable teenager, too, after seeing a particular film or being exposed to a particular sort of conceptual/mythological universe. Examples might include secret 'Oriental' underworlds of superhuman ninjas and mystical Shaolin monks with their ch'i and death touches, or perhaps that of ex-special forces agents, from James Bond or *The Man From U.N.C.L.E.* to the characters played by Chuck Norris, Van Damme, Dolph Lundgren, and more recently Matt Damon as Jason Bourne in the *Bourne* films, and beyond. Bruce Lee's pragmatic kung fu films occupy a very particular position here, of course, as we can see.

But, is Bruce Lee's 'influence' primarily an influence over 'impressionable teenagers'? Is it just related to some 'fact' about the 'adolescent mind', which all too 'easily surrenders to fantasy'? In any eventuality, what is the status of fantasy and what is the significance of such surrender? We will defer a consideration of whether fantasies can really be separated into neat categories, discrete boxes, such as those of 'success, sex and revenge', but rather entertain the possibility that any or all of these are intimately involved in subjectivity, or *subjectivization* (a notion we will consider in more depth in the following chapter). Of course, what this implies is that even when we are concerned primarily with fantasies of revenge, this does not necessarily mean that sex needn't concern us. As we will see through a consideration of fantasies about fighting (fantasy fighting as much as fighting fantasies) via examples from film, spectatorship and related cultural practices, regard and self-regard, sex and violence, cannot be disentangled.

This chapter will examine the topics of fantasy in relation to film and cognate or contiguous subjective and cultural practices in various ways. It will further the arguments of the previous chapters that fantasy and physical reality cannot be divorced, as even 'in what makes reality seem original to us, fantasy is at work' (Mowitt 2002: 143). As argued in Chapter One, fantasies are both social and psychic, and this frustrates the possibility of a simple or sharp distinction between objective and subjective, and indeed between the inside and the outside of the subject. Fantasies *supplement* the subject: they are an element from *outside* that is also at the heart of the *inside* (Derrida 1981; 1998). To reiterate Judith Butler's account, fantasies are actually dynamically linked with 'social norms' – the values and practices that 'are variously lived as psychic reality' (2000:

154). Accordingly, 'Norms are not static entities, but incorporated and interpreted features of existence that are sustained by the idealizations furnished by fantasy' (152).

The contingent, historicisable and performative element of these norms is something that Butler always takes great pains to emphasize. For, in Butler's understanding, *what* norms *are* and how fantasy interacts with and supports or produces them is always the product of complex contingent interactions, in terms of 'what is going on' in one's culture, in one's life, in the world, and so on. In this context, then, it is perhaps even more interesting to take seriously Brian Preston's swift and easy account of precisely why Bruce Lee entered into the Western imaginary so power-fully at the historical moment that he did. Indeed, Preston's account actu-ally has rather strong affinities with the sort of argument that might be made in the most academic of discourse analyses: it covers mechanisms that are impeccably 'discursive', it is related to history (to what 'is there', what is 'going on'), and it concerns 'something about people' (specifi-cally, the quite possibly universal functions of identification, fantasy and desire). For instance, in an interpretive account that is akin to the most theoretical of discourse analyses in all but style and tone, Preston's ac-count seamlessly articulates macropolitical events and processes with popular cultural interests and subjective identifications, tastes and prac-tices: Bruce Lee, he says, 'exploded onto the world stage just as the Viet Cong, the wee pajama-clad fighting tigers of a tiny Asian nation called Vietnam, were kicking big bad John Wayne America's butt' (2007: 76):

> The Americans armoured themselves in tonnes of brawny gleaming steel, and their terrifying modern weaponry dropped megatonnes of muni-tions and chemicals like Agent Orange, but they still proved no match for a bunch of guys hiding out in caves dug by hand under their bamboo huts. The politics of 'freedom' versus Communism became irrelevant in a mis-match like that – the underdog by default became the good guy. Then along came Bruce Lee, and suddenly every teenage North American boy with a testosterone-fuelled fantasy of being tough, of righting the wrongs of the world with pugilistic powers, was identifying with a lithe, agile Chinese man, all fists and attitude, barely five-and-a-half feet tall. Millions of young men flooded into Kung Fu schools that suddenly appeared out of nowhere to teach the new fighting techniques. Overnight, Asian martial arts was mainstream. Can't beat the Asians? *Become* the Asians. Bruce Lee was the public face of that coping mechanism.
> On the other side of the world, Bruce Lee was the public face of a ris-ing Asian self-confidence, the ice-breaker who showed Asians they could compete, and win, on the world stage. Bruce Lee was their first champion,

the David they shoved forward to face the best of the Philistines. He slew the Philistines, all right. They fell in love with him. (Preston, 2007: 76-77)

Thus, says Preston, 'I respect Bruce Lee's place in martial arts. I respect the influence he has had on nearly every martial artist who came of age in the last thirty years. Without Bruce Lee, would East have met West? Certainly not as soon, or as spectacularly' (2007: 77). Stephen Teo agrees, proposing that 'no other figure … has done as much to bring East and West together in a common sharing of culture as Bruce Lee', and that in Bruce Lee 'Hong Kong cinema found its most forceful ambassador; an Asian role model espousing aspects of an Eastern culture who found receptive minds in the West' (1997: 110). However, Teo argues, *in the East* the appeal of Lee integrally includes an indelible and active reference to a certain 'Chinese nationalism', which 'cannot be easily dismissed if one wishes to appreciate fully his appeal to Chinese audiences' (111). This remained 'a rather abstract and apolitical type of nationalism': 'an emotional wish among Chinese people living outside China to identify with China and things Chinese, even though they may not have been born there or speak its national language or dialects' (111). Indeed, Miller suggests wryly, even within China, 'the chief religion is not Taoism or Buddhism. Nor is it Confucianism or Maoism'; rather, the main 'religion among Chinese *is* Chinese, the religion of being Chinese, as being Jewish means more to those who are Hebrew than simple religion and ethnicity' (2000: 121-2).We will return to this recurrent idea about ethnic Chinese nationalism, in the final chapter.

Despite the fact that 'an anti-Western sentiment is more than apparent in his persona' (Teo 1997: 110), Bruce Lee could still remain appealing to Western audiences because, as Teo sees it, Lee 'went further' than merely espousing Chinese nationalism, 'overlaying what was essentially a humanist reaction against racism with a Chinese nationalist sentiment'. Rather, Lee's movies also emphasized themes of 'pride and anti-racism' (110). In other words, because they always staged a mismatch of innocent Chinese versus organised aggressors (a corrupt drug-trafficking employer, an aggressive Japanese institution in a colonial situation, a mafia-like gang in Rome, an evil Fu Manchu-esque drug trafficker with a private army on an impregnable fortress island), Lee's movies could also be enjoyed by those whose national, ethnic or colonial situation might literally be antithetical to Chinese nationalism. But, like capitalism versus communism, the politics of Japan, America, Britain or Russia versus China become irrelevant in a mismatch like those staged in Lee's films – 'the underdog by default became the good guy'. But does this mean that the *jouissance* of Bruce Lee revenge fantasies are thus able to function in a potentially 'universal' or 'universalizable' way for both Eastern and Western subjects? And does this mean that Eastern and Western subjectivity is 'essentially the same' (perhaps a sameness produced by sharing or investing in the same fantasy figure)?

Sick Men of Asia, and Other Animals: Or, Contingency, Universality and Narcissistic Violence

Bruce Lee's martial action might be regarded as culturally deterritorialized or deracinated. As Lee himself was fond of saying and writing, really how many ways can there be for two humans – each biologically the same, with just two arms, two legs, two hands, two feet and one head – to fight hand to hand and toe to toe? In other words, he regarded his approach as basically *universal* and *scientific*. (True, he regarded and often sought to champion China as the originator of kung fu, but – as we will consider more fully in Chapter Four – he equally sought to extricate himself from the stultifying constraints or strictures of non-scientific traditions and institutions.) But what kind of universalism or universality is this? For, rather than being 'universal' – or a claim to embody a universality – a quality that Ernesto Laclau characterises as a permanently deferred 'elusive fullness' (2000: 80) – it is perhaps easier to argue that Lee's martial arts (both the celluloid version and the taught version) have, in fact, been hegemonized, colonised or expropriated (or even, to use Derrida's term, *ex-appropriated*) by particularly *Western* ideas, principles and ideals: ideas and ideals that are liberal, multicultural, interdisciplinary, even antidisciplinary or anarchic. We will explore all of this more fully in Chapter Four.

First, we should explore the question of the universality or inevitability of fantasies about violence. Is positing such a fantasy as universal to *essentialize* a desire that is presumably biologically male? Is it to attribute an essential type of fantasy to an essential 'human nature' – one which is regarded therefore as 'essentially' violent and aggressive? Is it inevitable that, upon seeing a martial arts film or spectacle, men or women might henceforth be likely to fantasize about violence, as Preston does at one moment in his narrative when he imagines with relish the fantasy scenario of striding into the office of a newspaper that pulled out of publishing a story they'd commissioned from him, and kicking their asses in the manner of Bruce Lee?

My position is that one need not essentialize or construct a fantasy about the 'necessary' *character* or *contents* of a fixed, stable or essential 'human nature' in order to regard something like 'violence' as constitutive or inevitable. For instance, post-structuralist and post-Marxist paradigms propose the notion of 'antagonism' (and conflict) as not only inevitable, but also constitutive. Such approaches offer us a variety of ways out of or away from essentialisms about 'human nature' or 'male fantasy'. In such approaches, identities and institutions *themselves* are regarded as arising in response to antagonistic plays of forces (Protevi 2001). Indeed, antagonism and conflict are regarded as constitutive of identities. As Paul de Man puts it, 'violence' may be regarded both as 'self-constitutive' (1978: 24) and as inevitably entailing conflict with otherness. Subjects 'have to behave in such a potentially violent and authoritarian way' because 'this is the only way in which it can constitute its own existence, its own ground':

> Entities, in themselves, are neither distinct nor defined; no one could say where one entity ends and where another begins. They are mere flux, 'modifications'. By considering itself as the place where this flux occurs, the mind stabilizes itself as the ground of the flux, the *lieu de passage* through which all reality has to pass... (de Man 1978: 24)

Similarly, Fredric Jameson has insisted that the relationship between social and cultural 'groups is, so to speak, unnatural', always based on 'the chance external contact between entities' (qtd. in Chow 2002: 55). Reciprocally, what is also significant here is that other than through 'contact' with other groups, 'groups' themselves cannot otherwise be said to have an 'exterior' (and hence arguably no sense of 'identity' as such). They are not properly 'groups' before contact with that which they rub up against a surface of and decide they are not. There is no group before the antagonistic attempt to distinguish and distance a self from an other group. In Jameson's words, groups 'have only an interior (...) and no exterior or external surface, save in this special circumstance in which it is precisely the outer edge of the group that – all the while remaining unrepresentable – brushes against that of the other'. 'Speaking crudely then', he continues, 'we would have to say that the relationship between groups must always be one of struggle and violence' (qtd. in Chow 2002: 55). The reconceptualization of violence and conflict as factors that are *constitutive* of identity is an extremely important insight for any cultural study. Violence, antagonism and conflict are not secondary elements that might somehow be eradicated over time – as if violence might subside if people would only start to be nicer to each other.

Such insights are equally important for the study of Bruce Lee, of course, and in more ways than one. We might consider for instance the memorable moment in *Fist of Fury* when Bruce Lee affirms: 'Now you listen to me. I will say this only once. We are not sick men'. This comes at the culmination of Lee's famous battle in the Japanese school, the point at which he returns the offensive framed poster of the words 'Sick Men of Asia' to the Japanese School. The Japanese martial artists irreverently presented this offensive 'gift' to the Chinese School at the official funeral of the Chinese school's master. Seeking revenge for this outrageous act of disrespect, Lee has marched into the Japanese dojo, beaten every student and teacher, and forced two senior Japanese martial artists to do what they had earlier arrogantly vowed: namely, to 'eat these words' if any Chinese could beat them. Lee makes them do precisely this by shattering the frame and glass, tearing the poster out and stuffing handfuls of paper into their mouths and cautioning: 'This time you're eating paper. The next time it will be glass'. Revenge, a sense of justice, a sadistic *jouissance*, an assertion of identity, self-regard or self-love, and indeed actually the '*discovery*' (invention) of a certain identity *through* a violent encounter with an other: all of these are present here. As Davis Miller puts it:

> 'We are not the sick men of Asia,' Lee's screen character proclaimed to Japanese persecutors in *Fist of Fury*. With this single declaration (scripted by Lo Wei), several thousand punches and kicks, and an avenging tomcat-from-hell battle scream created expressly for this picture, Bruce Lee transcended pop idol status and came to be regarded as a messiah not only by millions of Hong Kong Chinese, but eventually by hundreds of millions of put-upon people throughout the world. (Miller 2000: 120)

Stephen Teo argues that while to Western viewers 'Lee is a narcissistic hero who makes Asian culture more accessible' (113), to Eastern viewers he 'is a nationalistic hero who has internationalised some aspects of Asian culture' (114). These two views may 'appear antithetical' (114), he suggests. But, to tackle this antithesis, Teo takes issue with what he regards as the exemplarily 'Western' argument – or, that is, an argument that he regards as being most often made by white Westerners – that 'Lee's narcissism is a trait which distinguishes him more than his nationalism' (1997: 113). Teo argues instead that, although simple (bodily) 'narcissism may well be one aspect of Lee's character through which an international audience gains access to eastern motives and behaviour', for a Chinese audience things are considerably different. For Chinese viewers, Teo asserts:

> Lee's narcissism is a manifestation of the anti-*ditou* [anti-shame] factor that galvanises characters into action in kung fu movies. Lee is literally putting his bravest face (and body) forward in order to show that the Chinese need no longer be weaklings. The physical art of kung fu entails the exertion of power and physique. Narcissism then ties in with Lee's urge to 'show face' *(biaomian)* as opposed to 'lose face' *(diaolian)*. (Teo 1997: 114)

For Teo, it is significant that the same signifiers function completely differently depending on the contexts of their reception. For Western audiences, Teo proposes, 'Lee's improvised action choreography ... earned him the title of postmodern hero' at the same time as 'his kung fu, part of the generic tradition of Chinese action movies, is innovative and exotic compared to the fisticuffs and armaments of Western-style action scenes' (119). On the other hand, he claims, 'Chinese audiences take pride in the image Lee projects as a superb fighting specimen of manhood who derives his status from "traditional" skills' (114). Indeed, for Teo it is the embodied fighting skills themselves that function in symmetrical yet diametrically 'opposite' ways – as exotic and novel for the west ('postmodern', says Teo; one might equally suggest 'mystical' or 'new age', as argued in the previous chapter), but as a 'traditional' source of pride for the east.

However, Teo's argument contains some significant problems. The first is that any such fantasy constructions as these surely ought to be construed as equally phantasmatic 'projections', one 'orientalist', the other 'nationalist', and both deeply ideological. The second is that even though he is unsatisfied with what he regards as the 'western' rationales for Lee's popularity, Teo nevertheless maintains the terms of the rigid taxonomical divide that he claims structure all readings of Bruce Lee. For, as Teo sees it, there is on the one hand a Bruce Lee in/for the East and, on the other hand, a Bruce Lee in/for the West, and never the twain shall meet. Teo finds this confirmed by the extent to which western viewers and critics have not adequately acknowledged Lee's Chinese nationalism. Yet, a problem remains in that Teo himself hesitates to reconcile the two different views at all. I would argue that this is because doing so would have to transform the terms and paradigms that structure Teo's work, especially as they congregate and condense around the concepts of narcissism and nationalism – Teo's key (yet uninterrogated) terms. Nevertheless, even though Teo does not take this step, the *terms* of his text can be taken to suggest that the nationalism interpretation could quite easily be combined with the narcissism interpretation, at least insofar as the nationalism is narcissistic and the narcissism is nationalistic. But Teo himself does not proceed to do this. Thus, rather than critiquing or transforming the terms of the problematic that he has identified, Teo's writing arguably simply reiterates and therefore, in a sense, confirms it.

It seems to me that Teo's refusal to relate the putatively unconnected interpretations of narcissism 'versus' nationalism derives from something that for Teo would be a problem: namely, the possibility that what subtends this putative East/West divide can indeed be identified by exploring the question of *narcissism*. Of course, in Teo's binaristic approach, making this argument will simply reconfirm how 'Western' my reading is. But it strikes me that one of the main reasons that Teo subordinates narcissism to nationalism in Bruce Lee is that he takes narcissism to refer, firstly, to 'the tendency of heroes to strike a pose in kung fu stance to evoke masculine sexuality', and secondly to refer to the 'homoeroticism, male bonding, [and] covert homosexuality [that is] part of the tradition of martial arts-kung fu films, particularly evident in the films of Zhang Che in the late 60s and 70s' (119). Both approaches to narcissism are of course very constraining. However, it remains the case that even if 'narcissism' were approached in these narrow senses, narcissism and nationalism could still be thought together as part of a productive understanding of the semiotics of nationalistic ideology. But Teo does not do this. The symptom of this is registered in the way that Teo claims to remain perplexed about Western critics' insistence on the significance of Lee's narcissism. 'What is not clear', he writes, 'is whether some Western critics offer a thesis of narcissism as a counter argument to Hong Kong critics' focus on nationalism in Lee's movies, or whether their attempts to rationalise Eastern culture has brought forth a claim of narcissism', a claim which might work 'to explain concepts such as nationalism and Lee's stand against racial prejudice' (119). Instead of choosing either option, Teo simply concludes his discussion with a restatement of the presumed opposition between nationalism and narcissism:

> To see Lee as a mere kung fu martial artist without taking into account his nationalist sentiments is to perceive Lee as Narcissus gazing in a mirror: the image reflected is an illusion without substance. It ignores the symbolism of the dragon in Lee's Chinese name, Li Xiaolong, which means Li, the Little Dragon. When the dragon looks in the mirror, it sees not Narcissus but the Chinese masses looking back. This is the substance behind the reflective theory of Hong Kong cinema – that it mirrors the aspirations of Hong Kong people, and reflects their psychological mind-set and behaviour. This is also the substance behind Lee's narcissism. With death, Lee achieved true mythic status, allowing him to be all things to all men: Narcissus gazing in the mirror or Little Dragon exhorting the Chinese to stand up and be counted. Lee achieved the distinction of being both Narcissus and Little Dragon, straddling East and West. (120)

Teo's tropology here is troubled, and troubling. He proposes that if we regard Lee as narcissistic, then this is not only to regard him as just 'gazing in a mirror', but it is also for some reason to regard that act as 'illusion without substance'. What is more, Teo's words are uncannily close to that of the Shaolin Abbot who instructs Lee at the start of *Enter the Dragon* that 'you must remember: the enemy has only images and illusions behind which he hides his true motives. Destroy the image and you will break the enemy'. Teo seeks to break this image of Lee as narcissist and to replace it instead with an idea of Lee *as* 'the Chinese masses'. How else could a dragon looking in a mirror see 'the Chinese masses looking back'? So, Lee 'is' the Chinese. This assertion seems rather more like an 'illusion without substance' than any act of looking in a mirror. Moreover, and more problematically, Teo claims this to be 'the substance behind the reflective theory of Hong Kong cinema'. So, cinema itself is here regarded as a 'mirror'. This mirror now reflects 'Hong Kong', however – or rather, 'the aspirations of Hong Kong people, and reflects their psychological mind-set and behaviour'. And *this*, we are told conclusively, 'is also the substance behind Lee's narcissism'. The 'substance' of Lee's narcissism is the metaphor of the dragon, and the cinema is a 'mirror'. Such a naïve and phantasmatic schema – a 'conclusion' which would seem to satisfy the ideologically nationalistic imagination more than anything else – clearly lacks and calls out for a fuller consideration of all of the key terms: narcissism (which is construed as subjective vanity), cinema (which is construed as a 'mirror'), nationalism (which is left empty, but is implicitly 'good'), and 'the masses' (which are a dragon).

Teo's reluctance to take seriously the notion of narcissism in Lee apparently devolves on his understanding of narcissism as *vanity* (and therefore, as feminine or feminizing). But is that all there is to narcissism? One apt way to broach this impasse is by turning to the perhaps unexpected question of the status of Bruce Lee's 'real' fighting ability.

Violence and Vanity

Perhaps the most frequently asked question about Bruce Lee is: How good a martial artist was he? Was he *really* good, or was it just all *show*? His students, acolytes and fans certainly thought very highly of him (to understate the matter quite considerably). But in the context of this discussion it is helpful to turn to the testimony of one of Lee's students, multiple-world champion martial artist Joe Lewis. Davis Miller comments that 'Lewis claims there were numerous times when he tried to get Lee to spar with him' (2000: 163). But, in Lewis' words, 'Bruce didn't spar anybody, except a couple of those guys who ran around sucking up to him'. Significantly, he asserts, 'I'll tell you right now, I never, ever, sparred with Bruce. It was never that open with Bruce, not once. Never the possibility of give and take, moment to moment, let's really get down and do it' (163). In other words, Bruce Lee would not 'reveal himself' or display his actual abilities fully in any recognised context. This is something that is deeply problematic to many people, and a strong contributory factor to what we will call in the next chapter Lee's 'undecidability'. Lewis puts it as such:

> 'Substitute the word "swimmer" for "fighter",' says Lewis. 'This was the greatest *swimmer* of all time. He would a beat everybody else, ever'.
> 'Was he?' I ask. 'How many times did he win the Olympics?'
> 'Aw, man, he didn't have to do all that'. That's what those JKD guys claim. 'He was *beyond* all that,' they say.

'Now here, this guy's never competed, never been to a swim meet, we've never seen him really swim. We don't even know how many swimming lessons he had, really.
Do you see what I mean?
'Put another word in place of "fighter", does all of it start to sound stupid or what?' (169-70)

Bruce Lee's reluctance to 'reveal himself' openly or directly is regarded by Miller and Lewis as based on the fact that 'Psychologically, he *needed* to be regarded – by himself and others – as a fighter'. But, asks Miller, 'was he a *real* fighter?' (168). For the definitive statement on this topic, he again turns to Joe Lewis, whose own competitive credentials are implicitly beyond question:

'Angelo Dundee never fought,' says Lewis, 'but he understands the science of fighting. Robert De Niro looks great as Jake La Motta in *Raging Bull*. When he's standing in front of a mirror, he throws some good-looking punches. I must've heard Bruce say a hundred times, "You can't swim without getting in the water, Joe". But, what Bruce did is he *thought* about sparring. Always analysing, always figuring something out. Partly to make himself look good because he understood fighting, partly to look good in movies. All the time standing on the shore watching other guys swim. People who do something over and over do it because they like it. Why do they like it? Because it empowers them, makes them feel special. Since Bruce wasn't fighting anybody who was good, why was it empowering to analyse all that karate and wrestling and boxing? If you're not gonna get in the ring and look good, then you want to *feel* good. And what's gonna make you feel good is when you know something – and people *believe* you know something. You want to understand Bruce Lee, what makes the boy tick. It's pretty simple – it's vanity, baby'. (168-9)

This is neat and tidy, and even quite persuasive. But Lewis's conviction that this psychological schema is 'pretty simple' is also deceptive in at least one regard. First of all, it actually comes as the conclusion of a rather complex movement, organised by an implicit argument, whose steps and movements imply our acceptance of a particular psychological character or 'profile'. A second level of complexity enters when one recalls the arguments and orientations of so much scholarship in the fields of post-colonial, film and cultural studies, scholarship that can easily be applied to the study of Bruce Lee, in which arguments are regularly made about entrenched cultural, historical and geopolitical reasons for the emergence of such a psychological structure in the first place. So, despite its conclusive rhetorical flourish, Lewis' 'it's pretty simple' may be rather more like Sherlock Holmes' claim that his amazing feats of deduction were 'elementary', when in fact they were fiendishly complex or convoluted.

In other words, if Lee's motivations are as Lewis suggests, related to vanity, the question is whether this vanity really is pretty simple. An important argument advanced by Rey Chow would tend to suggest that matters are rather more complicated. According to Chow: 'Contrary to the conventional associations of narcissism as an excessive selfishness', the Freudian understanding of this notion, from which so much follows to this day (including pop psychology), 'defines narcissism as an essential concomitant of life'. Therefore, rather than being 'a misplaced perversion', Freud argues that narcissism is 'simply the basic instinctual mechanism of self-sustenance' (Chow 2002: 139). In Freud's words, it is 'the libidinal complement to the egoism of the instinct of self-preservation, a measure of which may justifiably be attributed to every living creature' (qtd. in Chow 2002: 139). 'And, yet', Chow continues, 'as in the case of human sexuality in general, things are never that simple'. For, in the Freudian account, 'narcissism is something we have to give up at an early point in our lives'. Thus, 'though essential to the human organism, narcissism is something that tends to be blocked – and out of reach'. According to Freud, this is why 'we tend to be attracted to those who appear narcissistic – who appear somehow not to have been obliged to surrender that precious, intimate relation with the self that we ourselves have been obliged to surrender'. Hence, when we 'look with adoration on such still-narcissistic people, we are unconsciously reliving the part of ourselves that has been sacrificed' (Chow 2002: 139). Following this Freudian argument, Chow points out that narcissism, therefore (and indeed 'self-regard' *per se*), 'is the complicated result of the self's negotiations with the observing collective conscience' (140). In Freud's words, 'The institution of conscience was at bottom an embodiment, first of parental criticism, and subsequently of that of society' (qtd. in Chow 2002: 140). Thus, 'how we look at ourselves and how much we value ourselves, that is, depends a great deal on our sense of being watched, approved of, and loved by others' (140).

Now, although Chow tests the limits of these psychoanalytical propositions through a reading of contemporary ethnic and immigrant *writings*, her considerations of the cultural issues attendant to 'recognition' will nevertheless be familiar to us by now in the context of the analysis of Bruce Lee. Chow notes a familiar problematic – one that Lee was by all accounts intimately concerned with – namely, the oft-repeated 'affective complaint' that surfaces time and again among Asian American writers, that there is 'no corresponding image or reflection – what may be redefined as "regard" – in the culture at large of the truth of Asian American experience: Asian Americans, it is often pointed out, are simply omitted from mainstream representations' (141). She notes that a 'legalistic response to such a complaint might involve increasing the number of Asian American representations in the media and providing larger quotas for various ethnic groups in major professions'. But, she retorts, there are considerably more complex cultural questions than quotas at play here, and these can be conceptualised usefully 'in terms of narcissism'. Indeed, she proposes 'marginalization' itself (in the sense of 'the lack of proper societal representation, the absence of societal approval'), perhaps ought really to 'be redefined in terms of a narcissistic relation that cannot be developed'. Such a thwarted relation to an other (here, mainstream society) has knock on effects for 'the love of oneself', as it amounts to a 'need (imposed by mainstream society) to abandon one's narcissism'. Hence, 'every interaction with the social order at large by necessity turns into a painful reminder of this process of suppression and wounding' (141).

As such, Bruce Lee's 'vanity' may be not quite such a simple or individual matter. Or rather, one might say, *even if it is also* psychological and individual, Lee's symptom is one that is lived more widely, 'felt by an entire group of people'. This refers it to 'a transindividual issue of attachment and belonging', something which itself may be the 'symptom of a perceived narcissistic damage, an aggression that is felt to be directed by American society at large against the self that is the "Asian American"' (141-2). Thus, Chow asks:

> Would it not be necessary to locate the loss and wounding of narcissism more specifically at the transindividual level of ethnicity, so as to clarify that what the 'Asian American' feels she cannot love is not just any part of her but precisely her 'Asian Americanness' – a mark that is not reducible to a single individualized self (because the identity it designates is collective by definition) yet meanwhile is a fluid, historical sign of difference, something that cannot be positivistically pinned down and categorized once and for all (as a statistical reality, for instance) without being turned into the most objectionable kind of cultural stereotype? (142)

Bruce Lee's adorable hypertrophic narcissism was evidently rather more manifest and hard to avoid than thwarted. Similarly, as studies and discussions of Bruce Lee regularly suggest, his cultural politics at least can be firmly made sense of in terms of a certain conflicted or ambivalent moment or movement within the discursive dialectics of postcolonial identity politics.

However, like Teo, Ackbar Abbas too hesitates before any assertion of a narcissistic interpretation of Bruce Lee. Again, this is apparently because to admit to the presence or work of 'narcissism' would implicitly therefore be to 'feminize' Bruce Lee and, by extension, once again, to feminize diasporic Chinese identity *tout court* (at least *vis-à-vis* 'Western identity' – as if such a thing simply exists, or exists simply). Indeed, as Chow acknowledges, Freud did consider narcissism to be both 'passive and feminine' (Chow 1995: 134); so, deeming Lee narcissistic could therefore be the equivalent of feminizing him. However, rather than remaining within such a limited economy, Chow emphasizes that 'Freud states that narcissism is not so much a perversion in the pejorative sense as it is a means of self-preservation' (134). Moreover, 'if we disregard this sexual bias (which is obvious)... [w]e notice that those that he identifies as narcissistic share a common status, which is the status of the outsider – marginalized, mute, or powerless – beheld from a distance' (134). Thus, even though narcissism 'as we understand it in popular usage, is the "love of the self", if we return our consideration to the Freudian usage, it should not be regarded so much as 'a perversion in the pejorative sense as [being] a means of self-preservation'. Hence, argues Chow, we should 'defocus Freud's rigid sexual division between the male and female as anaclitic and narcissistic, and instead use his argument about narcissism for a *social* analysis that would include men as well as women as narcissists' (135):

> Narcissism, seen in terms of the 'outcast' categories in which Freud locates it, can now be redefined as the effect of a cultural marginalization or even degradation. The narcissist's look of 'independence' – a self-absorption to the point of making others feel excluded – to which Freud attributes an aesthetic significance must therefore receive a new interpretation in the form of a question: is it the sign of a lack or one of a plenitude? Is it the sign of insecurity or self-sufficiency? Once we introduce the dialectic of social relation here and understand the 'exclusionary look' as a possible result of (or reaction to) being excluded, it becomes necessary to think of certain forms of narcissism not in terms of independence but as the outward symptoms of a process of cultural devastation, which leaves

the self recoiling inward, seeking its connection from itself rather than
with external reality. (Chow 1995: 135)

A discussion of Bruce Lee in terms of postcoloniality, marginalization,
diaspora, ethnicity, and so on, is extremely fertile and rewarding. Reciprocally, it raises interesting questions about Westerners' investments in
these themes, identities and practices. Indeed, it casts light and points out
questions which arguably could recede from view or never appear at all
were it not for the perspectives opened up by such theoretical problematics and reading strategies as those offered in postcolonialism. So, what
might be the status of 'Western' interest in Bruce Lee-inspired or Bruce
Lee-led martial arts activities? Any such discussion should not be under-
taken in ignorance or denial of the importance of ethnic considerations, of
course. For, as Chow points out, 'Orientalism has many guises – both
decadent and progressivist, in the form of sexual adventures and textual
devotion, *and also* in the form of political idealization, fascination with
subaltern groups and disenfranchised classes, and so forth' (Chow 1998:
75). But it remains pertinent to consider the influence of Bruce Lee in
'the West', or for non-marginal and even hegemonic subjectivities – that
is, for subjects who would not necessarily be aware of or sensitive to any
question of ethnicity, simply by virtue of their own hegemonic and
largely invisible because unrecognised ethnicity. Ethnic matters are always implicitly present in these post-colonial waters, of course. But,
when it comes to such subjectivities and positions, Leon Hunt hits the nail
on the head when he observes:

> while kung fu's corporeal exhilaration seems to act on a 'universal' body,
> moving it to ecstasy through Bordwell's 'Motion Emotion', the genre
> sometimes seems ambivalent about its non-Chinese audience. As Stephen
> Teo (1997; 2001) has emphasised, there is an insistent strain of national-
> ism in the Hong Kong martial arts film, observable in a range of films
> from *Fist of Fury/Jingwu Mun* (1972) to *Once Upon a Time in
> China/Huang Feihong* (1991). Watching kung fu films as a white, West-
> ern fan (like myself) may involve a degree of identification with Bruce
> Lee or Jet Li, but it may also lead, at some point, to finding one's counter-
> part in the *gwailo* ('white devil'), either associated with imperialist op-
> pression or the American karate experts that Bruce Lee was fond of hu-
> miliating. I may not want to (and, simply, don't) identify with Chuck Nor-
> ris in *Way of the Dragon* – hairy back, not as cool or glamorous as Bruce –
> and yet part of me knows that the Lee/Norris coliseum fight embodies a
> patriotic structure of feeling that is supposed to at least partly exclude me.
> However, it is my left liberal 'postcolonial' self that recognises this exclu-
> sion; significantly, as a teenage Bruce Lee fan, I didn't feel remotely ex-
> cluded by his films. (Hunt 2003: 3)

So, rather than remaining focused on questions of ethnicity and postcoloniality, let us (re)turn to a (re)consideration of some of the psychoanalytic
and cultural questions that Bruce Lee's intervention raise 'elsewhere' and
'otherwise' – even if that elsewhere and otherwise is now none other than
the mainstream subjectivities of hegemonic white masculinity. To be
clear, this is not to proceed in ignorance or reactionary disavowal of the
work and insights of postcolonial approaches, but rather to reconsider
Bruce Lee's intervention into and in terms of some of the cultural factors
at play within contemporary Western hegemony without remaining entirely or compulsively within the orbit of the problematization of orientalism. Of course, as Rey Chow notes:

> in the contemporary studies of the non-West that derive their ethical impe-
> tus from Edward Said's *Orientalism*, the visual culture of postcoloniality
> is usually associated with European cultural hegemony – a hegemony,
> moreover, that is defined as Europe's dominating, exploitative *gaze*....
> Because it clearly establishes seeing as a form of power and being-seen as
> a form of powerlessness, this view of visuality, even though it is greatly
> reductive, has become the basis for much antiorientalist criticism. Ironi-
> cally, however, such a view of visuality also leads antiorientalist critics to
> focus their attention excessively on the details of the European 'gaze' – a
> gaze exemplified by film, ethnography, and tourism alike – and thus un-
> wittingly to help further knowledge about *Europe* rather than the non-
> West, in a manner that is quite opposite to their moral intentions. (Chow
> 1995: 12)

My own intentions at this point are, again, 'wittingly' rather than 'unwit-
tingly' Eurocentric.

There is no *essential* difference between 'us' and 'them'. This is so
whichever way sameness and otherness are culturally demarcated (Chow
2007: 31). There is no essential sameness, of course, also. Indeed, thinking in terms of 'essences' is arguably an intellectual, ethical and political
problem in itself (as we will discuss further in the next chapter). My interest here is rather in the observation that as it was arguably Bruce Lee
films that predominantly inspired and precipitated the rapid explosion and
continued growth of participation in martial arts in the West since the
1970s, so it seems appropriate to reconsider the ways in which martial
arts as myths and practices developed, in terms of fantasy and subjectivization 'here'. ('Where?' 'There!' 'Where?' Well, precisely!)

The Semiotics of the Spectacle

Now, even if a spurious transcontextual or typically Eurocentric pseudo-universal take on this topic will tend to overlook the ethnic, ethico-political matters that a postcolonial perspective will be able to identify, it is not the case that such Western interests, investments and involvements in the fantasies and cultural practices of 'Eastern' martial arts are free from (or can be disassociated from) 'political' questions and themes. Although at the margins – and hence at the disavowed heart – of the western interest in oriental martial arts, orientalism and postcolonialism do not exhaust all of the limits of the cultural and political issues attendant to them. Indeed, it is also possible to suggest that this type of cultural activity proliferated because of some specific areas of ideological contradiction and tension, related to globalisation, mediatization and its results: what Guy Debord once infamously called 'spectacular society'. Today, even though many may want to reject Debord's hypotheses (whilst often still using and relying on his terminology), Debord's pessimistic arguments about the 'society of the spectacle' nevertheless offer something of a paradigmatic statement of the problematics of what came to be called postmodernity. At the very least, there is an interesting potential account of the explosion of involvement in martial arts in a mediatized socio-cultural context.

This is particularly interesting because, according to Debord, the spectacle 'is that which escapes the activity of men'. The spectacle and spectacular social relations are all about passive *watching*. Yet many people become interested in and begin practicing martial arts after witnessing only spectacular cinematic displays of impossible martial arts performance. So, even if martial arts are (to all intents and purposes) 'originally' or '*originarily*' spectacular, even spectacular (relations to) martial arts are not *totally*, *necessarily*, *always* or *essentially* spectacular. They do exist in a spectacular form, constituted, disseminated, known and 'fed' by spectacles. But the other side of the coin is that their 'essence' is participation, and this stands in some tension with the sense of spectacle as that which totally 'escapes' activity. Martial arts always construct a subjectivity via the expedient of 'doing', and this is championed over what Debord calls the spectacular domination of merely 'having' or 'appearing' – although even in 'doing' and acquiring skill ('having') there is always an inevitable 'generalized sliding of having into appearing, from which all actual "having" must draw its immediate prestige and its ultimate function' (Debord 1991: Thesis 17).

Now, martial arts in the West first proliferated as karate (Krug 2001), as we saw in Chapter One. Karate remained dominant even after Bruce Lee arrived with his 'Chinese gung fu'. However, it was the Korean high-kicking art of taekwondo which became most popular in the wake of celluloid martial arts. It should be remembered that a large part of Bruce Lee's immediate impact was the popularising of amazing *kicking*, so although Bruce Lee was to become associated with kung fu, it is nevertheless apparent that Lee's flamboyant movie kicks were unlikely to be taught or even found in kung fu or karate schools, but rather only in the Korean art of taekwondo. As Leon Hunt notes:

> Since the early 1970s, the phrase 'Northern Leg, Southern Fist' [which referred to the distinguishing characteristics or emphases of Chinese martial arts styles] might be more accurately represented as 'Korean Leg, Chinese Fist'. Films like *Hapkido/He Qi Dao* (1972) and *When Taekwondo Strikes/Taiquan Zhen Jiu Zhou* (1973) varied the anti-Japanese theme of many kung fu films by having Chinese martial artists team up with Korean ones. Korean martial arts emphasise high, elaborate kicking techniques – they are more spectacular than even northern Chinese kicks. Wong In-sik, Chi Hon-tsoi, Huang Jang-li, and Casanova Wong were all Korean martial artists trained in either Taekwondo or Hapkido – along with Chinese Taekwondoists [*sic*] John Liu and Tang Tao-liang, they constitute what many fans call the 'Superkickers'. (Hunt 2003: 30)

As we have already seen, 1973 was the year in which the West was exposed to something like a coherent mythology of martial arts. This took the form of Bruce Lee's *Enter the Dragon*, the enormous success of which removed martial arts from a position of obscurity in the West and placed them within a far wider popular cultural intertext. Indeed, were one so inclined, it might even be reasonable to propose that prior to *Enter The Dragon* a crude behavioural psychological analysis could sufficiently describe the determining factors operating when a Western subject engaged in the practice of a martial art: factors such as an aggressive, working class environment, and so on (Toch 1972; Dickinson 1976). Either way, the practices were indeed effectively ghettoised. But today the membership of the most popular styles within the West, such as taekwondo, karate, jiu jitsu, judo, and – increasingly – capoeira and mixed martial arts arguably show no discrimination in terms of class, race, age, sex, or penchant for engagement in actual fighting outside of the dojo, dojang, kwoon or training hall. 'Behaviourally', this would seem to be inconsistent with a practice premised upon violence, battle, and war. So, paradigms such as behaviourism arguably fall down slightly here. Reciprocally, however, this is exactly where an approach to subjectivization informed by an awareness of a media saturated cultural context comes into its own. This is why a brief theoretical/experimental return to Guy Debord's enormously paradigmatic yet pessimistic model of such a society is still worthwhile, even if subsequent developments in media theory have 'taken the edge off' Debordian pessimism in various ways.

As discussed in Chapter One, many of the most popular styles in the West originally manifested themselves as hardly different from any sport, with a trophy-orientated approach to training apparent in their syllabi. Although the status and form of martial arts are constantly changing, it arguably remains the case that the sport-orientation remains dominant, even when the emphasis is putatively on 'reality martial arts' or 'ultimate fighting'. Most pre-black-belt syllabi in taekwondo, for example, overwhelmingly allow no strikes to any part of the body other than the front or side torso and head, even though there are a multitude of more 'effective' targets available for the incapacitation of an opponent. Arguably, the entire syllabus up to black belt level is overwhelmingly based on 'showy' techniques designed solely for the semi-contact arena (despite the rather amusing myth within taekwondo circles that its high flying kicks are an authentic ancient Korean strategy for kicking enemies off horses). Yet it is perhaps rarely – if ever – the case that those who enter any martial arts activity do so with the idea of sport in mind. Arguably, the sporting tendency emerges only when the practitioner comes to test his or her mettle against other trained fighters within a controlled environment. Yet, as testified by virtually every poster, flier, advert and leaflet for martial arts, the perceived impetus to train and the primary marketing alibi for martial arts classes is overwhelmingly that which is encompassed by the umbrella term *self defence*. This is different from most other sports, which can easily be entered into 'innocently', as a game. Indeed, most sports are introduced as a game. Moreover, one can be seen to be competent at sports without ever having been involved in an enduring student-teacher relationship. Yet one could never be seen to be a martial artist without having been involved with at least one institution or representative of a discipline who possess the authority to confer the once-mythical black belt upon the pupil. One could be seen as a 'fighter', but never a martial artist. The ideological connotations are enormously different.

In this context, even on a very cursory analysis, a film like *Enter the Dragon* introduces and manipulates a great deal of what came to amount to an enduring mythological universe of martial arts – or indeed, what semioticians, following Roland Barthes, would once have termed *martial artness*. This is a *myth* because, in Barthesian semiotic terminology, the structure of this cinematic text, in its plot and narrative devices, conforms to a dominant or 'readerly' mode, based as it is around hegemonically transparent, or ideologically intelligible oppositions of good/bad, hero/antihero, and the putative triumph of justice over injustice, despite the odds (or, rather, despite the numbers) being stacked against the agent of this justice. The primary motive force of the action is that the anti-hero is involved in large-scale crime – drug dealing and people trafficking. This is presumably because of the myriad negative connotations aroused in an audience interpreting within the dominant-hegemonic code, or a negotiated version of it. Thus, the hero (Lee) agrees to undertake the mission for these general reasons alone (after having been primed by the Shaolin Abbot, who tells Lee that Han has disgraced his Shaolin Temple). Moreover, Lee is then informed by his own father that among the anti-hero's henchmen is a man (O'Hara/Bob Wall) who was personally responsible for his sister's death. Thus, all areas of motivation are activated: social obligation, the 'Shaolin Commandments', familial duty, honour, and, of course, revenge.

The semiotic structure of the film is, thus, simple. It is 'readerly' and 'ideological' in many respects. This permeates the film: there are, for instance, basically four characters into which the film condenses a large amount of easily readable imagery (imagery that is *'lisible'*, in Barthes' terminology). Two of these are the hero (Lee) and the anti-hero (Han). Because these characters are located within an apparently 'alien' culture, the attention given to their depiction is considerably more extrapolated than the other two dominant characters, whose location is firmly within an intelligible North American code. The latter are Williams and Roper, each of whom is allotted a flashback scene which shows how and why it is they have chosen (or been obliged) to attend the martial arts tournament at which the action of the film takes place. These scenes also construct their iconic status. Briefly, Roper is shown to be an all-American entrepreneur-cum-gambler, whose frivolous lifestyle has led him into such debt that he has to attend the tournament as a means of escape – both as temporary respite from his pursuers and as a means of hopefully gaining some money to get out of his debt. Next, Williams is a hip afro-haired urban black from an unspecified ghetto. He is shown to be a respected graduate of a tough karate dojo, and we are shown his response to one incident of extreme police racial harassment: the extent of its injustice leads Williams to severely beat (and possibly even to have killed) two police officers. Accordingly, Williams is unavoidably 'politicized'. We see this when, faced with the sights of impoverished communities living in the waters around Hong Kong, Williams comments that ghettos are 'the same everywhere: they stink'. This is an immanently political observation which the white 'bourgeois' Roper defuses by replying, 'Same old Williams!' (We will return to the topic of such (immanent) politicization in the next chapter.)

Soon we are shown that these two were together in Vietnam, which explains their cross-class and interracial friendship and perhaps their martial arts training too. Together they represent ideological composites of one fantasy of US identity. They are each sides of the same mythological coin: the pursuit of pleasure and the defence of freedom and justice; playboy and (para)politician. The immediate function of the two is, of course, to ground the film within a recognisable interpretive context, a context which might introduce 'alien' features but which can still serve to 'rearticulate the existing symbolic order in ideologically orthodox ways' (Silverman 1983: 221). This is most recognizably fulfilled by their expression of unease and confusion in the alien context of the hyperoriental(ised) environment of the anti-hero's palatial 'island fortress'. So, this Williams/Roper relation contains cultural and racial stereotypes which are basically black/white, promiscuity/monogamy and conscience/frivolity. The ideological terrain entered by these characters is ostensibly that encompassed by the hero/anti-hero (Bruce Lee/Han) dialectic, but Williams and Roper serve to ground that strange and exotic otherworld within an 'ideologically orthodox' western 'symbolic order'. Within this tokenistic space, Bruce Lee is the 'positive' and more extrapolated (Asiaphiliac) component of this binary. Han is the Fu Manchuesque (Orientalist) signifier of pure negativity.

As is by now very familiar to us, the opening scene of the film has shown Lee engaging in competition combat, watched by an audience consisting of (hyper) Oriental-looking men seated in regimented and colour-coded rows, dressed in flowing robes. Presiding over this scenario is an aged man, adorned in an orange robe, with a long grey moustache and pointed grey beard. The combatants bow to him before and after the bout. This arrangement serves to facilitate the decoding of the context as unequivocally 'Chinese' for a Western spectator. But this is a very specific brand of Chineseness, becoming so by virtue of the old man presiding: his age, apparent serenity, position of dominance, grey beard, the deference with which he is treated, and even his very silence serve to denote the Wise Man. These signifiers are familiar within the Western repository of mythical stereotypes. This 'Chineseness' thus becomes that of ancient, ascetic, meditational mysticism. Yet, at the centre of this situation is a fight – the significance of which we considered at some length in the previous chapter.

After his victory, Lee triumphantly somersaults over a group of monks who apparently expected him to pass beneath their ceremonially joined and raised hands. Lee's unexpected action is greeted with laughter and applause. So the construction of Lee after this first scene is that of the proficient fighter, even champion, of a mystic Chinese institution whose totemic principle is that of wisdom as personified by the sage-figure. Lee is the exceptional peer of at least those others dressed in black, and is held in esteem and affection by them. The mystic/physical binary at play in this discursive construction is furthered in the next scene. This time the gaze comes from a British agent, Mr. Braithwaite; but now Lee performs in spite of and not for his observer. The (stereo)typically British Mr. Braithwaite is present to request the services of Lee – an agent of the British Empire requesting this mystic Chinese martial artist monk to aid it as a 'special agent' in this mission (a role which reputedly led to outrage among Hong Kong audiences, who allegedly slashed up movie theatre seats in protest at Lee playing the role of a British agent – a role which is of course distinctly different from his prior roles as rural Chinese bumpkin who beats up non-Chinese (and) organised criminals.)

As discussed in the previous chapter, in these early scenes of *Enter the Dragon*, aspects of Lee's behaviour appear eccentric, unexpected, and enigmatic, (apparently) especially for Western eyes. In his meeting with

Braithwaite, Lee interrupts Braithwaite's conversational flow, unsettling his sense of etiquette and confusing him slightly, by unexpectedly standing up from the table at which they have been drinking tea and saying, 'It's Lau's time'. As we have already seen, he proceeds to give the boy Lau a lesson, whose structure is again organised by enigmatic and confusing instructions, actions and interpretations: he first surprises Braithwaite by breaking off their meeting; then he surprises Lau by instructing him to kick him; he then slaps Lau for 'thinking', slaps him for concentrating 'on the finger', and again for taking his eyes off his opponent. We are shown all of this, then we are shown Braithwaite, who has been watching, nodding approvingly. If we don't quite 'get it', we nevertheless certainly 'get into it'. However, the behaviour of Lee's character in this 'teacherly' mode is not without some basis in fact. According to Avital Ronell, Zen teachers often liberally strike students who give the wrong answers to Zen koans, an act which arguably has various pedagogical functions. Ronell writes:

> A site of thinking beyond thinking, testing is not eliminated but takes place beyond the parameters of a test subsumed under codifiable attributes. The largely internal contest of koan is intended to secure an experience of extreme dispossession. But the themes and topoi of inside and outside, of internally and externally determined categories, do not mean much here except for the dependence that koan practice implies on concepts of opening. A draft for scheming radical exposure, the koan, offered by the teacher – the 'master' – is meant to 'open' the pupil to the possibility of Saying. The master is responsible for initiating the call of such an opening. Often this opening, which in no tradition escapes the suspicion of violence, is attained by the administration of a shock. Thus the master, in texts devoted to the koan, is frequently figured as beating, hitting, or slugging the pupil. The hit seals a sort of 'compliment' conferred by the attentive master, who prods the physical body for the purpose of uninhibiting a scene of contemplation, new and unanticipated. The shock is crucial to the experience of the koan: it stages the opening of thought exceeding itself in the jolt. (Ronell 2004: 62)[10]

---

[10] Significantly, Ronell continues: 'Although the temptation may exist to read such protocols of Saying in a mood of estrangement, one would be wrong to envision the choreography of violence as something foreign to Western forms of thinking about thinking. There is the Heideggerian *Stoss* (jolt) in *Being and Time* that, awakening to its own beat, still needs to be contended with; nor should one overlook the destructive passivities of Blanchot puzzling out Lévinas. Some passages of the *Infinite Conversation* or *The Writing of Disaster* stunningly converge with the sense of abandonment to which the koan consigns passive bodies, particularly where the koan burdens the student with the strictures of responsible Saying' (Ronell 2004: 62).

This scene constructs the bare essentials of what passes for Lee's 'character'. Even the simple addition of the unusual bow (right fist pressed into left palm) serves to enhance the encoded sign of Orientalness into a more specific Mystic Orientalness, by virtue of its unusual symbolic motivation. This mystic status is then complicated by Lee's command, 'kick me', and the fact that the lesson is apparently about fighting, right until the moment that it apparently becomes about apprehending 'heavenly glory' via non-linguistic 'emotional content' (the 'feel' of the kick, and the finger and the moon analogy), whereby the lesson is yet again metamorphosed at the interpretative level from an immediately graspable physical lesson into a mystical one. (We will consider the significance of the 'finger pointing to the moon' formulation in the following chapter, when we discuss Eve Kosofsky Sedgwick's analysis of its possible meanings.) Just when the pupil thinks he understands, Lee returns to the physical requirements of combat, even during the institution of the bow. This mythologising representation of martial artness embodied by Lee is reactivated several scenes later when he defines his style as 'the art of fighting without fighting', as discussed in Chapter One.

So the construction of Lee here appears, in the Western context (or intertext) to be a 'new' genre of hero figure, composed of pure opposites which combine to initiate a subjectivity of total harmony and perfection for the viewer to identify with. However, despite these novelties, the character played by Lee, his positioning – what semiotic analysis calls his manifest and latent functions – still does not seem to diverge from or develop away from the prevailing Western symbolic order. That is to say, the narrative is determined by Lee's actions, he occupies the central positions of camera interest, motivation, singularity, power and invincibility. In Lacanian terms, Lee is an 'ideal representation defining for the [viewing] subject what it lacks' (Silverman 1983: 177). In Lacanian terms, he is a metonymic embodiment of the phallus from which 'the Western symbolic order derives its coherence' (131). As an apparently British colonial native subject (although the Shaolin Temple is typically located in mainland China and I am not aware of a Shaolin Temple in Hong Kong), he is fetishistically novel. But a Foucauldian reading of Lee's status here might see him as an ultimate manifestation of 'bio-power', of the subject developed as an agent, and accordingly, despite the Oriental Warrior myth, a personification of 'the principle underlying the tactics of battle –

that one has to be capable of killing in order to go on living'; a principle which was significant for Foucault because he saw it as that which 'defines the strategy of states today' (1978: 137). Indeed, argues Foucault, 'bio-power was without question an indispensable element in the development of capitalism' (140-1). So, even at the birth of a yin and yang take on cinematic harmony in Western popular culture, Lee would arguably be at the centre of an essentially capitalist ideological 'tool'. In the Barthesian sense, Lee's 'martial artness' here is simply working as *myth*.

According to Barthes, myth functions best in its immediacy, and this is precisely what happens here. Whilst seeming on first glance to depict a radical new subjectivity, the subjectivity of Lee apparently remains fully embedded within what theorists used to call 'phallogocentric' cultural values: the principle of the phallus; the principle of the Law – indeed, says Foucault, 'The law always refers to the sword' (1978: 144); and representations which will appeal to the superego as 'ideal', hence showing the ego 'what it should be' (Silverman 1983: 135). It would be in this way that the subject 'not only learns to desire within the symbolic order; it learns "what" to desire' (177-8), and that this coercion is an ongoing interpellative process. But the fragility to analysis of the actual difference of this putatively new difference is largely irrelevant, for it is a myth in the Barthesian sense in that it 'essentially aims at causing an immediate impression – it does not matter if one is later allowed to see through the myth, its action is assumed to be stronger than the rational explanations which may later belie it' (Barthes 1972: 141).

It is at this point that a return to Guy Debord can be provocative. For one might use this perspective on Lee to propose that there are factors at play within contemporary society which actually *prevent* the removal of martial artness from its contradictorily flourishing position in the ever-changing repository of spectacular mythological fashions. These are factors that have enabled it to gain a position inside what semiotics calls the *langue* of myth rather than remaining an isolated *parole*, and they are factors which suggest that whilst the phenomenon was born as a spectacle and is fuelled by the spectacle, its character, at least at the manifest level, is also anti-spectacular. Any 'rational explanations' of this myth will serve rather to reinforce it than to 'belie it', for reasons that devolve on situating this particular spectacular myth within a conception of society as 'spectacular'.

Martial Myths and Spectacles

According to Debord, the media is what dominates the contemporary world. The media itself is dominated by discourses that constitute 'news' and 'current affairs', purporting to be urgent or immediate 'issues'. The substance of these discourses can be dissected variously, but for Debord they are to be regarded as a perennial bombardment of either: war, politicians' decisions, economic conditions, large-scale tragedy and injustice, crime, or the many forms of show-business attention. In Debord's notion of society as spectacular, the media presentation of political debate, economic commentary and show-business 'news' equal what he calls the purest form of 'noisy insignificance' – although any other class or instance of event or issue can join this party. Indeed, in many ways, all already have, insofar as they are mediatized. For, in being mediatized, 'issues' and 'events' are presented in their immediacy and externality: wars are spectator sports; injustice is only shown when it yields the freshest tragedies leaping out of the unregarded woodwork unexpectedly; and crime is simultaneously horrific and an addition to a statistic, thereby necessitating political reaction, media-comment, media-debate, until a newer issue allows media-disinterest, and the effective non-existence of the event.

This is a paraphrase of some of the social features described in *Society of the Spectacle* (Debord 1967/1995) and *Comments on the Society of the Spectacle* (Debord 1988/1990). In the latter, Debord proposes an account of the principal mechanisms at work in such a society. These are said to be, first, 'incessant technological renewal'. This translates into 'surrendering everybody to the mercy of specialists' – a feature operating in tandem with 'unanswerable lies' that has 'succeeded in eliminating public opinion'. Second is the 'integration of state and economy', serving to eliminate 'all former possibilities for independence' on the part of wage-earning experts and specialists, thereby making the 'ability to falsify [...] unlimited'. This assists the crucial 'decisive complement' of 'generalized secrecy' which 'stands behind the spectacle' – a mythopolitical instrument inherent to the integrated state/economy/spectacle, and its 'most vital operation'. Finally is Debord's notion of 'an eternal present', whose features we have just touched upon in the description of media-presentation – an eternal merry-go-round of inconsequentialities which reduces everything to a never ending cycle of pointlessness like, for example, fan discourse on football league tables, season in, season out (Debord 1988: 11-13). Together with such mechanisms of regulation, this society, Debord notes, is controlled by governments of immediacy: 'For the first time in contemporary Europe', he lamented in the 1980s, 'no party or fraction of a party even tries to pretend that they wish to change anything significant' (21). Significantly, perhaps, Debord identifies the date of May 1968 as that which first clearly illustrated the hold that the 'integrated spectacle' gained over 'reality'. The political disturbances of this time have been 'thoroughly coated in obedient lies', he proposes. With this procedure now instituted as standard, the implication is that the capacity for individual or collective political potency is nil; where it might exist, the potential for political agency is effectively foreclosed by the domination of society by spectacular relations. (Baudrillard, of course, would go on to call this the reign of hyperreality in the era of simulation.)

According to Debord, the specific nature of the power particular to the spectacle is that of 'separation'. The manifest form of separation is achieved through the commodity: the archetypal consumerist commodities, the car and the television, separate people from each other in myriad ways, of course. But for him, this spectacle, which 'permeates all reality', succeeds in creating 'lonely crowds' (13) of people who are only and 'always watching to see what happens next'. According to Debord, such people, indeed such a society, will 'never act' (14). This dystopian view of the contemporary situation and the political impasse is not, of course, unique. During the same period of time as Debord expressed his 'Comments' (the late 1980s), many others were expressing the same pessimism, if not the same sense of failure and doom and gloom. At around the same time, Richard Harland described the plight of the subject within this socio-political system in Althusserian terms. Harland proposed that there was a deeply debilitating political paradox around the ways that the terms 'individual' and 'society' had come to be articulated. The terms 'individual' and 'society' are, Harland argued, the key terms which organise much political rhetoric, particularly of that era, and they came to be related in such a way as to delegitimize *any* political action. That is, says Harland, 'individual' and 'society' were rhetorically deployed by power (in the political contexts of the Thatcher or Reagan governments) such that:

> with the interests of the separate individual [represented as if] on the one side, and the interests of society as a whole [represented as if] on the other, there is no room for the interests of groups and classes that are larger than the individual but smaller than the whole. In our present system, specifically, it is unionized labour and political interest groups that are excluded. Thus, the bonding together of individual human units of labour is made to appear factional within society as a whole, and an unnatural surrender of freedom on the part of the separate individual. (Harland 1987: 46)

In other words, the depressing position voiced by Debord, Harland, and others, is that there is a prevalent ideological force of coercion which militates against the belief that anything of major social consequence can fundamentally be changed. This is of course the view which holds that 'the way things are is the only way they can be'; that all that a person can do is spectate and consume. Wars, economics, and politics can only be regarded, not stopped, influenced or changed. Injustice and tragedy can only have money thrown at them until they seem to go away (Žižek calls this 'interpassivity'). Show-business is the ultimate ideal, yet it resides at the level of a pipe-dream, consumed ubiquitously.

But then there is crime. Crime is unique, presented as the perennial threat, the social disease. It is that which threatens to undermine stability everywhere – the stability of the social 'order', of our everyday lives, of our possessions, and of ourselves. Crime is sold by the spectacle as threat. It is consumed by the subject as a personal threat. The archetypal crime of theft is sold as a treachery (against what theorists used to call the 'phallologocentric', individualist, capitalist/consumerist ideal – even though it is in a sense the perfect realization of that ideal). The threat of theft in Freudian and Lacanian theory would be a form of castration threat, and the removal of any 'objet petit a', however sophisticated, will be traumatic for the subject. Similarly, a crime against the subject's body (or, indeed, mind) will be an assault on a 'sense of self' – again, a castration threat or attempt. For any subject sensing such a threat, this will be a cause of what Freud famously termed 'unpleasure'.

The Martial Arts Pleasure Principle

Any threat constitutes a cause of what Freud referred to as 'tension'. In the Freudian model of the psyche, the strongest and originary impetus for any mental activity is the desire for the eradication of unpleasure. In this model the subject 'is' an interacting system of unconscious, preconscious, conscious, and mnemic forces. The primary processes are those, originary in effect, desiring the immediate absence of unpleasure, and these exist in repressed form under the secondary processes of the preconscious, within the constituted subject. The preconscious is more dynamic and complicated (that is, less immediate/'primal') than the unconscious; indeed, says Silverman, it 'is "born" of disillusionment with the solutions provided by the unconscious' (1983: 59). That is, it is linguistically structured, marking the ascent to the acquisition of language. The distinction between the two arises when the acquisition of language necessitates the repression of all that does not fit into a place within this structure. Freud describes this process in terms of the Oedipal crisis; Lacan of course describes the Oedipal crisis as synonymous with language acquisition, because it is linguistically structured. In Silverman's take on Lacanian theory, when the infant (*every* infant) first 'recognises' its image in the mirror stage, as a first symbolic recognition of self, this is immediately a misrecognition, for 'to know oneself through an external image is to be defined through self-alienation' (158). This introduction to 'self' simultaneously presents the subject with an 'ideal image' and the realisation of incompleteness deriving from the newly-formed sense of something Other. This lack is enhanced by the introduction to language, where the subject occupies only one linguistic position among many. At the point of completion of the Oedipal crisis further complications can be added:

> When the child internalizes the image of the parent of the same sex at the end of the Oedipal crisis, it compounds mis-recognition upon mis-recognition. The result can only be a brutalizing sense of inadequacy both for the male and female subjects – for the former because he can never be equivalent to the symbolic position with which he identifies, and for the latter because she is denied even an identification with that position. (191)

This is to say that, from this sort of psychoanalytic-semiotic perspective, the subject can be considered to be always-already 'fully contained within a predetermined narrative' (Silverman 1983: 136). The question of *how* 'predetermined' or immutable the cultural narratives within which sub-

jects 'find themselves' are – and hence whether all subjects are constituted according to Freudian or Lacanian structures – remains debatable.
Certainly the Freudian account of subject formation has been subject to a
great deal of criticism, a lot of which is organised by the accusation that
Freud passes off parochial factors as universal (i.e., not every subject is
formed in a European Victorian bourgeois household). But perhaps the
most pertinent aspect of this brief reiteration of the psychoanalytic account of the impetus to mental activity is the claim that the subject will
strive for unpleasure to be removed.

At this point, such a theoretical conception of the subject might be
productively relocated or reinserted into the society of the spectacle.
Thus, the subject can be regarded as ideologically castrated, an agent of
no fundamental socio-political potency (in the Lacanian sense of not being the 'phallus' as that which can 'designate all of those values which
are opposed to lack' (182-3)). Yet, at the same time, the subject has become aware of a threat whose manifest form is of socio-political birth and
also personal threat. Accordingly, the psyche will desire the removal of
this unpleasure, and an immediate impetus will be to affect some style of
escape. Such a solution may take the form of hiding from society, in-
doors, behind locks, alarms and insurance policies (and presumably in
front of a television), or the avoidance of dangerous areas, ghettoising the
spectre. Unfortunately, such solutions may not create a complete enough
real or 'hallucinatory gratification' (Silverman 1983: 77), for two reasons.
The spectacle presents the threat as insidious and ubiquitous, rendering
notions of escape and tranquillity impossible; and anyway, all of these
constraints and limitations serve merely to create a newly constituted
source of unpleasure. More commodities with which to frustrate the spectre constantly become available, but they only serve to reinforce and reactivate the unpleasure. Such expedients as these are immediate and devoid
of any holistic informing aspect. That is, the solutions lack any inherent
propensity for the consistent and final eradication of an unpleasure, as the
threat takes the character of that which at any time and anywhere could
leap out of nowhere with the intention of robbing, raping, hurting or killing the subject. So the problem is social, society cannot contain it, and
society 'cannot' be changed. The only solution for a subject with such a
perspective must therefore derive from an individual ability to wield the
power in this instance. The ideal would be physical invincibility. Here we

return to the myth of martial artness: 'Enter the Individualist Invincibility Ideal', so to speak.

Interpellating the Dragon

Anyone who enters the karate dojo, taekwondo dojang or kung fu kwoon will do so armed with myriad ideas, beliefs, hopes and fears about the activity being entered into: they will already be participants in the myth of martial artness. The force of this myth, its hold on them, must not be underestimated, and cannot be overstated. To reiterate Silverman's observation again: 'The subject not only learns to desire within the symbolic order; it learns "what" to desire' (177-8). This of course also proposes that 'even desire is culturally instigated, and hence collective' (130). The instigation of such a type of desire as that which martial artness 'promises' to satisfy is born, as argued earlier, of the castration threat from the extant cultural depictions of the social world. But, unlike most myths, martial artness actually gains strength from its simplicity. This is not least because the cinematic birth of martial artness represents an extension of a continuing tradition of the construction of the phallic (therefore apparently whole, potent, complete, powerful) hero. However, all other types of construction of the phallic hero rely upon the utilisation of some other entity as the source of their potency – most commonly the gun. So any such potentate and any subsequent mythology (cowboy-ness, soldier-ness, police-ness, etc.) contains the flaw that the hero is not, *in himself*, the organising principle, the coherent 'paternal signifier' (131). However, the martial artist hero does not suffer from this drawback: the power, the agency – the phallus – *is* the hero-figure's physical reality. And this invincibility is clearly *methodically* attained, and therefore attainable, by the simple expedient of dedicated training. There is no illegality, but a simple (fantasy) causality. Learn martial art: become invincible. Not only this, but the myth, at the very moment of its introduction to the West, arrived with a massive and seductive quantity of Eastern mysticism surrounding and embellishing it with legends and traditions of the enormous physical prowess to be achieved. The truth content of this is secondary to the impact of such a mythological armoury, the force of which seemingly becomes embodied within the person of the martial artist.

Writing in the early 1990s, British martial arts writer Geoff Thompson accounted for the phenomenon of the explosion of martial arts in the UK like this:

> 20 years ago karate (and all martial arts for that matter) was veiled by a curtain of mysticism and mystique. If you practiced it as an art form, for exercise or purely as a means of self defence, it went without saying that the mysticism extended itself to you, automatically labelling you with the tab of being a 'dangerous person'. Competence in self defence was of course an inevitable by-product or at least everyone thought so. Talk of registering one's hands with the police as 'dangerous weapons' was commonplace and known karateka were given an extremely wide berth by would be antagonists. (Thompson 1993: 19)

It is interesting that Geoff Thompson also attributes the martial arts 'explosion' to Bruce Lee films, and it is of course largely predictable that he blames them for a corresponding decline in quality in actual martial arts practice – 'All of a sudden everyone and their dog was a black belt (or at least they wore one)' (19), he observes. Nevertheless, whether real, fake, authentic, fanciful, ancient, modern or postmodern, in entering the martial arts club as a student, the subject becomes involved with the production of discourse, and thus bound up within a discursive network of both power and knowledge. In 'any society', writes Foucault, 'there are manifold relations of power which permeate, characterize and constitute the social body, and these relations of power cannot themselves be established, consolidated nor implemented without the production, accumulation, circulation and functioning of a discourse' (1988: 93). Indeed, it is well known that, for Foucault, discourses are bound up in the production of knowledge and the exercise of power: 'There can be no possible exercise of power without a certain economy of discourses of truth', just as 'we are subjected to the production of truth through power and we cannot exercise power except through the production of truth' (93). In this respect, the structures and experiences of the martial arts lesson are exemplary and intensive sites of discipline, as well as the production of discourse – even of notions of truth.

The typical taekwondo lesson, for instance, will be structured in this way: The class is lined up in a hierarchy of rank signified by belt colour. Before the class stands the instructor. All bow as a sign of respect for the activity and its embodiment in the instructor. Next follows aerobic and flexibility exercise in which the students are expected to push themselves. Formal movements and sequences of movements depicting highly stylized and abstract attack and defending scenarios are then practiced, and also set-, step- and 'free'-sparring with a partner, the function of which is the development of skill within a controlled environment. The class will finish with more warming-down exercise, and culminate with another bow to the instructor. Such formats and experiences – and all martial arts classes will be organised by elements of this sort of structure – can stand as an adequate 'reality test' for the subject, despite the controlled, stylized (often superfluous, spectacular) and abstract form the lesson takes, and even though many forms of martial art may well measure up to 'real-combat' as the picture of a light would compare to a real light for utility in a darkened room (but making such a generalisation as this about any system is always going to be a moot point). Still, this is largely irrelevant to the criteria of the subject's probable reality test. For the state of affairs is clearly that a trained practitioner *could indeed* kick an opponent in the head in exactly the same way that Bruce Lee 'does' on the screen – and this will be enough, especially as the untrained subject could not execute such kicks. Similarly, of course, the bodily stress and psychological investment in the session and sense of empowerment, sustained by fantasy, will activate the adrenal gland and the subject will invariably experience an endorphin and adrenalin 'high'. This is significant for it will serve as fuel for any conscious or unconscious 'hallucinatory gratification'. Moreover, as the subject progresses in visible rank and physical ability, the belief may become that of an ascent to the possession of power – and a 'real' power at that, because it is at the level of somatic reality.

Of course, what often goes unnoticed in such a process or interpellation is the *institutionalisation* of the subject. Bruce Lee purported to want to extricate martial arts from this process of institutionalisation or institutional stultification. And we will turn our attention to this in some considerable detail in the following chapter. But at this point it should suffice to recall the extent to which Lee regarded such formats as 'formal' martial arts syllabi, moves, patterns, kata, drills and forms as restrictive and fanciful abstractions, reductions, distortions and distances away from the reality of combat. Hence, rather than advocate a 'way' or a 'style', Lee sought to institute 'using no way as the way' and 'having no limitation as limitation' in his own martial art of jeet kune do.

Jeet kune do means the 'stop-fist way', or 'way of the intercepting fist'. According to Bruce Lee's senior student, Dan Inosanto, the term 'jeet kune do' was thought-up in 1968. John Little, however, dates the term's first occurrence to Bruce Lee's notebooks from 1967. According to Inosanto, the birth of jeet kune do happened 'in the car' in 1968 (Inosanto 1980: 66-7). But his tidy 'origin narrative' may be contestable, especially as several other figures offer different dates for the inception of the term jeet kune do, and several others also claim to have been present at the moment of naming. This says something about the foibles of memory and fantasy, perhaps. But whatever its historical status or degree of reliability, Inosanto's narrative is instructive in its emphasis on jeet kune do as 'our main concept'. Indeed, Inosanto subsequently modified the term 'jeet kune do' and almost always says or writes 'jeet kune do *concept*'. His point is that, in contradistinction to the names of martial arts styles – with their fixed syllabi of traditional forms, patterns or kata, etc. – the term jeet kune do was initially intended to refer to a guiding principle, rather than a fixed form.

The literal meaning of jeet kune do, then, is the 'stop-hit'. 'Jeet' is a concept that is found in other Chinese martial arts, too, but it is not necessarily actualised in the same way as a fencing-like 'stop-hit'. Jeet can also take the form of an interruption of the other's rhythm that is not premised on intercepting or parrying their attack. Indeed, as we have seen, Miller and others have called this original principle 'naïve', at least to the extent that it presumes the opponent will not be able to anticipate or interrupt your stop-hit or that your own direct linear attack will not be – no matter how fast – predictable and hence stop-hittable or otherwise counterable. It is helpful to remember that when it comes to styles, tactics and strategies, martial arts are ultimately rather like the game of 'rock-paper-scissors': one may take the other by surprise, but there will always be something that trumps your manner of attack or defence, especially if one can see or predict what is coming. Hence the problem at the heart of Bruce Lee's proposition that 'there is no such thing as a style if you totally understand the roots of combat': this is a highly moot point. For there *are* such things as styles and they *have* been used in combat. The question of what a non-style should or 'must' look like or how a principle should be actualised is a difficult one to answer. Bruce Lee's own fullest answer reputedly takes the form of the incomplete, posthumously re-leased film, *The Game of Death*.

The Symbolic Structure of *Game of Death*

The remains of the footage for *Game of Death* suggest that Lee's 'phi-losophy' of fighting, or the message he intended to deliver, was some-thing to do with freeing oneself from the limitations of traditional disci-plinary institutions in the martial arts. This is allegedly why Lee wears the garish yellow tracksuit: in being yellow, and skin tight, it reflected no known martial arts garb of the time, thereby allowing Lee to avoid asso-ciation with any particular style. But it was of course *very yellow*: a fact which is doubtless significant in any semiotic analysis. For, some com-mentators have suggested, in discussions of other elements of such films as *Crouching Tiger, Hidden Dragon, Hero* and *House of Flying Daggers*, 'yellow' is not only a shorthand for East Asians – referring as it does, often pejoratively, to skin colour – it is also a particular coding of a trans-national identification of 'Chineseness'. Indeed, it may even be signifi-cant to note, as Chow points out in a discussion of *The Last Emperor*, that in China until the 20th Century, 'only the emperor [could] wear yellow' (1991: 11). So, whether Bruce Lee wearing such a *very yellow* yellow whilst starring in his own authored and directed film signifies freedom from association with a martial style, transnational Chineseness or his own status as emperor of martial arts is an interpretation that is up for grabs. Indeed, there is no reason why it could not or should not be all at the same time.

As performed in the choreography of *Game of Death*, freeing one-self from institutional limitations is dramatised in the ascent through the Pagoda, in which Bruce Lee and his allies are faced with evermore de-manding opponents. In order to demonstrate this, Lee's allies are of course dispatched one by one before Lee belatedly intervenes in each case. Such a sacrificial structure is the device by which the lethality of each opponent is demonstrated. It also justifies Lee's subsequent venge-ance. Thus, Lee proceeds up the levels of the pagoda. At the very top he encounters Kareem Abdul-Jabbar, an extremely tall, very black, sun-glasses-wearing nemesis. Many commentators have noted that Abdul-

Jabbar 'mirrors' Lee in that he does not wear the insignia or trappings of any known martial style, nor is his fighting style clean, crisp or orthodox according to any of the usual conventions: his kicks and hand strikes are 'direct' and not at all 'flashy'. Thus, it is said, Abdul-Jabbar's fighting style is equivalent – indeed, identical – to Lee's own. In fighting Jabbar, Bruce Lee is said to be fighting another jeet kune do spirit – someone who has 'transcended' style. *Game of Death* tells us: the supreme style is no-style, and the name, conventions and 'look' of this supreme non-style is that of jeet kune do.

Throughout his earlier battles in the pagoda, Lee has overcome his opponents by revealing the weaknesses and limitations of their styles: too stiff, too rhythmic, too predictable, etc. He has adapted his own fighting style in order to break into and break through their defences. The other clearest example of this 'lesson' in Bruce Lee's films, of course, can be seen in his fight with Chuck Norris's Colt in *Way of the Dragon* (1972): as we have seen, this is a fight in which Lee is forced to move from a formal 'grounded' style to a much more dynamic and (to borrow Muhammad Ali's term) 'floating' style in order to best the karateka. So, what is Abdul-Jabbar's stylistic weakness and limitation? Interestingly, because Abdul-Jabbar is massively larger than Lee, and is also represented as practicing an equivalent 'no-style', the film encounters a difficulty. For, if Abdul-Jabbar reflects something like the spirit of jeet kune do, then Lee evidently could not come up with an actual weakness within his own (no)style, or, that is, *within his own argument*. So Lee has to look *outside* for a weakness. Thus, we learn by chance that Abdul-Jabbar's character is photosensitive. This is why this dark man is in dark glasses in the dark. When Lee notices the effect on his opponent of sunlight shining through some broken windows, he realises he can best this opponent simply by opening the pagoda up to the light of day. Hence, Abdul-Jabbar can't fight all that well anymore because he has been blinded by the light.

On a conceptual level, what this *deus ex machina* also reveals is that Bruce Lee could not come up with a way for jeet kune do to be the truly democratic and emancipated fighting style that he imagined it to be. For, as the pagoda scenes clearly and unequivocally show us, in jeet kune do, the bigger, longer, heavier, stronger fighter will simply be able to beat the smaller fighter. This is hardly 'using no way as way' or having 'no limitation as limitation'. This is rather more '*Size is no limitation? No way!'* For, in order to demonstrate the 'superlative' character of jeet kune do, Lee needs the larger and more physically advantaged fighter to have a contingent limitation. Hence, he is photosensitive. But this is not a structural or systemic limitation. It is simply a chance feature associated with that particular individual. At best, the jeet kune do justification for this device could only be that the jeet kune do practitioner will be able to exploit any limitation in the opponent or context. But what happens when the limitation arises that one's own size, speed and strength meets a greater size, speed or strength? Bruce Lee evidently had no answer better than 'the more adaptable fighter will win'. But this is only so on the premise that the larger, stronger fighter has a random limitation.

Moreover, we should pause to consider this: not only does Lee make Abdul-Jabbar's nameless character photosensitive, he also makes him black. Of course, Lee hasn't 'made' Abdul-Jabbar black. Rather, he chooses to make the *character* of the ultimate level of opponent black (and, we might reiterate, apparently nameless). Quite what we might want to conclude about this usage of a black man to play an ultimate enemy who dwells in the dark, behind dark glasses in a dark room, hidden from the light of day, to be beaten by a small yellow man in a yellow suit remains to be established. But the matter that interests this discussion here, primarily, is that despite Bruce Lee's fantasy of realising a superlative 'rational' martial principle, what he arguably devised was what one of the 'classics' of tai chi ch'üan regards as entirely typical of virtually all traditional martial arts styles: 'There are many other styles of martial arts, but they are nothing more than the strong bullying the weak' (Wile 1996: 15). That is: most martial arts are based on *winning by being stronger*. But this is hardly a superior principle. What it advocates is 'nothing more than the strong bullying the weak'. As one martial arts instructor explained to Brian Preston:

> There's a saying: *Go Weak for Technique; If You're Strong, You're Wrong*. Strength is the wrong way to learn; you always need to practise as if your opponent is stronger than you. You need to be thinking, this is a technique by which I can beat a stronger man. If you're relying on strength in practice, that day that you come up against someone stronger and bigger than you, you'll actually have no technique against him. For sure you'll lose the battle. But if you train by picturing that people are always going to be physically stronger than you, then the opponent's strength doesn't matter. (Preston 2007: 81)

Indeed, it is apparent that Lee implicitly advocated such a principle. We can infer this from his regular reiteration of the idea enunciated in *Enter the Dragon* about expanding when the opponent contracts, contracting when the opponent expands, and having such sensitivity to the interplay of forces during an encounter that when the moment for launching a strike arises it can be taken by the sensitive body without the active involvement of the mind. Doubtless, Lee's awareness of this principle derives from his sensitivity training in wing chun 'sticky hands' – a drill with a partner in which one's responses to the other's moves, resistances, and efforts are trained to a point of great sophistication.

Be Like Water: Bruce Lee's Bamboo from *Kill Bill* to *Fight Club*

Bruce Lee himself regularly formulated this principle in terms of the injunction to 'be like water'. This sentiment was recorded within many of his written archives, as well as in television interviews and in accounts of his lectures and conversations by his friends and students. Don't be rigid. Be like water. Don't be beholden to limited and limiting conventions and postures. Flow – as and when and wherever necessary. Move around and onwards, relentlessly. Find the cracks; exploit them. Fill the space. Etc., etc. This is sterling stuff, of course. But what would it look like? As the bully at the start of *Enter the Dragon* legitimately demands, 'Show me some of it!' If Bruce Lee's answer finds its cinematic representation in his incomplete, self-written, directed and produced labour of love, *The Game of Death*, it is because in this film the footage shows Lee finding his opponent's weaknesses and 'flowing' into them. As Lee proceeds up five levels of the pagoda, he faces increasingly difficult opponents – the ultimate being of course the towering Kareem Abdul-Jabbar. But it is in Lee's fight with the Filipino martial artist, played by Dan Inosanto, that Lee's aqueous philosophy finds its best cinematic realisation.

In the fight, the Filipino kali/eskrima master wields two demonstrably lethal sticks. We have already seen him dispatch one of Lee's allies. In response to this, however, Bruce Lee chooses to brandish nothing more daunting than a length of flexible bamboo. Of course, as every good pseudo-Taoist knows, where there is flexibility, therein lies the 'strength' to overcome rigidity. So, Lee proceeds to 'interrupt' his opponent's fighting rhythm. Inosanto, that is, is set up to represent both literal rigidity (in his solid sticks), and also the rigidity of traditional institutional styles (he literally beats out traditional Eskrima/kali rhythms with the sticks). This rigidity, then, is represented through the predictability of rhythm and the inflexibility of straightforward strength. Lee interrupts Inosanto's rhythm with whips and cracks from the bamboo; strikes that are not devastating but are nevertheless bothersome enough to disrupt and open Inosanto up · to further intrusions and more substantial attacks from Lee. Lee's 'broken rhythm' breaks the other's rhythm, by finding the gaps and interstices.

This is an interesting 'lesson'. Indeed, reiterations of it can be detected running through many other martial arts films. For instance, Tarantino gives a distinct nod to it in *Kill Bill, Volume II* (2004), when Beatrix Kiddo fights Elle Driver in Budd's trailer. Because of the confined space, Elle cannot unsheathe the much-fetishized Hanzo sword. She keeps trying to unsheathe it, but it keeps bumping into the ceiling. Kiddo, however – exemplifying the very spirit of the opportunistic and pragmatic jeet kune do of *Game of Death* – is not so fixated on the necessity of the sword. Rather, she snatches an extendable aerial and, exactly in the manner of Lee with his bamboo in *Game of Death*, interrupts her opponent by stinging her repeatedly with the flexible weapon of convenience.

Whether such an intertextual similarity between *Game of Death* and *Kill Bill* is chance or intentional is up for grabs, of course. But, seizing on the allusions and references to *Game of Death* in *Kill Bill*, Brian Preston proffers the following theory: there is a poetic justice to *Kill Bill*, he argues. For in it a symbolic or metaphoric Bruce Lee kills the character who usurped or gazumped Bruce Lee's intended star vehicles. Beatrix Kiddo of course wears the yellow cat-suit of Bruce Lee in *Game of Death* and is accompanied extra-diegetically by the theme tune of *The Green Hornet* on her O-Ren Ishi-i murder mission. Similarly, David Carradine – the eponymous 'Bill', who everyone hates, for always-unspecified reasons – comes replete with the flute that he first carried in *Kung Fu* and *The Silent Flute*. Both of these were films that Bruce Lee had actually co-conceived and co-written with James Coburn and Stirling Siliphant, the former materialising during Bruce Lee's lifetime and the latter appearing posthumously in 1978. The fact that Carradine starred in *The Silent Flute* after having also starred in the TV series *Kung Fu* – both of which were ideas of Bruce Lee's, and which he had hoped to star in himself – could be regarded as an injustice compounding an injustice. Way to kick a man when he's really down, you might say. We might add to this the observation that the Crazy 88s, the henchmen of O-Ren Ishi-i that Kiddo/Lee dispatches, are dressed as Kato, the character that Lee played in *The Green Hornet* (smart suits and 'Kato masks'). Thus, suggests Preston, thanks to Tarantino, Lee finally gets his 'revenge', albeit in deferred, displaced, metaphoric and symbolic form.

However, perhaps the best Hollywood response to or representation of the injunction 'be like water' via a 'flexible' weapon is that in the final fight scene of *Fight Club* (1996). The scene in which the lead character (Edward Norton) fights his imagined friend Tyler Durden (Brad Pitt) contains myriad references to Bruce Lee films, in very many ways indeed. But from the point of view of our current discussion, the most appropriate intertextual allusion arrives at the point when Norton snaps the aerial off a parked car and proceeds to try to whip Tyler Durden with it. Pitt/Durden takes the first sting and retorts with an indignant – incredulous – shout of '*What*?!' – as if to say 'what the hell do you even think you are trying to do with that ridiculous non-weapon?' Pitt proceeds to barge through Norton's flailing whips and strikes, smash his opponent's face into the wall and return to the straightforward work of beating him down. This perhaps passes a certain comment on Lee's advocation of the bendy bamboo over the heavy and hard stick. Given the sheer intertextual overloading, overcoding and overdetermination of this fight scene by references to Bruce Lee films, moves, sounds and strikes, it seems unlikely that this reference is not fully knowing and intentional, even if the ability to 'see' it or the predisposition to draw it out requires something of an investment in the intertextual relations between fight choreographies.

If some readers find this connection between these elements of *Game of Death* and *Fight Club* untenable, it will perhaps be because of my suggestion that the traces of *Game of Death* that I am locating (or placing) in *Fight Club* might have been placed their *intentionally*. This would be a reasonable hesitation. And indeed there is no reason to regard the recurrence or reiteration of thematic, dynamic, dramatic and choreographic elements across texts as 'intentional'. But to me, in this respect, it seems overwhelmingly to be the case that in many respects *Fight Club*'s Tyler Durden is constructed in part by way of strong references to Bruce Lee. In the concluding fight with Norton, Durden makes Bruce Lee catcalls, strikes Bruce Lee ready-stances (weight mainly on back leg, torso angled slightly away from the opponent, body leaning ever so slightly – cockily – back, hands formed as if mimicking the holding of an invisible telephone, with thumb and little finger depicting the shape of the telephone, etc.). Furthermore, at one point, when Durden stamps down on the fallen Norton, he pulls the same facial expression as Lee does when stamping down on O'Hara in *Enter the Dragon*. Of course, in *Enter the Dragon*, Lee has stamped on O'Hara's head or neck and thereby killed him, whereas in *Fight Club* Durden has stamped on Norton's leg or foot, and this is immediately followed by the comical event of him pulling off Norton's shoe and beating him with it. This comical, ironic, intertextual, parodying take on Bruce Lee semiotics in *Fight Club* is therefore strongly in evidence. In one earlier scene, as mentioned earlier, Durden is also seen practicing (badly) with a set of nunchakus.

Bruce Lee's Nunchakus

One of the strongest indexes of the interest in and the influence of Bruce Lee has always been the nunchaku. According to Inosanto, Lee was interested in this martial arts weapon long before it became popular amongst martial artists in the west; indeed, it was surely his use of it in films that popularised it among martial artists and cinemagoers in the first place. The possible reasons for this interest – both Bruce Lee's interest, and martial arts fans' interest – deserve consideration. For, the origins, history and martial status of the nunchaku is – as usual – shrouded in uncertainty and controversy. But a little more is known about its recent popular cultural history. This relates ineluctably and chiefly to Bruce Lee's use of them in *Enter the Dragon* (1973). According to the website of the British Board of Film Classification, in 1975, 'Following reported outbreaks of violence involving martial arts weaponry, BBFC Director James Ferman enforce[d] a blanket ban on all sight of nunchaku and shuriken (throwing stars)'.[11] This is said to have been closely related to or compounded by the 1970s 'crazes' for subcultural gang violence informed by or not entirely alien to the penchant for exotic weaponry as seen in *A Clockwork*

---

[11] http://www.sbbfc.co.uk/printtimeline.asp?t=violence_weapons

Orange (removed from circulation in 1973) and such other films as *Warriors* (1979). However, a closer inspection of the reasons given for the expurgations of nunchaku (rather than shuriken) scenes from films available to British eyes is quite revealing. For one of the main reasons given for their censorship was not that nunchaku-wielding youths were hurting *others*, but that teenage boys were hurting or killing *themselves* in their bedrooms, gardens and garages whilst practicing with them.

One significant thing about nunchakus is, of course, the ease with which they can be fabricated: two bits of wood held together by a short length of cord, rope or chain, and away you go. Another thing about nunchakus is their metonymic or symbolic function: thanks both to Bruce Lee and thanks to their enduring exoticism (they are, after all, a bizarre twirling, whirling sight to behold), they surely signify 'martial artness' through and through. Furthermore: although – or perhaps because – the prospect of swinging bits of wood rapidly around so close to one's head and body is so daunting at first, it is nevertheless relatively easy to gain the appearance of competence or expertise very quickly. Thus, a hundred times faster and easier than learning how to do flashy kicks, punches and blocks, or an adequate range of successful locks or throws (and ten thousand times faster than learning correct distancing, timing, relaxation, rhythm and flow to make such techniques work), the nunchaku can offer a very fast way to gain some teenage 'cultural capital' or kudos. In a few hours of practice, you can learn to whiz nunchakus apparently proficiently around you, behind you, in front of you, across your back, around your waist, and you can even hit (moveable) targets, such as leaves on tree branches to practice your lethal accuracy. (It is foolish – bordering on suicidal – to hit a hard, rooted target, as the nunchaku will rebound unpredictably if its course meets a hard obstacle.) You may of course get it ever so slightly wrong, crack yourself in the temple and kill yourself. But if your peers and maybe even some chicks are going to see you twirl and whirl them 'nunchucks' like Bruce Lee, and if they may even be impressed by your antics, surely the risks are well worth it... Playing with nunchakus will even quickly condition your grip, forearm muscles, biceps, triceps, deltoids and trapezius muscles, so you'll start to 'look the part' too.

Thus, unlike many other weapons or aspects of martial arts training, nunchakus 'do all the work for you'. Off-putting at first, the inexperienced will be impressed by your courage in using them. Easy to brandish, the free end of the sticks will swirl exponentially faster than your own wrist rotates, so you will look like greased lightning and can bask in their speed as if it is your own. What other martial arts weapons do this for you? With swords and staffs you have to learn a form that involves all of your body, specific stances, grip changes, timing, balance. Unlike other hinged, jointed or cord weapons, nunchakus are short enough to be kept at arms length: you can twirl them very fast and even keep them far enough away from your nose, jaw and temple so as to pose no threat to you yourself. Thus, with no lessons and no requirement for martial or fighting ability, nunchakus enable their twirler to look the part. But what is that part? Their status and credibility among martial artists is disputed. As with most things martial, of course, there is a sense in which they *always possibly could* be valid and valuable weapons, but 'in reality', the stakes are perhaps just too high: the brandisher is as likely to come off as injured as his or her assailant, largely because the lethal end of the weapon is basically out of control for most, if not all of its movement, and it is always going to bounce back relatively unpredictably after a strike or other contact.

Why did Bruce Lee champion this weapon? The reason is likely to involve all of the above: exotic, unusual, relatively easy to learn but difficult to master, impressive – indeed, *spectacular*. But there is another dimension to the nunchaku which is likely to have played a part: its (disputed) historical status as being an Okinawan but also/originally Chinese weapon of the underdog, the peasant, the farmer – particularly under the Satsuma daimyo interdiction against the carrying of bladed weapons. For the Chinese (diasporic) narcissistic nationalist Bruce Lee, anything associated with kicking Japanese, British or Russian butt was likely to appeal. Like the scream and the courting-catcall, the exposed hyper-lean and striated torso, adorned with as-if clawed-off fingernail scratches of skin, the nunchaku is the final fetishistic partial object to encapsulate Bruce Lee. Lines of sound, lines of striation, lines of muscle, lines of vein, red lines of slash and scratch marks, and the two lines of nunchaku linked by a taut line under tension characterise Bruce Lee. Add to this his jeet kune do insistence on the importance of the straight line of attack – best foot and hand forward, direct attack to the nearest target in order to get straight in and directly finish the job – and Bruce Lee becomes all about straight lines. Moreover, the extent to which the nunchaku is both immediately producible from everyday materials, its historical significance as the weapon of the underdog, the way in which one can quickly look flash but perhaps never be able to 'master' or effectively use the nunchaku, add layers of significance that enable this fetishistic supplement to exemplify the ethos (and not just symbolize the look) of Bruce Lee's anti-institutional interdisciplinarity. Moreover, it exemplifies the peculiarity of a 'turn east' that is also a turn to postmodern self-invention. The strange logic or peculiar philosophy underpinning this double-movement is what we will examine in the following chapter.

Chapter 4
Fighting—Philosophy

Finding a truth in one discipline and then applying that truth to an entirely unrelated discipline is a hallmark of Lee's genius: he saw the connections where others did not.
- John Little (in Lee 2001: xiv)

[T]o link is necessary; how to link is contingent.... But there exist genres of discourse which fix rules of linkage...
- Jean-François Lyotard (1988: 29)

He says JKD has no technique. My wife says everybody in the sixties talked that way.
- Dan Inosanto (in Miller 2000: 107)

Filming Philosophy: Like a Finger Pointing Away to an Icon

According to Daniele Bolelli, 'we only need to examine the concepts at the root of Jeet Kune Do, the martial art created by Lee, to see how fundamental philosophy was to Lee's approach to the martial arts' (2003: 157). At the same time, however, after a brief account of the most formulaic elements of many martial arts films, Bolelli argues that 'Lee's four movies (five if we include the posthumous *Game of Death*) contain all the defining elements of martial arts films. Philosophy, on the other hand, seems to be (literally) missing in action' (178). The key word here is 'literally'. Bolelli cannot detect anything philosophical in Lee's films because he is looking for it in words alone: his notion of the philosophical is logocentric – focused on words. Thus, Bolelli trades in a very particular notion of philosophy and the philosophical: 'Generally speaking, movies are not the best form of media to convey philosophical ideas' (178). He proposes:

Martial arts movies, in particular, are not exactly famous for their philosophical depth. Fast-paced action scenes and spectacular stunts are the staple

> of this genre in which the plot is often little more than a pretext for the
> fighting sequences. Since audiences usually do not watch martial arts
> movies for their fine intellectual content, producers often save on the un-
> necessary expenditure of a decent screenwriter by recycling the same plot
> over and over. (178)

On the one hand, this seems to be a reasonable observation. Yet, on the
other, Bolelli can also equally reasonably observe that although Bruce
Lee was an action hero first, he nevertheless 'added to this role an aesthetic beauty and a philosophical depth which were lacking' in other male
action heroes (155). For Bolelli, this testifies to the fact 'that his appeal
relies on something deeper than a popular infatuation with Asian fighting
styles' (156). Indeed, to support this claim he quotes Lee's widow, Linda
Lee Cadwell, when she asks rhetorically: 'What is this something about
Bruce Lee that continues to fascinate people in all walks of life? I believe
it is the depth of his personal philosophy, which subconsciously, or otherwise, projects from the screen and through his writings' (qtd. in Bolelli
2003: 156).

We have already considered aspects of this 'projection' of a 'philosophy' onto the screen in Chapter Two. Similar to that discussion,
Linda Lee Cadwell's claims here suggest that to be able to regard films as
philosophical, a notion of 'philosophy' – or at least of 'communication' –
that is somewhat other than logocentric will be required. For, the logocentric focus on words as if they are the exclusive medium of philosophy, or
any other kind of communication, can lead to an impasse – an inability to
'see'. Specifically, this will take the form of a mind/body dualism. We
can see the kinds of effects that this can have, in Bolelli, when he writes:

> ...in order to find any sign of philosophical life in Lee's first two movies,
> *Fist of Fury* and *The Chinese Connection* (a.k.a. *The Big Boss*), one needs
> the gift of a very fertile imagination. As an explanation for this complete
> lack of philosophical substance in the works of a man who was so im-
> mersed in philosophy, we need to remember that in 1971 Lee was still not
> particularly famous as an actor. For this reason, it is logical to assume that
> he did not have much power to influence the scripts of the first two mov-
> ies. In fact, as soon as Lee gained great fame, philosophy entered into his
> films. In his next (and last) two movies, *Return of the Dragon* and *Enter
> the Dragon*, glimpses of Lee's philosophy manage to come out in between
> action sequences. (Bolelli 2003: 178-9)

So, in the most traditional of manners, Bolelli regards the philosophical as
existing primarily as *words*. Yet Bolelli also has an inkling that philosophy can be communicated by being 'translated' into other realms, regis-

ters, modes or mediums, becoming a kind of aesthetics. For despite representing philosophy as linguistic, Bolelli nevertheless goes on to note that:

> In a final fight of *Return of the Dragon*, Lee again inserts a small philoso-
> phical element. Like all movie heroes, Lee begins the fight by losing. At
> this point, however, unlike the heroes of other movies, who usually rely
> only on willpower to come back and win, Lee changes his fighting style to
> suit the situation. Lee's opponent, on the other hand, is bound to only one
> form of fighting and is therefore unable to change. This lack of flexibility
> proves fatal and Lee goes on to soundly defeat his opponent. In this scene,
> the Taoist emphasis on being able to change to suit the circumstances and
> on having no form in order to be able to assume all forms are the keys al-
> lowing Lee to win what started out as an unfavorable fight: a perfect ap-
> plication of the principles of Jeet Kune Do. (179)

Similarly, Bolelli sees (yet, one might say, in pseudo-Zen manner, does
not 'realise') the philosophical dimensions of the lessons in *Enter the
Dragon*. As he writes:

> If in *Return of the Dragon* Lee timidly began introducing philosophical
> themes, in *Enter the Dragon* he added more philosophical fuel to the fire.
> The very beginning of the movie sees Lee in a temple teaching martial arts
> to a young pupil. In this dialogue, Lee uses plenty of Zen sayings (a para-
> phrase of the famous 'The wise man points at the moon, but the fool looks
> at the finger') and stresses Zen ideas such as relying on intuition more
> than on absolute rationality. (179)

In contrast to Bolelli, Miller regards Lee's penchant for such aphorisms
as rather less than philosophical, arguing instead that Bruce Lee 'created
his wisdom from Chinese clichés (the "pointing finger" analogy is an example)' and noting that Lee also 'adapted at least one of Mao Tse-tung's
credos. "Absorb what is useful; reject what is useless", Mao said. Lee
expanded this to include, "Add specifically what is your own"' (Miller
2000: 115). Similarly, in a discussion of *No Retreat, No Surrender* – a
film in which 'Bruce Lee' returns from the grave to train the put-upon
teenager, Jason – Meaghan Morris notes that such ideas as the 'emphasis
on being able to change to suit the circumstances' are as much stock
'clichés of martial arts cinema, as [they are] of many self-development
regimes' (2001: 182). Basically, 'brutes and bullies, in these films, are
inadaptive':

> In innumerable films opposing 'fluid' to 'rigid' styles of fighting *(Dragon,*
> the *Kickboxer* and *Bloodfist* films), strong, flexible bodies to muscle-
> bound hulks *(Rage and Honor, Bounty Tracker, Best of the Best 2)*, hu-
> mane to fascist authority *(Showdown, Sidekicks, Only the Strong, Watch*

the Shadows Dance), and improvisational to mechanistic training *(Rocky IV, The Karate Kid, Best of the Best)*, the point of a pragmatic aesthetic pedagogy is always to shape a socially responsive as well as physically capable self that can handle new experience … and creatively engage with strangers. (Morris 2001: 182)

So, the 'philosophy' of Bruce Lee as manifest in and through his films may be neither all that unique nor all that philosophical, and rather more formulaic and clichéd. However, Morris argues that all of these formulas (which are indelibly 'stamped on' such films as *No Retreat, No Surrender* from its 'opening scene, when Jason whirls out of the stiff routine of his father's karate class') are not simply generic clichés but amount rather to 'the trademark ethic of the experimental art of Bruce Lee' (2001: 182). Although these themes may now have become clichés, it is safe to say that it was with Bruce Lee that they forcefully emerged in martial arts and action cinema. Indeed, Morris arguably gets right to the heart of the matter when she proposes that, if regarded as 'a hard-edged allegory of the text as a reflection of its own creative process', then:

> *No Retreat, No Surrender* could plausibly be seen as a Hong Kong film that cleverly accessed a US market by retelling the classic Hollywood success story ('Outsider makes good'), using Bruce Lee, the ultimate migrant cross-over star, as its *mise-en-abîme* of accomplishment. The film's canny makers clearly understood Lee's special role in US martial arts film culture: neither a 'body' nor a generic action hero, Lee is first and foremost an iconic film teacher. In a mythology still being elaborated by countless martial arts magazines and by 'secrets of Jeet Kune Do' videos and books, Lee figures as both a great martial arts teacher who struggled against adversity to become a great film star *and* an exemplary martial artist who used film as a pedagogical medium – on both scores, inspiring others to do likewise. (178)

If Morris hits the nail on the head, by moving discussion of Bruce Lee 'the film icon' into the *practical, cultural* realm, Bolelli on the other hand could be said to run directly into a brick wall by construing philosophy as *words* and *arguments*. Bolelli's ultimate conclusion is that although 'Lee's films were hardly full of philosophical dialogues, we can also see how, as Lee gained fame and influence, philosophy gained a more prominent role in each new movie' (2003: 181). But we should not yet regard Morris's proverbial 'nail' as *fully* nailed. Nor should we recoil from Bolelli's wall, rubbing our head. For Bolelli's discussion exemplifies a prevalent tendency of thought and analysis, and a wider-ranging locus or chiasmus of questions and issues.

Bruce Lee's Body of Philosophy

Discussions of Bruce Lee 'and philosophy' often begin with expressions of amazement about Lee's *physicality* and his *visual* impact. However, they inexorably move from the opening 'wow' about Lee's body into the whys and wherefores of his written words. Thus, although these discussions are often based on an implicit attempt to articulate 'philosophy' and 'body' (through visuality), they are often organised in terms of the very mind/body dualism that the attempt to think body and philosophy *together – through* each other – initially promised to transform. This is perhaps why so many writings that claim to include studies of Bruce Lee's 'philosophy' either collapse into odes of straightforward hagiography or celebrations of a rather saccharine self-help ideology.

This is not simply to subscribe to the rather arrogant idea that 'popular' studies of Bruce Lee are limited when it comes to discussing philosophy or when it comes to discussing Bruce Lee as a cultural phenomenon. In other words, this is *not* to be understood as a problem arising when 'lowly laypeople' try to handle the complexities of 'high philosophy'. In fact, some of the most limited writing about popular culture hails from the academic field of philosophy, just as surely as some myopic writing about academic philosophy comes from fields such as cultural studies. Rather, the problem here is one inherent to all attempts to relate or articulate 'philosophy' and 'culture', especially in terms of such a contestable multimedia object or text as Bruce Lee. For, a discussion of a philosophy or theory of fighting is one thing. A discussion of a philosophy of fighting derived from a still-controversial mediatized martial entrepreneur of unverifiable martial status who was the first Asian male lead of a major Hollywood blockbuster in a tumultuous and still unclear cultural period is quite another. Indeed, neither discussion would encompass the range of Bruce Lee's field of influence. For, studying Bruce Lee is not just a matter of focusing on fighting and all things bodily. Nor is it just about assessing an argument ('mind'). As Bolelli points out, there is a need to contextualise and historicise. There is also – perhaps chiefly – a need to take into account what Chow calls 'the process of magnification and amplification that is made possible by the film medium, which, as it were, makes the spectacle spectacular, the demonstration monstrous, and thus underscores the significance of a technologized visuality' (Chow 1995: 6). Indeed, the interdisciplinary requirements demanded here are not only daunting – encompassing as they do so many disciplinary problematics, from philosophy to film to culture to cultural translation, etc. – but also fundamentally impossible to satisfy in a way that could please everyone, from every discipline or field encountered. As Mowitt emphasizes, the fundamental problem with interdisciplinary work is that it is ultimately impossible for people hailing from different disciplines to agree on how interdisciplinary work should be done 'properly' (Mowitt 1992; 2003).

Daniele Bolelli attempts to bridge the traditional philosophical mind/body impasse that he has inadvertently tangled himself up in by attempting to articulate Bruce Lee's written philosophy with his martial training practices and bodily movements. In doing this, Bolelli seeks to differentiate and distinguish what he calls the 'appeal' of Bruce Lee from that of other action movie stars and celebrities: 'Lee's role as a tough, lonely hero who fights injustice wherever he meets it is certainly appealing to vast segments of the public' (156). What we should also note is the significance of the word 'appeal', which not only strongly refers to *attraction*, of course, but also denotes the sense of *call, hail* and indeed therefore *interpellation*. 'Lee has something else to offer' (156), Bolelli proposes. This is why Lee both appeals, hails, or calls out to, *and* offers or *promises* something. He was first 'merely' an action hero, certainly. But Lee 'added to this role an aesthetic beauty and a philosophical depth' (155). Thus, claims Bolelli, 'his appeal relies on something deeper than a popular infatuation with Asian fighting styles' (156). He quotes Linda Lee Cadwell's assertion that the 'certain *je ne sais quoi*', the certain 'something about Bruce Lee that continues to fascinate people in all walks of life … is the depth of his personal philosophy, which subconsciously, or otherwise, projects from the screen and through his writings' (156). Bolelli notes that the 'same feeling is echoed in the comments of Lee's own students', and he quotes Kareem Abdul-Jabbar's contention that 'Lee was a teacher first of all' who 'taught philosophy and tried to spread knowledge and wisdom', which is 'why he took on the martial arts establishment the way he did' (156). Bolelli also quotes Daniel Lee's assertion that Bruce Lee's was 'a different approach to martial arts instruction'. According to Daniel Lee, 'We studied philosophy with Bruce because he had philosophy as his underlying theme and direction. He was really my mentor in showing the linkage between philosophy and martial art. They're inseparable' (qtd. in Bolelli 156).

So, perhaps the first cluster of questions about 'Bruce Lee and philosophy' are those of whether he *had anything* that could be called a 'philosophy', and if so (or if not) what that was. (The second cluster of questions relate perhaps to adjudicating the significance of this 'thing'.) Deciding this will not be easy, not least because decisions about what may be considered to be 'philosophy' will never be natural or neutral. Indeed, according to Jacques Derrida, 'the question of knowing what can be called "philosophy" has always been the very question of philosophy, its heart, its origin, its life-principle' (1995a: 411). As Derrida sees it, many people simply 'confuse philosophy with what they have been taught to reproduce in the tradition and style of a particular institution, within a more or less protected – or rather, less and less well protected – social and professional environment' (411). 'What is more', he continues, 'I am always surprised or amused when I see someone, in the name of a discipline, calmly classifying a discourse – for example philosophical or nonphilosophical. I recognize that this can be of use, but what use, and to whom?' (413)

So, the term 'philosophy' can either be hugely vague or suffocatingly particular. It can be taken to mean *anything* or it can be deployed to designate *only* what this or that school of philosophers say philosophy 'is', or what they philosophize philosophy 'as', or what *they* read, think about and 'do'. This is at least one of the reasons why, since the 1970s, it has become common in UK, US and other anglophone universities to replace the word 'philosophy' with 'theory'. Moreover, says Chow, 'we should remember that what is often called "French theory" is really philosophical writing that departments of philosophy, under the sway of Analytic Philosophy, tend to reject as philosophy proper' (2006: 18). Of course, both 'philosophy' and 'theory' here are calculated to signify an intellectual practice that is distinguishable from 'ideology', or unexamined cultural beliefs. The point is that theory or philosophy is imagined to be analytical, self-reflexive, critical, and so on. By implication, then, everything else may implicitly be presumed to operate by just blindly falling into ideological line or at best trading in the terms and concepts that circulate in a given historical conjuncture, or 'cultural' time and place. Needless to say, however, just because one may have taken great pains to define one's own efforts as properly philosophical or thoroughly self-aware and theoretical, and therefore in opposition to ideological/'bad' practices which are not properly rigorously self-aware, critical, etc., there is nevertheless no guarantee that one's efforts *are* entirely non-ideological. Anyone can accuse anyone else of being a symptomatic expression of the operations of an ideology. Indeed, exchanging such accusations has become the stock in trade of many academic discussions. Deciding who or what is ideological and who or what is otherwise 'reliable' or grounded on firm (non-ideological) foundations has become more and more difficult – perhaps even *undecidable*.

The Undecidability of Bruce Lee

Some thinkers and theorists have gone so far as to propose that *undecidability* is the very problematic of (post)modern knowledge. From structural linguistics to science, today's primary methodological problem, says Sam Weber, is undecidability – the undecidability of every claimed interpretation, every claimed relation, and in fact every claimed fact:

> the world of contemporary science emerges as one of Doppelganger and of ambiguous 'choices', in which 'time operates more by repetition than by duration', and where reality appears as a 'spectrum of numbers' or even as 'a double play of writing'. And yet, in this spectral world, choices must still be made and identities established, no matter how provisional, probabilistic, and aleatory these may be. It is the inevitability of such decision making, in a situation marked by irreducible ambiguity, that gives rise to a thinking nourished not only by ambivalence, but also by anxiety. (Weber 1987: xii)

In cultural studies, discourse analysis, film studies, and beyond – in fact, throughout the fields of the contemporary arts and humanities – knowledge about social and cultural reality has come to be construed and established by proposing that reality is unavoidably text-like, constructed and articulated, hegemonically, discursively, and so on. This has been very enabling for thinking about the relationships between cultural practices and fields, including film and questions of politics, institutions, ideologies and ethics. Indeed, thinkers from Lyotard to Laclau, and even Derrida and beyond, view the 'contingent articulation' of such nominally heterogeneous areas as film and politics as a real chance for rethinking ethically and politically consequential change (Lyotard 1984; Laclau 1989; Derrida 1996: 84). As we have seen in the previous chapter, one of the most popular versions of this position is expressed by Giroux, who regards such cultural productions as films to be 'public pedagogies because they play a powerful role in mobilizing meaning, pleasures, and identifications' (2002: 282), or as 'public discourses that address or at least resonate with broader issues in the historical and sociopolitical context in which they are situated' (279). However, viewed accordingly, the problem now becomes that 'there is no reason why anything is or isn't potentially articulatable with anything' (Hall 1996: 146). With this observation, Stuart Hall points to the fact that the contingency and undecidability of articulation poses an insurmountable challenge when trying to establish knowledge, one that ultimately returns to haunt and menace even the celebrants of contingency and articulation. For, if everything is *contingent*, then *everything* is contingent, including putative 'knowledge' about contingency. The contingency of articulation ultimately casts doubt on *all* knowledge establishment. So, the crisis that Hall discerns in deconstructive cultural studies is a version of the one that Weber finds haunting science and all (post)modern knowledge-establishment: it all 'inevitably entails the effort to determine the indeterminable' (1987: xiii).

Weber is ultimately following Derridean deconstruction and other tendencies of poststructuralism in his study of science, knowledge and institutions. His argument is that because of developments in science, philosophy, theory and even linguistics, the problem of interpretation/undecidability has become general. Derrida argues that once you reach a realisation of undecidability, then the 'strongest responsibility' becomes to make 'as clear and thematic as possible' the 'political implication' of all interpretation and all knowledge establishment itself (1992: 22-23). For, 'an institution', he argues, 'is not merely a few walls or some outer structures surrounding, protecting, guaranteeing or restricting the freedom of our work; it is also and already the structure of our interpretation' (22-23).

The Derridean insight is that 'the interpretation of [*anything*] is only produced by simultaneously proposing an institutional model, either by consolidating an existing one that enables the interpretation, or by constituting a new model to accord with it'. *All* interpretation – of *any-thing* – requires that the interpreter 'assume one or another institutional form'. 'This', Derrida adds, 'is the law of the text in general'. However, interpreters are not 'subjected passively' to the dictates of an institutional form; and all interpreters' 'own performance will in turn construct one or several models of community'. But nor is interpretation 'free': reading, or interpretation, cannot be extricated from the complex snares of the institutions, practices, and protocols of the contexts within which it occurs. Nor is reading or interpretation 'natural', or necessarily 'true'. Rather, it is always in some sense institutionally located and (over)determined. Indeed, Derrida goes further: *institutions themselves* are not simply free or unconnected from other social and cultural tendencies and institutions. Rather, they too are complexly ensnared, imbricated within, and complexly articulated to yet other institutions. There is a fundamental complexity and textile-like interimplication between institutions, the acts within and of them (that are never simply 'within'), and other contexts, sites and scenes. Derrida puts it provocatively: 'When, for example, I read some sentence from a given text or in a seminar … I do not fulfil a prior contract, I can also write, and prepare for signature, a new contract with an institution, between an institution and the dominant forces in society' (21-22). It is the 'political implication' of this complex textuality that Derrida demands should be made 'as clear and thematic as possible' in terms of 'the most classical of norms': In *all* reading, interpreting, or establishing, Derrida contends, we must 'acknowledge that an institutional concept is at play, … a *socius* implied, repeated or displaced, invented, transformed, menaced or destroyed'. Hence his pointed affirmation that an institution is 'not merely a few walls or some outer structures surrounding, protecting, guaranteeing or restricting the freedom of our work', but 'also and already the structure of our interpretation' (22-23).

It is because of the complexity of articulation and hence the undecidability of interpretation that Stuart Hall similarly points out that 'it has always been impossible in the theoretical field of cultural studies … to get anything like an adequate theoretical account of culture's relations and its effects' (1992: 286). This is so no matter how culture is theorized, conceptualized or understood – 'whether it is conceived of in terms of texts and contexts, of intertextuality, or of the historical formations in which cultural practices are lodged' (286). As such, a question about the 'relations and effects' of Bruce Lee may strictly speaking be impossible to answer decisively. Indeed, in light of the 'methodological' challenges posed by an acknowledgement of the contingency and undecidability of articulation and of establishment or interpretation, the questions of 'Bruce Lee and philosophy' should refer us primarily to the supposedly 'secondary' matter of interpretation itself.

The Interpretation of Bruce Lee

Bruce Lee's 'art and philosophy' has often been regarded as a singular occurrence: the unique production of a 'genius'. The polar alternative is to regard it as expressive of a particular historical and cultural movement. Bruce Lee's principal biographer, John Little, prefers the former interpretation, arguing for instance that the 'hallmark of Lee's genius' was that 'he saw the connections where others did not' (Little in Lee 2001: xiv). The opposite interpretation is to deem Lee's interdisciplining and deconstructing as exemplifying a cultural tendency. For instance, Nicholas Royle has suggested that 'what is happening today', in general, across all manner of fields and contexts of 'society, politics, diplomacy, economics, historical reality', and so on, is quite simply the generalised deconstruction of more and more institutions (2000: 11). *Deconstruction happens*. In itself, this can be interpreted in various ways too. For instance, whilst many deconstructionists regard deconstruction to be an intensification of questions related to justice and exclusion, Timothy Bewes argues, on the contrary, that 'deconstruction is produced by capitalism – by the anxiety towards the effects of capitalism, and by the uneasy perception that those effects are irresistible' (2001: 93). Indeed, he proposes that:

> The revolution ratified by deconstruction, in fact, is the capitalist one, which effects the gradual anonymization and *atomization* of society. This revolution lacks any 'end' other than itself: it involves, as the *Communist Manifesto* puts it, the 'constant revolutionizing of production, uninterrupted disturbance of all social conditions, everlasting uncertainty and agitation'. (92)

Elsewhere, I have argued that deconstruction can nevertheless be understood as, in Derrida's words, a 'kind of questioning' which 'tries to politicize and democratize the university scene' (Derrida 1995: 410; See also Bowman 2007; 2008). Whether Bruce Lee's interventions can be re-

garded as 'deconstructive' in the same way as *academic* deconstruction
and post-structuralism remains to be decided. Doubtless, Lee's spectacular cinematic entrance is responsible for much that might be regarded as
culturally deconstructive, however. We may, for instance, recall one last
time Bruce Thomas' biography of Bruce Lee in which Thomas points out
that it is all because of Lee that he, 'an Englishman ... was able to begin
learning a Chinese martial art from a Welshman' (2002: xii). As we have
seen, Thomas claims that Bruce Lee therefore 'bridged cultures', as well
as 'revolutionized the martial arts, taught a fierce philosophy of individualism, became a film icon and remade the image of the Asian man in the
West' (xi). The irony is that so successful was Bruce Lee in this regard
that Bruce Lee himself and kung fu are now, basically, *ordinary*. This is
so even though outside China and diasporic Chinese communities, it is
largely thanks to his films that what became known as 'kung fu' is even
known about at all. Bruce Lee and kung fu have become – arguably
thanks to Lee's spectacular cinematic simulation – immensely globally
familiar, and have touched and continue to touch millions, albeit with a
virtual, constitutively mediated, yet particularly 'concentrated a contact
that remains infinitely remote from any touch' (Heidegger 1971: 16).

As we have also seen throughout the previous chapters, what
Bruce Thomas' opinion expresses here is particularly telling: Bruce Lee,
he says, both revolutionised and popularised the martial arts, both
'bridged cultures' and 'remade the image of the Asian man in the West',
and so on. And this, implicitly, is a good thing. What is perhaps most significant is that implicitly residing here also is a view that has been most
formalised, theorised and advanced by those working in cultural studies,
postcolonial studies, discourse analysis, and so on: that *all* culture (from
physical culture to film), in its contingency, is effectively political. Stated
in reverse, however, this can also be taken to mean that the putatively
radical insights of deconstructive cultural studies are, in a sense, ordinary.
This is precisely why the likes of Slavoj Žižek disavow cultural studies
and retreat into a stalwart Marxist perspective, viewing all anti-
essentialism and multiculturalism as mere indices, symptoms and signs of
the success of capitalism's ideology (which is currently, to Žižek's mind,
that of neoliberalism).

In a Žižekian interpretation, as we have seen, all the multicultural
hybrid, east-meets-west identity-performativity of Welsh wing chun mas-

ters and spectacular Asian-American pseudo-Shaolin celluloid stars 'inspiring' countless imaginary and actual, factual and phantasmatic encounters, interventions and events across the world actually indicates nothing more than the deceptive deconstructive simulacrum of global capitalism. Again, for Žižek, if Protestantism was the necessary ideology of industrial capitalism, then the western appropriation of Taoism and Buddhism equals the necessary ideology of postmodern 'late capitalism'. In this picture, such phenomena as Bruce Lee's 'art and philosophy' (jeet kune do), Derridean deconstruction, and cultural studies could count as exemplary – indeed, sublime – objects of ideology. In this picture, then, despite all appearances to the contrary, and despite any apparent ethico-political improvement, reduced racism, cultural hybridity, apparent meetings of east and west, or anything else, all that we meet in Bruce Lee (and deconstruction) would be the deleterious 'deterritorialisation' of commodification and ideological fetishization (Žižek 2001: 12-15). This, for Žižek is the power of capitalism's 'real abstraction' (the power, that is, of money). And this is why Žižek lumps together and disdains so much multiculturalism, deconstructionism, new ageism, cultural-studies-ism and postmodernism as all being equivalent expressions of capitalist neoliberalist ideology. In this paradigm, Jacques Derrida and Bruce Lee – or at least their progeny – could be said to meet. And the political implication seems clear: deconstruction and Bruce Lee are equivalent lapdogs of neoliberalism; both culture and academia are 'political' or have 'implications' only insofar as they are hapless indices or symptoms of capitalism's unfettered reign.

This is not, perhaps, a very happy-sounding interpretation of Bruce Lee (or deconstruction or cultural studies). But it does at least serve as an interesting foil for the most utopian hagiographies of Bruce Lee (and deconstruction and cultural studies). Yet perhaps we need not let it get us down. For one must remember that although Žižekian and Marxian discussions use words like 'capitalism' as if they signified pure evil, one must also consider the fact that Žižek's peculiar Marxian/Hegelian/Lacanian determinism seems consistently to compel him to discredit that with which he is nevertheless fascinated: 'superstructural' phenomena like film and popular culture. And we should also remember that although it is very easy to evoke grand overarching entities like 'capitalism', our discussion of Bruce Lee – like *any* discussion of culture

– is principally a discussion of the relations between texts, discourses, interests, investments, fantasies, institutions and practices. Thus, in one sense, we should perhaps not rush headlong into dramatic conclusions about capitalism before considering the micrologies of that which is instituted.

For instance, to characterise Bruce Lee in terms of 'capitalism' may not be unlike *Enter the Dragon*'s Shaolin Abbot's characterisation of him in terms of 'spiritual insight'. That is to say, the very terms of the discussion may send us off looking for a red-herring. For, in *Enter the Dragon* and in jeet kune do, what subtends all of this is not 'spirituality' but rather matters to do with *discipline*, in a (post-)Foucauldian sense. Noting as much is to introduce a third term which complicates and subverts the smooth functioning of the former terms, so that questions like 'is Bruce Lee a symptom of capitalist ideology or not?' or 'is Bruce Lee spiritual or not?' become complicated in such a way as to suggest that the implicit premises of their initial formulation require transformation. Indeed, focusing on the institutional in this way is arguably the only way to gain access to *the object*, rather than gaining access to a smoothly functioning mechanical argument about 'capitalism'. In *Enter the Dragon*, Lee's character is the highest production-point of Shaolin *discipline*. Even though *Enter the Dragon*'s Shaolin Abbot mischaracterises Lee's 'talents' as being 'now at the point of spiritual insight', in actual fact this point, the route to it, and everything about it, can more usefully and more reliably be regarded as *disciplinary*. Indeed, in *Enter the Dragon*, from the student Lau to the compliant Lee versus the renegade Han, *vis-à-vis the institution*, the matrix is clear. Just as the Hong Kong audience disliked Lee's lapdog character in this film, so Bruce Lee the martial artist actually disliked all institutional strictures, calling institutional martial arts 'the classical mess', 'the fancy mess' and 'organised despair'. Instituting his inter- and anti-disciplinary jeet kune do was an approach to martial arts that sought to be '*an institutional practice for which the concept of the institution remains a problem*' (Derrida 2002: 53). This is Derrida's very definition of deconstruction, which Wlad Godzich renders like this: institution 'is the target of deconstructive practice' (1987: 162). Specifically, we might say, the target of deconstruction is what might be called *the political implications of disciplinary philosophy's institution of 'the essence'*. John Protevi explains:

> That the basic problem of deconstruction, even in Derrida's technically de-
> tailed readings of phenomenology, is thus basically political is clear: the
> names of philosophers as signatories are indices of texts which are indices
> of real history. The role of presence in the West is the target; philosophy
> texts are only paths to this target. The long-debated relation of philosophy
> and politics, the difference between the history of the West and the history
> of metaphysics, is thought by Derrida under the rubric of 'force'. (Protevi
> 2001: 20)

'The institution' – in terms of styles, systems, institutes, and rule-bound
practices of any form – was also the wider target of Bruce Lee's theoriza-
tions. We should thus turn our attention to this in more depth.

The Essence of Bruce Lee

Engaging with the problematic of 'institution' is essential to any cultural
study (Derrida 1992; Hall 1992; Mowitt 1992; Bowman 2007). Likewise,
tackling the topic of institution is simply unavoidable in any consideration of Bruce Lee. His critique of institutions ('styles') has always been
regarded as central to his intervention. At the same time, Lee has been
called *original*, a *genius*, an *originator*, and a decisive point of *origin* for
a wide range of things, including jeet kune do, the popularisation of
cross-training, a scientific approach to martial arts, 'American' freestyle
karate, the widespread move towards mixed- or no-holds-barred-martial
arts, and much in the way of self-help ideology (Inosanto 1980; Little
1996; Miller 2000; Thomas 1994). At the very least, he has been deemed
to have started a veritable revolution in both martial arts training and in
film fight choreography (Miller 2000; Hunt 2003). Bolelli puts it like this:
'Bruce Lee took old ideas and applied them in new, original ways' (2003:
159). Rather more problematically, he proceeds to illustrate this with the
claim that Lee 'took Taoism and Buddhism and applied them to the competitive, ego-driven world of movie-making, to the martial arts and to his
own daily life'. Quite what 'Taoist movie-making' might entail is left
unspecified. But Bolelli's point is that 'in the process, he drastically al-
tered the Western perception of Asian cultures, and inspired many martial
artists to explore the philosophical dimension at the root of their physical
practice' (159). Furthermore:

In the 1960s and early 1970s, Lee's philosophical stance, popularized through his writings and his movies, was an antiauthoritarian slap in the face to the dogma and immutable tradition that still dominated the way most people practiced martial arts in the West. Although ... he was not the first to challenge the dogmatism of some martial arts schools, he was more visible and more radical than anyone who had come before him, and therefore was also in a more powerful position to affect the prevailing perceptions of martial arts' practice and philosophy. (Bolelli 2003: 159)

Thus, to Bolelli, Lee's 'originality' took the form of a particular, timely and well-placed intervention into a specific context, rather than being a matter of apparently self-contained, autonomous, autochthonous and timeless genius. Indeed, Bolelli goes so far as to propose that Bruce Lee ought to be regarded as having 'made great philosophical contributions even though he clearly did not commit to paper a single original philosophical idea' (158). In this account, then, Lee is to be regarded as an *interlocutor*, a transformative *articulating link*, or a *cultural translator* from one realm, culture or context to another. His 'originality' takes the form of the success of 'his' intervention.

I italicise 'originality' and 'his', here, because despite Bolelli's contextualisation of Lee's intervention, there are nevertheless a number of problematic connotations that are all too easily attached to ideas of 'origins' and 'originality', which it seems prudent to identify: ideas like purity, newness, genius, uniqueness, and so on. These connotations are what thinkers like Derrida would term metaphysical 'traps', or what many, following Judith Butler or Ernesto Laclau, have called 'essentialisms'. By this what is meant are manners of thinking organised by efforts to find 'essences' – the essence of something's 'being', or its supposedly simple unitary self-contained points of origin or origination. To be sure, Bolelli takes pains to operate according to a more subtle understanding of origins, originality and genius. (But a different form of essentialism clouds his account, as we will see, in the Orientalist rhetorical structuring of his discussion in terms of East/West, Taoism/Confucianism, and Ancient/Modern.) Before turning our attention specifically to Bolelli, in this context there are perhaps two (becoming-three) essentialisms to be acknowledged: first, *the essentialism of origins*; second, *the essentialism of the originator's (original) genius*; and third, the ways in which these two essentialisms recur, mutually reinforcing each other, by each creeping back into efforts to account for the other.

The essentialism of origins is the presumption of a single, unitary, simple point of origin. On this matter (so to speak, that of the 'original essentialism'), hopefully the sheer weight of the scholarship, research, analysis and argumentation across so many fields for at least the last several decades now has done enough to enable us to discredit automatically any ideas or claims about 'pure and original origins' in the realms of *any* 'identity'. This includes claims about the 'essences' of ethnic, national, regional, class, gender or other constructs, as well as notions of identity that are implicitly essentialist in their very formulation, such as the notion of 'race'. For, *all* identity is always already a partial, incomplete, complex *process*; a multiple, hybrid, discontinuous, ongoing *original copy*; and therefore neither 'pure' nor self-contained, neither self-sufficient nor internal, and certainly not residing as an essence somewhere. Therefore, of course, *any* 'identity' is not really '*an* identity' as such at all. The word 'identity' denotes singularity, unitarity, indivisibility, and self-sufficient completeness. But current approaches to the subject understand identity as anything but essential, unitary, complete or indivisible (Derrida 1998: 33).

Some of the problems that arise in the wake of thinking in terms of positive essences take the form of such '-isms' as ethnocentrism, nationalism, racism, sexism, and so on. These 'isms' are characterised by the logic which holds that any Group A ('us') is/are essentially *this* (i.e., superior), whereas Group B ('them') is/are essentially *that* (i.e., inferior). The deconstruction of this type of thinking is now intellectually – if not culturally or politically – widespread. Its highpoint took the form of the movement that came to be known as 'PC', or 'Political Correctness', a discursive constellation that we will have reason to discuss more fully in due course. (The 'other' of PC – namely, essentialist, xenophobic, homophobic, etc. types of belief and thought – continues to proliferate and precipitate in many forms of prejudice.) As will come to be significant in our consideration of PC, Bolelli argues that the way Bruce Lee regarded it was like this:

> Since there can be no concept of 'we' if there is no 'them' representing the antithesis of everything that 'we' stand for, group identity inevitably is built on opposition to something. It is not a coincidence that patriotism always runs stronger in times of war. (Not surprisingly, in Lee's mind, patriotism, just like any other value emphasizing the power of the group over the individual, is among the diseases to be eliminated.) (Bolelli 2003: 170)

Unfortunately, a belief that this binary group logic can be 'eliminated' is somewhat problematic. Indeed, such a belief is actually an example of precisely the same kind of 'violent' logic as that to which it claims to be opposed (Chow 1995). Trying to 'eliminate' this or that 'other' is, surely, still an effort *to eliminate an other*, or to eradicate a kind of otherness. Even if it is the effort to eliminate those who are opposed to others or their otherness, this is still in itself an opposition to otherness, still an effort to eliminate an other. According to thinkers from Debray to Žižek, this tragic convergence of 'inclusive' utopian universalism with a logic of elimination of the other is arguably the point at which PC ideology meets neoliberalist ideology (Žižek 2001, 2002). A tolerant regime or ethos cannot tolerate intolerance.

If arguments about 'us' and 'them' tend to be based on a claim of a fundamental difference at the historical or temporal origin, we would seem to be faced with a different issue when confronted with the question of the essences of 'new things': this seems to be not a question of 'origins' but a question about the production of the new. This might not seem to be a question about origins *per se*. But it is. Indeed, in the face of the New, essentialist thinking is faced with a dilemma. The question in both cases is: where did the (new) essence of the new thing come from? Either the essence of the new thing has been conjured up out of nowhere, like a kind of alchemy (dreamt up or produced almost magically by the mind of a 'genius'), or it is not really a new essence in itself, but rather the most recent manifestation of some older and more enduring essence. If we hold the former opinion, then we are participating in a kind of hagiography or deification of the creator. If we hold the latter opinion, then the quest for the essence leads to a problem of infinite regress, wherein the (supposedly) 'new thing' is regarded as really just a modification of a prior essence. This refers the matter backwards, into a (mythological) imagining of times past. It also just defers or displaces the question. Where did this essence come from *originally*? At some point it must have been dreamt up by a 'genius'. Hence, in such a line of reasoning, the dilemma between the 'creating genius' who invents something 'entirely new, out of the blue' and an infinite regress back to a former time of creation are 'essentially' the same thing: both cases tend to regard the origin as being inextricably bound to the intentional creation of a genius.

This schematic sketch or caricature of essentialist thinking is relevant because it illustrates that even if it is the case that essentialisms about pure and unitary historical origins have been widely deconstructed, both academically and culturally, it is nevertheless the case that essentialism still threatens to return in answers to the question of what makes something 'original' – especially given the connotations of 'unique' and 'new' that the word 'original'. For, in the question of what makes something original – even if this is posed as a question of what its *essential difference* is from other things – this can easily be approached as a question about essences rather than *differences*, or what is produced by *relations* and *relationships*. Again, one would hope that the hold over thought and scholarship of such essentialisms as beliefs in the purity of origins as much as those of 'authorial genius' have been weakened, if not entirely eradicated by the overwhelming impact of feminism, deconstruction, post-structuralism, post-colonialism and postmodernism on many disciplines. But it is important to note that challenging and dislodging beliefs in the purity of (historical) origins is a lot easier than doing the same for (Cartesian) beliefs in the 'original genius'. Hence, we can have the situation in which, for instance, on the one hand, Bruce Lee's interdisciplinary borrowings and productive recombinations can be rather easily recognized and accepted as interdisciplinary constructions rather than essences. But at the same time, on the other hand, what persists – what returns – is the belief that the person who is doing this borrowing, interdisciplining and recombining is a unique, singular, creative genius.

The Institutions of Bruce Lee

Arguably, Bruce Lee actually tried to deconstruct a belief in essences. However, in doing so, Lee simply reinstituted a different version of essentialism. In the influential article 'Liberate Yourself from Classical Karate' (1971), for instance, Lee insisted that, contrary to many of the mythical martial art creation legends that many practitioners still believe in, 'we must recognize the incontrovertible fact that regardless of their many colourful origins (by a wise, mysterious monk, by a special messenger in a dream, in a holy revelation, etc.) styles are created by men' (Lee 1971). As such, he continues, 'A style should never be considered gospel truth, the laws and principles of which can never be violated. Man, the living, creating individual, is always more important than any established style'. To argue his point, however, Lee fabricates a creation myth of his own:

> It is conceivable that a long time ago a certain martial artist discovered some partial truth. During his lifetime, the man resisted the temptation to organize this partial truth, although this is a common tendency in a man's search for security and certainty in life. After his death, his students took 'his' hypotheses, 'his' postulates, 'his' method and turned them into law. Impressive creeds were then invented, solemn reinforcing ceremonies prescribed, rigid philosophy and patterns formulated, and so on, until finally an institution was erected. So, what originated as one man's intuition of some sort of personal fluidity has been transformed into solidified, fixed knowledge, complete with organized classified responses presented in a logical order. In so doing, the well-meaning, loyal followers have not only made this knowledge a holy shrine, but also a tomb in which they have buried the founder's wisdom. (Lee 1971)

Lee emphasises the contingency of origins and actually italicizes the word 'his' in order to suggest that singular authorship or ownership are problematic ideas. So this account goes some way towards deconstructing the essentialisms of origins and of original genius. But Lee then falls back into another version of the same belief in the importance of the original creative genius: it is regarded as a brief beacon which institutionalisation ultimately extinguishes and abuses in trying to honour: 'the well-meaning, loyal followers have not only made this knowledge a holy shrine, but also a tomb in which they have buried the founder's wisdom'.

It is clear that Lee identified with this position of the founder, regarding himself as someone who had a special kind of insight and even the anti-institutional wisdom to pre-emptively address the problem of instituting jeet kune do. As Davis Miller notes:

> Shortly before his death, Lee closed his Los Angeles, Seattle and San Francisco schools and demanded that his art not be taught by the three 'authorized' *jeet kune do* instructors, Dan Inosanto in Los Angeles, James Lee in Oakland, Taky Kimura in Seattle, or by any of Lee's other pupils.
> George Tan explains Lee's motives. 'He felt no one was qualified. A lot of people who hung out with Bruce, especially during his Hollywood years, were weak men. Most of his students were guys he could use as moving, breathing punching bags. The exception was Jimmy Lee but he died before Bruce. Bruce knew the lack of quality in his students and teaching would come back to haunt him'. (Miller 2000: 143-4)

Because of his fame, in Lee's case, the problem of institutionalisation is amplified: 'with Lee's death and the success of *Enter the Dragon,* former students, most of whom wanted honestly to perpetuate Lee's teaching methods, also recognized that considerable money could be made by claiming to be heirs to Lee's art', says Miller (144). George Tan formulates it in Lee's own terms: 'Bruce knew this would happen. It's like Christianity or most any other thing. First, along comes an innovator. He dies and the guys left behind are followers' (qtd. in Miller 144). Miller laments: 'In the post-Lee years, *jeet kune do* has become much of what Lee sought to change in the martial arts: it pretends to be free-flowing, but is structured, systematic, formulaic, unintentionally worshipful, paralysingly dogmatic' (144). Moreover:

> 'Lots of these JKD people sit around and play office politics,' Tan says, 'fighting each other for what they can make by marketing Bruce's bones as icons. [The irony is that] Bruce was a revolutionary. He did his best to knock down the whole office building and grind up the bones of everybody inside. He's the guy who wanted to take a wrecking ball to the very *idea* of having an office building'. (Tan as qtd. in Miller 144)

Thus, what Lee attempted to institute might be regarded as an *anti-institution*: *a guiding idea*, one which would productively, creatively, and generatively disrupt or deconstruct existing institutional arrangements. This was clearly regarded by Lee and his subsequent interlocutors as the pinnacle of anti-authoritarian, anarchic, anti-institutionalism. However, the ambivalent effort of (not) instituting a 'guiding idea' rather than an institution can only be regarded as anti-authoritarian, anarchic, anti-institutionalism if institutions are conceived of as being *opposed* to guiding ideas; or only if, as Wlad Godzich puts it, we 'think of institutions as apparatuses, that is, as constituted bodies with their internal procedures and delimited field of intervention' (1987: 156). However, Godzich suggests, surely 'an institution is first and foremost a guiding idea, the idea of some determined goal to be reached for the common weal' (156). This guiding idea, if it really catches on and starts to guide, is destined to institute. Thus, we might say: Bruce Lee's antiauthoritarian, countercultural, individualist anti-institutionalism *opposed* guiding ideas to institutions:

> But an institution is first and foremost a guiding idea, the idea of some determined goal to be reached for the common weal; it is this goal that is sought according to prescribed behaviour and the application of set procedures. The idea itself is adopted by a group of individuals who become its

public possessors and implementers. This group then becomes the institution as a result of the combining of the guiding idea with the set procedures. The members of the group are shaped by the guiding idea they seek
to implement and the procedures they apply; they adopt common behavior, develop similar attitudes, all of which tend to unify them into a determinate and identifiable group and give the institution its distinct unity.
(Godzich 1987: 156)

Thus, Lee's anti-institutional impulse is arguably also the strongest impulse towards institution, the strongest force of institution. The counter-
point, however, would be that institutions are 'fundamentally instruments
of reproduction, not in the simple mechanical sense, but rather in that
they ensure that regulative processes take place so as to contain what otherwise could threaten to turn into anarchic proliferation' (157). Bruce
Lee's intervention arguably then sought to exploit the paradoxes and vi-
cissitudes of institution, by using the 'guiding idea' or declared *raison
d'être* of *all* martial arts institutions against their current entrenched
forms. This was to reactivate the impetus to 'anarchic proliferation' –
something that all institutions try to contain in order to preserve their present forms. Accordingly, this impetus ought to be regarded as neither
original nor copied but, to use Derrida's term, 'originary': both constitu-
tive/productive and de/constructive at the same time. Such an originary
institutional/anti-institutional impetus could and would of course produce
many different potential forms and contents of institutions and activities.

What Bruce Lee popularised was what he regarded as a 'scientific'
or pragmatic search for efficiency in martial arts. His procedure involved
exposing an existing form to a guiding idea – questioning the current institutional form by way of the ideals implied by the guiding idea. Of
course, this 'science' took the form of a rationalised or rationalistic approach (one that desired to be fully Rational), involving a 'four-step
methodology': '1. Research your own experience; 2. Absorb what is useful; 3. Reject what is useless; 4. Add what is specifically your own' (Bolelli 2003: 175). This rhetoric sounds very slick. But, aside from the fact
that this supposedly rational and universal method is actually derived
from one of Mao's sayings, there are in any case any number of aporias
and problems with it. First is the assumption that this rationale *is* rational.
For (second), is it really possible to *know*, or to *decide*, with certainty,
what might be 'useful' and what might be 'useless', in advance of having

studied a particular style for the requisite period of time in order to have mastered it? Can one know in advance? How does one decide?

Thirdly: although this is all part and parcel of an engaging humanist and individualist critique of institutionalisation, the problem with Bruce Lee's pragmatic, ostensibly anti-theoretical, anti-institutional stance is precisely that: it is a stance; necessarily both an interpretation and a pose; simultaneously an honest interpretation and an affectation. For, like so many anti-institutional projects, Lee evidently misrecognises the fact that *his* understanding of what he calls the 'actual reality of combat' is precisely that – *an* understanding, and moreover, one which 'stands under' his overwhelming identification with the principles of one particular theoretical paradigm – namely, the strategies and principles of wing chun kung fu. For it is wing chun theory and practice that provides the foundation for the guiding principles that Lee internalised and took to be 'natural', inevitable and necessary, which is why Lee takes 'simple and direct' to mean necessarily using short, quick, straight lines and economy of motion when fighting. However, like self-proclaimed 'pragmatists' and 'realists' of all orders, what Lee does here is to represent one theory as necessarily true, as 'not theoretical' but as 'really practical', really real, and to deem other orientations 'flowery' and 'artificial'.

Nevertheless, 'what this translated to in practical terms', argues Bolelli, 'was a radical departure from the methodology normally used by martial arts schools' (2003: 171). For, 'rather than following the standard curriculum of an established style, Lee began advocating a form of cross-training aimed at picking the best from different martial arts styles' (171). Inevitably, then, 'Lee moved away from the Wing Chun style that he had learned in Hong Kong from Yip Man and established his own "non-style" of Jeet Kune Do' (171-2). But the principles which guided the decision-making and selection processes of identifying and 'picking the best' arguably remained firmly rooted in the *paradigm* of wing chun. The 'move away' from the wing chun appearance was governed by a 'cross-training' interdisciplinarity that was nevertheless driven by Lee's understanding of the wing chun principles of efficiency and economy of motion.

Adjudicating Lee's grasp of these principles is not the aim here. Rather, what is prime is the *actuality* of relationships and articulations, the *productivity* of differences and particularities of understandings and interpretations (including misunderstandings and misinterpretations), and so on. Lee himself had something to say about such 'distortion' and de-velopment. To return to his own hypothetical scenario of an original gen-ius whose 'well-meaning, loyal followers' go on to make 'this knowledge a holy shrine, but also a tomb in which they have buried the founder's wisdom', Lee proposed:

> ...distortion does not necessarily end here. In reaction to 'the other truth', another martial artist, or possibly a dissatisfied disciple, organizes an op-posite approach – such as the 'soft' style versus the 'hard' style, the 'inter-nal' school versus the 'external' school, and all these separate nonsenses. Soon this opposite faction also becomes a large organization, with its own laws and patterns. A rivalry begins, with each style claiming to possess the 'truth' to the exclusion of all others. (Lee 1971)

To reiterate, Lee's theory is thus based on the hypothesis that at the origin is a spontaneous, vital, 'living' genius who has an enabling 'partial in-sight'. In attempting to preserve this insight, 'his' disciples go on to hon-our it, but succeed only in suffocating it, by interring it, constructing tight strictures in a self-defeating effort to preserve the original. Thus, it was Lee's aim to re-awaken the essential vitality of the spontaneous, free, creative, creating individual, by knocking down the institutions which have stultified this spontaneity. This theory is encapsulated in a plaque which reputedly greeted visitors to one of Bruce Lee's kwoons, which read: 'In memory of a once fluid man, crammed and distorted by the clas-sical mess'. This peculiar wording allows for several possible interpreta-tions. One is that we should remember an original spontaneity that has been lost. Another is that the reader is looking at their own tombstone: by entering *this* kwoon, the old you is going to be killed – you, the once fluid person who became crammed and distorted by the classical mess, are go-ing to be purged and purified here. This is about death, purging, purifica-tion and rebirth: return to the origin, return to the essence, through de-stroying the institutional distortion. As he wrote:

> To reach the masses, some sort of big organization [comprising of] domestic and foreign branch affiliation, is not necessary. To reach the growing number of students, some sort of pre-conformed set must be es-tablished as standards for the branch to follow. As a result all members will be conditioned according to the prescribed system. Many will proba-bly end up as a prisoner of a systematized drill.
> Styles tend to not only separate men – because they have their own doctrines and then the doctrine became the gospel truth that you cannot change. But if you do not have a style, if you just say: Well, here I am as a human being, how can I express myself totally and completely? Now, that

way you won't create a style, because style is a crystallization. That way, it's a process of continuing growth.

To me totality is very important in sparring. Many styles claim this totality. They say that they can cope with all types of attacks; that their structures cover all the possible lines and angles, and are capable of retaliation from all angles and lines. If this is true, then how did all the different styles come about? If they are in totality, why do some use only the straight lines, others the round lines, some only kicks, and why do still others who want to be different just flap and flick their hands? To me a system that clings to one small aspect of combat is actually in bondage.

This statement expresses my feelings perfectly: 'In memory of a once fluid man, crammed and distorted by the classical mess.' (Lee, n/d)[12]

Thus, Lee simultaneously discounts the possibility of totality ('Many styles claim this totality.... [But] then how did all the different styles come about?') *and* claims it as his own ('To me totality is very important in sparring.... To me a system that clings to one small aspect of combat is actually in bondage'). He critiques 'styles' in the name of a transcendent 'no-style', and 'ways' in the name of a perfectly fluid 'no-way as way'. Through the critique of style (institution), Lee sought a return to some kind of original (fantasy of) fluidity, or at least the hypothesis of a totally free and totally open, spontaneous, reactive and transcendent physicality. A finer version of countercultural hippy rhetoric would be difficult to find. And this informs all of Lee's thinking.

The Time of Bruce Lee

This is more than tangentially relevant to a consideration of Bruce Lee because, as Bolelli proposes, if Bruce Lee can be regarded as having a philosophy, then this 'philosophy of jeet kune do' might actually be regarded as 'the archetypical martial art of the 1960s' (2003: 181). Bolelli does not represent this as a problem as such, nor specifically as the problem of 'ideology'. Yet what would being 'the archetypical martial art of the 1960s' signify? Bolelli captures the potential problem (whilst introducing some more) when he asserts:

The importance of the context in which ideas came to light is sometimes downplayed in the study of philosophy. For example, if most of Lee's philosophy is derived from Asian sources that are thousands of years old, one may guess that the context in which Lee lived did not con-

---

[12] Bruce Lee (n/d) http://www.fightingmaster.com/masters/brucelee/quotes.htm

> tribute much to the articulation of his philosophy. The assumption is logical but, as logic often goes, terribly wrong.
> In its philosophical outlook, in fact, Jeet Kune Do is the quintessential martial art of the 1960s. It is not simply because the 1960s were the decade in which Lee came up with the main concepts of his new approach to martial arts. Rather, Jeet Kune Do is the embodiment in martial arts form of many of the wild, revolutionary ideas that characterized the sixties. (Bolelli 2003: 181)

Now, at the same time as introducing some highly problematic essentialisms by counterposing putatively 'ancient', putatively 'Asian' ideas with all things modern and Californian, Bolelli nonetheless situates Bruce Lee's ideas within a certain milieu or zeitgeist. As he puts it: 'At a time when no forms of established authority went unchallenged, it seems only natural that even the field of martial arts was destined to experience some drastic change' (182-3). Thus, he continues, 'It was in this receptive context that Lee stepped up with his radical form of Taoism and Zen' (183). Indeed, Bolelli paints Lee as almost perfectly exemplary of 1960s countercultural ideals when he recounts:

> Lee's highly unconventional personal background (an interracial marriage with a young white woman, his willingness to teach anyone regardless of ethnicity, the match fought against a Chinese martial artist sent to stop Lee from divulging martial arts 'secrets' to non-Chinese, the fact that he had never received a formal teaching license) united with his equally unconventional philosophy and his public role as an actor allowed him to become the man who was to take the spirit of the sixties into the martial arts world. The philosophy of JKD can therefore be seen as the gift (or the curse, depending on your point of view) of the alchemical mixing of Taoism, Zen Buddhism, the antiauthoritarian culture of the 1960s, and Bruce Lee's own personality. Regardless of whether we agree with Lee's approach or not, his example remains as an open invitation to do one of the healthiest things that anyone, martial artist or not, can do; questioning one's own beliefs. (183)

According to the Žižekian critique that has often entered our discussions so far, Lee's 'philosophy' may simply therefore be expressive of an 'ideology', in the pejorative sense. Indeed, in Žižekian terms, even Bolelli's account and argument could be said to be 'ideological', not only because it is based on several unquestioned beliefs about Bruce Lee interpreted according to a belief in the 'inherent' or 'essential' value of 'questioning one's own beliefs'. For, without even considering the implications of the celebration of questioning beliefs without actually doing so, the belief in the value of questioning beliefs can be regarded as one that may itself be historicized and interpreted as an ideological injunction that has arisen as a consequence of capitalism's deconstruction of 'all that is solid', to echo Marx and Engels' critique of the deconstructive effects of capitalism. Moreover, asks Chow, 'can such self-referentiality, however patient and vigilant, in any way help ameliorate the problems of social inequity and injustice, or does it simply become – and continue to derive its legitimacy as – such inequity and injustice's symptom?' (2006: 11-12) In other words, extolling the value of 'questioning one's own beliefs' *sounds good*, but extolling something as a value is neither to actually do that which is extolled, nor is it to question why it is to be valued nor what consequences or significance it has or difference it makes.

Nevertheless, as Bolelli sees it, 'we only need to examine the concepts at the root of Jeet Kune Do, the martial art created by Lee, to see how fundamental philosophy was to Lee's approach to the martial arts' (157). For Bolelli, the larger project of 'questioning one's own beliefs' in the field of martial arts necessitates the rejection of the very idea of 'martial arts style with its codified set of unique forms and techniques' and the advocation of 'the elimination of styles in favor of a constant process of individual research aimed at finding the techniques and training methods that best fit one's needs' (157). Thus, whenever a 'practitioner of JKD finds something effective along the way, or decides that a certain technique does not work for him/her, he or she is free to change the art'. This is why he concludes that 'clearly, more than a new martial art in the traditional sense of the word, Jeet Kune Do appears to be a philosophical principle applied to the martial arts' (157). This 'philosophical principle' is 'antiauthoritarian', a type of 'nearly anarchist thinking', which 'points out that Lee may have more in common with philosophers like Feyerabend, Lao Tzu, and Krishnamurti than with entertainers like Jackie Chan, Sammo Hung, or Jean Claude Van Damme' (157).

Whether or not any of this is yet a 'philosophical principle', ideas (or themes) like questioning beliefs and championing 'individual research' do seem to resound with something of the ethos and injunctions of the European Enlightenment, just as the advocation of what might be called Lee's 'antidisciplinary interdisciplinarity' (the rejection of *one* approach in the name of selecting and recombining elements from *several*) is reminiscent of a Lyotardian interpretation of cultural and academic procedures in postmodernity (Lyotard 1984). Indeed, Bolelli takes great pains to paint Lee, 'the creating individual', as a Nietzschean proto-

Feyerabend. That is to say, in Bolelli's account, Lee employed an approach to martial arts that implicitly had affinities with Paul Feyerabend's closely contemporary approach to science – namely, a belief in epistemological anarchism. The title of Feyerabend's most in/famous book is *Against Method: Outline of an Anarchistic Theory of Method* (1975/1993), and Bolelli attempts to make direct connections between Lee's method and that advocated by Feyerabend. Of course, Bolelli's comparison is retroactive (Feyerabend's epistemological anarchism was publicised after Lee died). But the point for Bolelli is that both share an 'extremely open-minded approach willing to adopt any method showing promise for delivering the desired results'. It begins by 'acknowledging that any method possesses strengths as well as weaknesses' (174) and it 'utilizes a method's strengths' whilst trying to avoid 'being bound by [its] weaknesses' (175). Thus, says Bolelli:

> Following this line of thought, Lee argued that no fixed formula could capture the flow of existence. What worked yesterday may not work today. What the old masters discovered was one way to fight, not necessarily the only one, or even the best one. Different conditions call for different approaches. To Lee, an endless process of trial and error was therefore preferable to establishing one day's intuition as an immutable law. Instilling in his students the ability to adapt to any situation made much more sense to Lee than teaching them a fixed method of fighting. (173)

As such, 'to Bruce Lee, the apologists of particular martial arts styles, irrespective of which style they belong to, are all wrong' (167). The basis of their mistake is that 'by turning personal intuitions and sound principles into absolute laws equal for everyone, all styles are guilty of turning partial truths into the only Truth and thereby failing to see the complete range of possible truths' (167). Thus, it is chiefly his 'antiauthoritarian, nearly anarchist thinking' which is presented as key to Lee's 'philosophy'.

Postmodern Buddha Syndrome: The Interlocution of Bruce Lee

But, says Bolelli, although 'Lee's philosophy may have been his greatest contribution', it is nevertheless the case that 'Lee did not come up with any original ideas': 'The entire philosophy so passionately espoused by Lee derives from the writings of other people' (157). Indeed, Bolelli continues, 'Even if we limit ourselves only to the field of martial arts, Lee's approach is not entirely new' (158). Accordingly, rather than regarding Lee as being uniquely new or universally original, Bolelli proposes that we should regard him as a highly influential *interlocutor* or *cultural translator*. Thus, argues Bolelli, the suggestion 'that someone made great philosophical contributions even though he clearly did not commit to paper a single original philosophical idea is not as absurd as it may sound':

> For example, Alan Watts, who is considered by some as one of the most important philosophers of the twentieth century and who greatly inspired Lee, did not invent anything new either. His books (…) are based almost entirely on Taoist and Buddhist ideas. However, despite being clearly derivative, his writings beautifully convey the essence of Taoism and Buddhism in a completely new, original way. Although the topic and the conclusions found in Watts' books are not new, the freshness of his style, analogies, anecdotes and examples infuse new life to them. Furthermore, the way in which Watts adapted Taoist and Buddhist philosophies to a Western mentality is a splendid illustration of philosophical creativity. (158)

Comparing Lee to Alan Watts like this implies that – just like Watts – Lee translated 'Oriental ideas' into English. However, surely it is significant that many of Lee's 'Oriental ideas' were actually appropriated directly from the writings of Alan Watts himself. Thus, this comparison with Watts seems both lopsided and a little harsh on Watts. For, Lee did not simply translate from Eastern to Western terms, but rather 'translated' many of Watts' ideas into discourse about martial arts topics.

Moreover, what Bolelli literally proposes is that the ideas Watts largely introduced into Western popular consciousness through his best-selling interlocutions, interpretations and cultural translations were somehow 'already there', *before* his introduction of them. But if they were already there, then what did Watts do? For Bolelli, 'in a similar fashion', Bruce Lee 'took old ideas and applied them in new, original ways'. Specifically, he claims that Lee 'took Taoism and Buddhism and applied them to the competitive, ego-driven world of movie-making, to the martial arts and to his own daily life' (159). Quite *how* or in what way Bruce Lee could be said to have 'applied' such ideas as 'Taoism and Buddhism' to 'movie-making' and 'his own daily life' is not clear. Nor is it clear how these could be said to be 'old ideas'. But for Bolelli what is crucial is that in Bruce Lee's approach, epistemological anarchism meets radical individualism as 'ancient' Chinese Taoism meets 'modern' American pragmatism and Buddha meets Nietzsche: Bolelli directs our attention to Nietzsche's words in *Thus Spoke Zarathustra*, '"This is my way; where is yours?" – thus I answered those who asked me "the way". For the way – that does not exist' (qtd. in Bolelli 2003: 175). He proceeds to compare Lee's teachings to those of the Buddha: 'Buddha himself invited his followers to find out the truth for themselves without depending on anything or anyone, not even on his teachings' he begins; and continues, noting that 'in a similar spirit' Bruce Lee wrote 'jeet kune do is merely a term, a label to be used as a boat to get across: once across, it is to be discarded and not carried on one's back' (175-6). After making these grandiose comparisons, Bolelli moves directly to a rather grand-sounding conclusion: 'In this way, Lee resisted the temptation to turn his own intuition into dogma, downplayed his own self-importance as a teacher, and encouraged people to make up their own theories and become their own teachers'. For, asserts Bolelli, 'the essence of the epistemological anarchism that he espoused was in creating one's own method by taking bits and pieces from different sources, and recombining them into a new format' (176).

There is sufficient reason to question the validity of much of this. Furthermore, just as these movements, connections and formulations evince a rather problematic individualistic postmodernism, it is even more problematically 'supported' by such carefree declarations as 'just as Taoism argued that rules are necessary only for those who are too stupid to make the right choice on their own', so 'epistemological anarchism holds that absolute laws are an obstacle to genuine understanding' (175). Moreover, as well as constructing Bruce Lee's thought in terms of Feyerabend, Nietzsche, Krishnamurti, Buddha and Taoism, Bolelli goes on to represent this as an approach that is constituted in terms of an opposition. Specifically, Lee's jeet kune do is represented as being opposed not only to 'traditional' martial arts but also to Confucianism. Confucianism is for those who are 'too stupid' for Taoism. Tradition is for those who are too stupid for postmodernism, and so on.

Bolelli puts it like this. 'Lee derived his entire philosophy from Taoist and Buddhist sources'. But he also made a 'break' with Chinese tradition. By way of clarification, Bolelli argues that 'Since earlier I remarked that Lee derived his entire philosophy from Taoist and Buddhist sources, readers may get the mistaken impression that Lee's approach was consistent with Chinese traditions. [Yet] Nothing could be further from the truth' (159). Unfortunately, at this point Bolelli does not stop to ponder the implications of Lee's reliance upon such English Language interlocutors as Watts in his dissemination of 'Taoist', 'Zen' or 'Buddhist' ideas. Rather, he prefers to describe the *entirety* of Chinese culture and thought as if it proceeds solely according to two opposing camps: Taoism (which is represented as superior) and Confucianism (which is represented as inferior). He further subdivides Taoism and Buddhism into two factions: first, 'traditional', 'popular forms of Taoism and Buddhism' (which are again represented as inferior) and, second, what he calls 'Philosophical Taoism' (which is, again, reciprocally, superior). Thus, he proposes, despite aligning Lee with an 'ancient' Taoist wisdom that is thousands of enduring traditional years old, *Lee's* Taoism is actually an 'element that contributes to distance Lee's approach from Chinese tradition'. For:

> Chinese thought, in fact, has been heavily influenced by another philosophical current which is even more antithetical to Lee's worldview than popular forms of Taoism and Buddhism: Confucianism. Whereas the philosophical Taoism and the Buddhism embraced by Lee can be subtle and paradoxical, Confucianism offers the security of precise formulas and simple, straightforward rules. Philosophical Taoism requires great sensitivity to be grasped. Confucianism is very easy to follow. Philosophical Taoism mocks rigid laws. Confucianism reveres them. Confucian ideology dictates the rules of proper behavior, establishes the reciprocal, but unequal obligations between family members, regulates the relationship between citizens and state authorities, and oversees every possible aspect of public life. In other words, the very matrix of Chinese society was and still is saturated with Confucianism.
>
> In Lee's philosophy, not a trace of Confucianism can be found. Rather, as we will see more in detail later, Lee stood in firm opposition to the most dogmatic aspects of Chinese tradition cherished by Confucianism. By rejecting Confucianism and choosing to embrace the antiauthoritarian viewpoint of philosophical Taoism, Lee allied himself with the fringe-dwellers, the outcasts, the mavericks, the philosophical outlaws, the misfits of Chinese culture. In fact, although some of the principles of philosophical Taoism have been incorporated into Chinese culture, its radical nature makes it appealing to only a minority of people and sets it apart from the traditions on which most of Chinese society is based. (161)

Bolelli thus explicitly aligns a suitably deracinated 'ancient' Taoism and Zen (as understood by Lee through the works of writers such as Watts) with modern 1960s Californian antiauthoritarianism. Confucianism (and all actually-existing Eastern Taoist institutions), on the other hand, equals the status quo and therefore 'the bad': 'If we move from the way in which Lee presented Jeet Kune Do to the actual contents of the art, the chances of raising Confucian enthusiasms decrease even further', writes Bolelli. 'Lee's philosophy, in fact, amounts to a declaration of war against the conservative, dogmatic tendencies encouraged by Confucianism' (163-4):

> Rather than revering the way of the ancestors and accepting their conclusions as absolute truths, Lee encouraged individuals to question everything and find out for themselves. Whereas Confucianism valued obedience and conformity, Lee emphasized creativity and freedom. As Lee himself wrote, 'Art lives where absolute freedom is, because where it is not, there can be no creativity' (Lee 1975). Lee's commitment to individual freedom and empowerment placed him in opposition to any tradition requiring uncritical loyalty to authority. (164)

Now, whilst Bolelli makes prudent gestures to attempt to historicise ideas, the problem is that he reverts to a straightforward orientalism, first when it comes to regarding 'China' and all things 'Chinese' and second in the way he attributes to Lee an *essential* Taoism. These are both gestures that Rey Chow deems part of 'allochronism': a gesture which construes and represents China as *always* ancient, mystical and Confucian. Rather than following Bolelli in this, the most pertinent observation to follow would have to be the suggestion that *Lee's Taoism was not at all out of step with the times and the place of 1960s West Coast USA*. If anything, then, Lee was marching in time to the beat of a countercultural turn east; at the very least, he was capitalising on it. This is precisely why both Miller and Preston regard Lee's representation of himself as a kind of authentically mystical wise oriental monk could be so successful in the first place.

The Bruce Lee Industry: Enlightenment as Mass Marketing

Indeed, Preston is scathing about the very idea that Bruce Lee had a philosophy or any philosophical import whatsoever, suggesting instead that his impact has been primarily on Western martial arts practices and Western films. In fact, Preston goes on to argue that the 'philosophication' of Bruce Lee was simply the result of a marketing opportunity within the 'Bruce Lee industry'. At the same time, of course, as we have seen, Preston can still maintain that without Bruce Lee, 'East' would not 'have met West ... as soon or as spectacularly' (77). But however much the 'impact of Bruce Lee's movies has been profound', he asserts, 'it's all based on the visuals. The impact of his words? Nil' (78):

> I've seen, Bruce Lee's movies: they're not great, but his physical presence is unforgettable. I've read his collected writings: *snooooze*! They're mostly rehashes of Taoism and Buddhism 101, often lifted from youthful essays he wrote in his college days at the University of Washington in Seattle. (Preston 2007: 78)

Preston makes these polemical points in an attempt to redress what he thinks of as 'the worst excesses' of 'the Bruce Lee industry' (78). This industry, at least its publishing division, is arguably dominated by John Little, whose exclusive access to Bruce Lee's notebooks and other archives has enabled the steady but sustained release (and re-release) of Bruce Lee notes and quotes. These have been organised, ordered, reordered, packaged and repackaged under ever-changing titles and covers for many years now. And it is through this hagiographic process, Preston suggests, that interlocutors such as Little have 'changed' Bruce Lee 'into something he was not' (78). He offers two claims made by Little (1996) as examples of 'the worst excesses' of this hagiographic transformation. First, says Little: 'Certainly the case can be made for Bruce Lee having "awakened" to his own Buddha nature and, perforce, having become enlightened, or a Buddha'. Second, he claims:

> It could be argued convincingly that Bruce Lee was not only one of the greatest martial artists of all time, but also, given the scope, breadth, depth, and enduring impact of his words on such matters, one of history's greatest spiritual teachers or bodhisattvas. (qtd. in Preston 2007: 78)

We have seen this slide into hyperbole in the argument of Bolelli too, of course. It is not uncommon. But: 'Come on, John, get a grip', exhorts Preston in response to these hyperbolic claims: 'Perhaps if he'd lived to a ripe age, if he were still alive today, he would have buttressed his physical reputation with a deeper philosophy, and evolved into some kind of sage' (78-9). 'But he didn't', Preston reminds us. In fact:

> He died suddenly, at thirty-two, in the bed of a Hong Kong actress named Betty Ting Pei, while his wife and children waited for him across town. He died restless, unfulfilled, still consumed with worldly ambition, still driven by ego to become the biggest movie star on the planet, to taste sweet revenge against racist Hollywood for its initial rejection of him as a leading man. That's hardly the way a Bodhisattva bids goodbye to this earthly tumult. (78)

The implication here, then, is that Bruce Lee's particular penchant for making assertions or using tropes, terms and formulations that sound broadly Buddhist or Taoist may not actually have been coherent or connected with any sort of practice. Indeed, George Tan argues that:

> Bruce liked to use the word 'Tao'; he used it over and over... And the commonly held view is that Bruce was sort of Taoist. The truth, in a lot of ways, is he was more Confucian. Taoists surf the waves; the basic idea of Taoism is to accept the world as it is. Taoists don't blow their horns in traffic. Confucians manipulate the world – they think it's here to serve them, not much different from the way Christians believe they reign over everything else. Bruce is a guy who believed he had somewhere to go and he had to get there quick. He wasn't about to let anybody get in his way. Bruce was a Confucian in Taoist clothing. (qtd. in Miller 115-6)

Indeed, moving even more precisely into the specificities of the cultural context and milieu within which Bruce Lee moved, Miller suggests that 'Bruce's philosophizing came when he needed to develop an image, a device to market his martial art. He realized that there was more to be made from philosophizing than from getting punched in the face' (114). This breezy observation is perhaps highly significant, particularly when it comes to considering how and why anything like Bruce Lee's 'philosophy' caught on. For, during the late 60s and early 70s, Lee taught many 'notables in the film community', including James Coburn, Blake Edwards, Stirling Siliphant, Joe Hyams, Steve McQueen, Lee Marvin, Elke Sommer, Sharon Tate, Roman Polanski and Warner Brothers president, Ted Ashley (113). Thus, Miller suggests, it was almost inevitable that Bruce Lee was going to become regarded as 'the ideal of the martial monk, the wise man of gung fu' (113).

Yet, Miller observes, Lee's 'philosophy' was just as much a bricolage as his martial art: just as 'Lee had incorporated elements from gung fu, boxing, judo, karate, et cetera, into his fighting methods, he looked to the writings of popular 1960s sages to develop "his" philosophy' (114). Bruce Lee was 'taken with Zen rebel Alan Watts and anti-mystic J. Krishnamurti' just as much as he 'also created his wisdom from Chinese clichés (the "pointing finger" analogy is an example)'. Moreover, he adapted 'at least one of Mao Tse-tung's credos'; namely: 'Absorb what is useful; reject what is useless'. Miller points out that Lee merely 'expanded this to include, "Add specifically what is your own"' (114). But, overall, Miller points out, 'Aphorisms attributed to Lee, which are now echolaliacally quoted by his widow, students and numerous followers, were lifted directly from Krishnamurti's work' (114). At the same time as pointing this out, however, Miller tries to reassure us that his observations are neither meant to be cynical nor negative:

> To say that a person was not a great thinker, that he claimed others' thoughts as his own partly as a marketing ploy, is of course neither uncommon nor a crime. Nor do I mean to suggest that Lee didn't take these 'non-ideas' seriously. After all, he'd been interested in philosophy as an adolescent, had majored in it at university, and later collected such books about it by the hundreds, as well as any and all new and old volumes he could find about martial arts, boxing, wrestling and film-making. Lee's martial library consisted of thousands of books, many of which were long out of print and rare, which he annotated and cross-annotated with personal training notes. (114)

Like Preston's, the point of Miller's critique is to attempt to burst the bubble of mythologizing and hagiography that has supposedly obscured Bruce Lee's 'real' import. Of course, as we have seen, it is arguably a mistake to look for this 'real' if we want 'real' to mean something distinct from fantasy and mythology. Indeed, it seems important to point out that one of the further implications of Miller's critique is that the ridiculous claims made *about* Bruce Lee are in a sense smoothly continuous with the persona Lee himself sought to construct for himself. As such, fans and enthralled disciples alike are, like Little or Bolelli, merely taking Bruce Lee's own efforts to their logical connotative limits: *Bruce Lee was invincible. Bruce Lee was superlative. Bruce Lee was enlightened. Bruce Lee was a Buddha. Etc.*

In contrast, Miller too tries to ground his assessment of Bruce Lee's 'philosophy' historically. As such, he acknowledges that it was a very avant-garde, even trailblazing intervention – 'ahead of his time', as the expression goes. But this expression deserves to be unpacked. For, the claim that something was 'ahead of its time' can be taken, for instance, to support Derrida's (1994) argument that our experience of time itself is *always* 'out of joint'. For, if trailblazing *is* really trailblazing, then this trail will always have been blazed too soon to be recognized as what it will – retrospectively – come to be regarded as (or 'come to have been', to use a Derridean phrase). The 'final meaning' of something is 'always in the post', Derrida points out: never having fully arrived yet, here and now, decisively or definitively. For, 'time' is not simply lived in the present: dreams of past and future orientate activities; the past is written on the basis of selections made after, often long after, the event; events are understood retrospectively, always provisionally, always subject to revision and reinterpretation. Indeed, both the present and the future are often fantasised on the basis of a fantasy mythology of the past (as many, including Bruce Lee's own, fabrications and fabulations about the mythic origins of martial arts testify). Thus, those who may be (or may come to be, or – to use one of Derrida's preferred tenses – *may come to have been*) retrospectively regarded as having been 'ahead of their time' arguably have an *undecidable* status: for did they sow the seeds of what followed? Or, in being recognised 'belatedly', have they simply had contemporary values projected retroactively upon them? As Miller observes:

> In the years since Lee's death the notion that we can be whatever we want, that we can liberate ourselves, has become the stuff of corporate advertising, of the self-help genre of non-writing, of government-sanctioned propaganda, of half-hour infomercials. In the early 1970s the concept of self-actualization seemed shining and new. (116)

If what Bruce Lee preached once seemed radical and emancipatory but now seems saccharine and ideological, can he in some sense be called to account for what 'the concept of self-actualization' has since become? Indeed, did he *actively* contribute to this discourse in the first place? Or was he himself already some kind of *expression* of an emergent discourse? Such judgements seem harsh. But there is in a sense a temporal undecidability to Bruce Lee. For, agency is determined by conditions that are not of our choosing: an ethos, a topos – a contextual ground or orientation. Yet, as thinkers like Derrida and Žižek have pointed out, one cannot simply understand a historical context without thinking that context in terms of the interventions made by agents and agencies themselves. For, interventions may transform contexts.

This is the time-honoured conundrum of subject and structure or free-will versus determinism. The Foucauldian contribution to the thinking of agency and intervention is clarifying in this regard. As Foucault puts it:

> Power... is never localized here or there, never in anybody's hands, never
> appropriated as a commodity or piece of wealth. Power is employed and
> exercised through a net-like organization. In fact, it is already one of the
> prime effects of power that certain bodies, certain gestures, certain dis-
> courses, certain desires come to be identified and constituted as individu-
> als. ... The individual is an effect of power, and at the same time, or pre-
> cisely to the extent to which it is that effect, it is the element of its articula-
> tion. The individual which power has constructed is at the same time its
> vehicle. (Foucault 1988: 98)

All of this adds an extra twist to Miller's observations about Bruce Lee's
self-help philosophy/ideology. But is this 'extra twist' an extra tasty dash
of flavour? Or is it a twist of the judgemental knife? In other words, is
Bruce Lee's 'philosophy' to be regarded as *revolutionarily emancipatory*,
or is it to be regarded as an exemplary case of what has become the
hegemonic ideology of individualism – self-aggrandizing deluded 'inter-
passive' identity tourism? Is it indeed a heady 'new' cocktail of the ancient and the modern (perhaps therefore exemplarily 'postmodern')? Or is
it perhaps something altogether *other*?

On the one hand, Lee's anti-institutional rhetoric acknowledges the
interpellative power of institutionality. But on the other, in his thought,
'institution' *qua* 'the status quo' is simply represented as the negative to
be opposed to the potential positive of 'the individual', who might man-
age to free themselves of the shackles of their institutionalisation and return to a state of nature. Jeet kune do is, then, a kind of theory of false
consciousness. Ultimately, says Miller:

> Like all of us, the 'limitless, formless' Bruce Lee was an ambiguous char-
> acter driven by his biology, his culturization, and his time: the 1960s and
> 1970s, that phase when self-invention – the notion that you can cut your-
> self loose from psychic and physical moorings and float free, beyond the
> pull of gravity – seemed most possible. (Miller 2000: 107-8)

Hence Lee's many poetic formulations, such as: 'How can there be methods and systems to arrive at something that is living?'; or 'To that which
is static, fixed, dead, there can be a way, a definite path, but not to that
which is living'; or 'Do not reduce reality to a static thing and then invent
methods to reach it'; or 'True observation begins when one sheds set patterns, and true freedom of expression occurs when one is beyond systems'; or 'Knowledge is fixed in time, whereas, knowing is continual.
Knowledge comes from a source, from accumulation, from a conclusion,

while knowing is a movement'; or 'Jeet Kune Do favors formlessness so that it can assume all forms and since Jeet Kune Do has no style, it can fit with all styles. As a result, Jeet Kune Do utilizes all ways and is bound by none and, likewise, uses any techniques or means which serve its ends', etc. (Bruce Lee as qtd. in Bolelli 2003: 173-4).

This very rhetoric itself is telling. As Lee's friend and senior student Dan Inosanto put it: 'He says JKD has no technique. My wife says everybody in the sixties talked that way' (qtd. in Miller 107). But the point, says Bolelli, is that:

> rather than being an organized system, Lee's Jeet Kune Do was meant to be a laboratory where fighting theories and techniques could be put to the test. Students could experiment with them without being bound to follow any unless they wished to. The words written around the very symbol of JKD stand as the catchy slogan for Lee's methodology, 'Using no way as the way; having no limitation as limitation'. (Bolelli 2003: 174)

Advocating that the individual regard themselves a kind of Kantian self-legislating scientist in a laboratory of experimentation, seeking a return to the supposedly godlike or pre-lapsarian state of a true, unfettered and essential spontaneous nature, was one of the key contradictory interpellations organised by Bruce Lee. That is to say, if on the one hand Lee advocated a kind of *rationalised interdisciplinary approach*, on the other hand Lee's rhetoric and imagery simultaneously proposed that the *superlative state of nature* was already to be found in an allochronistic return to Taoism. This double movement exemplifies precisely the logic of what Rey Chow calls 'primitive passions' – or, an 'interest in the primitive [that] emerges at a moment of *cultural crisis*' (1995: 22):

> As the predominant sign of traditional culture can no longer monopolize signification – that is, as democratization is forced upon it – fantasies of an origin arise. These fantasies are played out through a *generic* realm of associations, typically having to do with the animal, the savage, the countryside, the indigenous, the people, and so forth, which *stand in* for that 'original' something that has been lost.... This origin is now 'democratically' (re)constructed as a common place and a commonplace, a point of common knowledge and reference that was there prior to our present existence. The primitive, as the figure for this irretrievable *common/place*, is thus always an invention after the fact – a fabrication of a *pre* that occurs in the time of the *post*.... This *exoticizing* of what is at the same time thought to be generic and commonplace characterizes the writing of history *within a culture* as much as the writing between cultures such as the practices of orientalism...
>
> In a culture caught between the forces of 'first world' imperialism and 'third world' nationalism, such as that of twentieth century China, the

> primitive is the precise *paradox,* the amalgamation of the two modes of signification known as 'culture' and 'nature'. If Chinese culture is 'primitive' in the pejorative sense of being 'backward' (being stuck in an earlier stage of 'culture' and thus closer to 'nature') when compared to the West, it is also 'primitive' in the meliorative sense of being an ancient culture (it was there first, before many Western nations). A strong sense of primordial, rural rootedness thus goes hand in hand with an equally compelling conviction of China's primariness, of China's potential primacy as a modern nation with a glorious civilization. This paradox of a *primitivism that sees China as simultaneously victim and empire* is what leads modern Chinese intellectuals to their so-called obsession with China. (Chow 1995: 22-3)

This paradox can be seen encapsulated in Bruce Lee's rhetoric and imagery, all of which is condensed in the famous jeet kune do badge – constructed from the yin-yang/t'ai chi symbol encircled by two arrows moving in opposite directions, supplemented by the legend 'Using no way as the way; having no limitation as limitation'. Thus, Lee's hailing was double: a call to a (post)modern deconstructive antidisciplinary interdisciplinarity in the name of a New Age 'Taoist' imaginary (or rhetoric).

As such, Lee's 'marketing' of himself is hardly *just* marketing. Rather, as Stephen Chan has argued of Japanese identity *vis-à-vis* the West, it is arguably the case that, in terms of a Chinese identity *vis-à-vis* the West:

> in order to have a view of self before the West, i.e. to have a self that would directly confront and seek to manipulate the Otherness imposed by the West upon them, the Japanese had to construct a stereotype of themselves *for* themselves. In this way, they became, 'samurai'. In [Hiroshi] Yoshioka's terms, they had to colonize themselves, to prevent too easy a colonization by others. (Chan 2000: 69)

For Chan, such a perspective 'of course, is very neat'. But to him it 'proposes a nuanced breathing space between Said's (or indeed Bhabha's) views of Orientalism on the one hand, and the somewhat cheeky counterpointing of this by a group of scholars who talk of the East's "Occidentalism"' (69-70). This allows Chan to suggest that Asians 'simultaneously orientalize *and* occidentalize ourselves, particularly those who, by accident of birth and by the deliberateness of constant travel, traverse and inhabit and (frankly) *play with* borderlines' (70). This can be regarded precisely as Lee's 'survival strategy' – a peculiar kind of 'resistance', akin to what Freud called 'egological resistance': a survival strategy which 'integrates the symptom into the ego and seeks a benefit in the illness' (Derrida 1998: 21). In his discussion of Freud's notions of resistance, Derrida adds (in parenthesis): 'Let me say in an aside that I wonder who does not do that' – i.e., who does not seek such a self-benefit in the face of a problem – and 'what ego does not institute itself and does not last by means of this form of resistance, and on what confused concept of illness one is relying when one describes this ruse as an interesting singularity' (21-2)? Rey Chow goes further, providing the following account of such a situation:

> For those groups on the side of non-white cultures, the problem presented by multiculturalism remains one of tactical negotiation. Negotiating a point of entry into the multicultural scene means nothing less than posing the question of rights – the right to representation and the right to culture. What this implies is much more than the mere fight (by a particular non-white culture) for its 'freedom of speech', because the very process of attaining 'speech' here is inextricably bound up with right, that is, with the processes through which particular kinds of 'speeches' are legitimized in the first place. To put it in very simple terms, a non-white culture, in order to 'be' or to 'speak', must (1) seek legitimacy/recognition from white culture, which has denied the reality of the 'other' cultures all along; (2) use the language of white culture (since it is the dominant one) to produce itself (so that it could be recognized and thus legitimized); and yet (3) resist complete normativization by white culture. (Chow 1998: 12)

This complicated situation, born of the complexities of looking at and being looked at, of regarding whilst being regarded, judging whilst being judged, being placed and placing, decided and deciding, etc. (in a dissymmetrical power situation) calls out to be considered in terms of *interpellation*. On this subject, Chow notes:

> For readers acquainted with Louis Althusser's argument in the classic essay 'Ideology and Ideological State Apparatuses', an ethnic person's practice of internalizing a cultural stereotype of herself may conveniently be explained by way of what Althusser calls interpellation. Whereas Althusser's frames of reference are religion and the state – so that the hailing of 'Hey, you!' is either from the church, the police, or the various apparatuses of civil society – in the realm of ethnic politics, the 'Hey, you!' is, we may argue, issued in the form of what Jameson calls 'community interdependence' – that is, the ensconcing of the individual within the confines of her ethnic ghetto. Moreover, the ethnic is being hailed not only from within the ghetto but also predominantly from the outside, by the cultural critics (the zoo gazers) who are altruistically intent on conferring on her and her culture a radical meaning, one that is different from the norm of their own society. (Chow 2002: 108)

This complex cultural logic of interpellation demands serious attention.

The Interpellation of Bruce Lee

It may be true that the Bruce Lee Hagiography Industry does indeed scrape the bottom of the barrel in tying to find 'Bruce Lee wisdom' that might be (re)packaged and published – ransacking college notes and personal jottings. But despite Brian Preston's claims it is nevertheless the case that Bruce Lee's published writings could be said to have had an oftentimes profound and both locally and perhaps generally significant 'emancipatory' impact, at the same time as and supplementary to his visuality. Indeed, the two realms are not distinct or discrete. Once again, Davis Miller's account of his own first encounter with Bruce Lee is illuminating, and in fact warrants some consideration here. For, just as he recalls the exhilarating experience of first seeing Bruce Lee, Miller's recollection of his first reading of Bruce Lee's written words presents them as being as revolutionary a moment as seeing Bruce Lee for the first time in *Enter the Dragon*.

Soon after first seeing Bruce Lee on screen, Miller finds a copy of Lee's influential article, 'Liberate Yourself from Classical Karate' in the September 1971 issue of *Black Belt Magazine*. Miller recalls that he 'found in it' both 'China' and 'a wisdom alive and new' (2000: 43). In experiencing the article, though, it was, again, the visuals that first arrested Miller: 'I studied the pictures a long, awed time before I read the words' (44). In the pictures, Lee sparred with 'a robot-looking-type, into whose head and body were being chunked punches and kicks rocketed from impossible-seeming angles. Impossible in that I'd seen no one else who could've conceived of them, much less done them' (43). And this *appealed* to Miller. Indeed, throughout this account, Miller emphasizes the interpellative call that he became ensnared by: 'Leave all preconceptions behind', Lee 'said' to Miller: '"Leave your protective shell of isolation", he told me, "and relate directly to what is being said"' (44). Using the pejorative nickname he had been given whilst at school, Miller continues: 'Foetus, he was calling, come out, come out, wherever you are' (44).

These words describe in some detail Miller's interpellation. This interpellation is a complex event. It is a transformation which is premised on a response to the visual image that caught Miller's phantasy, arrested his desire, and 'coloured' his reading. But the interpellation happens *through* his reading – at the same time as his reading – *at the same time as it effectively determines what he has read 'in' the article.* So we should follow the movement of this account closely:

> 'I am concerned with the blossoming of a martial artist,' Lee wrote, 'not a Chinese martial artist or a Japanese martial artist. A martial artist is a human being first. As nationalities have nothing to do with one's (basic) humanity, so they have nothing to do with martial art...
> 'Fighting, as is, is simple and total', Lee continued. 'It is not limited to your perspective or conditioning as a Chinese or Korean martial artist. True observation begins when one sheds set patterns, and true freedom of expression occurs when one is beyond systems. Regardless of their many colourful origins (by a wise, mysterious monk, by a special messenger in a dream, or in a holy revelation), styles are created by men. A style should not be considered gospel truth. . . Man, the living, creating individual, is always more important than any style'. (44)

Miller reads these words, which are apparently 'literally' only about fighting (although more is being claimed about a notion of a 'basic' universal humanity than about fighting), and finds in them the possibility of a radical imaginary leap, a transformative identification:

> In that moment, for the first time ever, I wasn't nothing. It no longer bothered me not to be just like other kids. For the first time I felt like something and that something (someone!) had been named. There was nothing wrong with being different. Being different could mean being an individual. I was an individual! Or, at least I could become one. When I began living. (44-5)

The words 'Man, the living, creating individual, is always more important than any style' are taken by Miller to be a plausible (utopian) statement of the virtues of 'difference' and 'individuality'. This 'positive' is achieved by opposition to a negative: 'styles' – institutions:

> 'At best, styles are parts dissected from a whole. Divisive by nature, styles keep men apart rather than unite [*sic*] them.'
> Lee was referring specifically to systems of martial art: tae kwon do, karate, kung fu, judo, kendo, but I took the term (and Lee's article) allegorically, to apply to any conditioning, any training, any capsulization, any categorization, any habit. 'Style' could mean religiosity, ethnicity, any prejudice. It might mean 'lifestyle' or any other way of thinking or being. It could mean idealizing a person, notion or situation; it could mean regarding one region of the world, or people who live there, as being better than another. It might mean making a big fucking deal out of Christmas or a stupid fucking football team or using 'good' goddamn table manners or most any ole construct. It might even mean feeling that to make it through

> the day you need a clean, mean ride with a full tank of gas and have to wear snazzy trousers and hard-starched shirts. (45)

Miller 'gets' *this* message: the anti-institutional countercultural message. Free your mind and break away from tradition. Break on through to the other side. There is no spoon. And so on. As in *The Matrix*, like in countercultural ideology tout court, those who are not awakened and liberated are perceived de facto as 'against' the free spirits:

> Then. It began seeming like one tiny dumb joke, finally; all of it. Everything I'd perpetrated on myself for half my life. Wallowing in the romance of sorrow, in the joy of melancholy. Blaming my lot on my mother's death, on God, on people, on the world. I'd closed myself off to almost everyone and everything around me and to myself, although I stayed so deeply inside of me. Inside of me in pretty unfortunate ways.
>
> I'll not do it any longer, I declared right at that moment. I choose not to frame myself, not to encapsulate myself, not to 'live' in a shell any longer. Nor will I adopt a 'lifestyle', choose somebody else's way, to replace my shell. I'll not join anybody's colony; not select a side; choose neither to believe nor to disbelieve; not step along; not be a passenger.
>
> I choose, instead, to live a life. Foetus will punch and kick his way out of his shell. (45-6)

Phantasy solution. Perfect. And all decided *before* Lee's 'philosophy' has even apparently been fully articulated. Miller recounts its decisive coordinates, in a passage that is so important it deserves to be quoted at length:

> 'Look around the martial arts', Lee continued, 'and witness the assortment of routine performers, trick artists, desensitized robots, glorifiers of the past. Life is constant movement – rhythmic as well as random. Life is continual change, not stagnation. Instead of choicelessly flowing with this process of change, many "masters", past and present, rigidly subscribe to traditional concepts and techniques of the art, solidifying the everflowing, dissecting the totality'.
>
> I finally saw my own Japanese/Negroese isolationist rituals for what they were, then. At best, I'd chosen to 'live' parts of the LIFE available to me, to limit my experiences, to solidify the everflowing, to choose the security of my cage, to settle for a niche, over the vast, vast world open to us.
>
> 'Lacking boundaries', Lee wrote, 'combat is always fresh, alive, constantly changing. Consider the subtle difference between having no form and having no-form. The first is ignorance; the second, transcendence. Through instinctive body feeling' – Foetus, get back to what you once were, he was saying, what you are – 'each of us knows our own most efficient and dynamic manner of achieving leverage, balance in motion, economic use of energy. Patterns, techniques and forms touch only the fringe of understanding'.

> These were ideas (non-ideas?) I'd not previously heard. 'These para-
> graphs are, at best, a finger pointing to the moon', Lee concluded. 'Do not
> take the finger to be the moon or fix your gaze so intently on the finger as
> to miss the beautiful sights of heaven'.
>   He'd used similar lines in *Enter*. I'd not understood them when I saw
> the, movie. Reading 'Liberate Yourself from Classical Karate', I felt that I
> did. I admired his presumptive non-presumptiveness, his pretentious non-
> pretentiousness. But what struck me most was the implied belief that peo-
> ple should have a grace, a fluidity, of personality and of thought and of
> movement. To have less is to be not quite human, not quite alive.
>   Lee intimated that these properties are innate – and that we've forgot-
> ten them. Most importantly, his body stated in movement, these attributes
> can be recovered and honed. 'Yes', I said aloud. A rounder, cosmic Yes!!
> roared up from my gut. (46-7)

This is a beautiful account – an anatomy, even – of a non-canonical but
exemplary instance of interpellation. The basic structure of interpellation
takes the form of 'Hey, you there!' 'Yes?'; the point being that when the
police officer or teacher hails us we recognize ourselves as subject to
their authority. However, in Miller's account of interpellation by Lee, it is
also, of course, an exemplary polemical anti-institutional manifesto.

The Lesson of Bruce Lee

These two realms – the realms signalled by *interpellation* and by *institution* – are closely connected. As Sam Weber argues in *Institution and Interpretation* (1987), 'the function of establishing identities, of imposing
determinations and of enforcing lines of demarcation, can be conceived
only as an effect of what we call "institution" and of "institutionaliza-
tion"' (Weber 1987: xiv). But the ramifications of this run deeper than the
supposed institutional *surfaces* of society. Rather, as John Mowitt puts it,
in our modern disciplinary societies even *the subject* is not prior to discipline but rather 'arises' in and through discipline. Disciplines – all disciplines – are primarily engaged in what Mowitt calls 'the social production
of subjectivity' (1992: 37). We see this in a pure and hyperbolical sense
in *Enter the Dragon* and other discourses that fetishize discipline, of
course. But this interpellatory contact permeates perhaps all of the displaced, deferred, reticulations and articulations of institutional social
space. We might relate this to the questions of this interpellation's historical, ethico-political, philosophical/ideological status by considering an
argument advanced by Slavoj Žižek:

> when, three decades ago, Kung Fu films were popular (Bruce Lee, etc.), was it not obvious that we were dealing with a genuine working class ideology of youngsters whose only means of success was the disciplinary training of their only possession, their bodies? Spontaneity and the 'let it go' attitude of indulging in excessive freedoms belong to those who have the means to afford it – those who have nothing have only their discipline. The 'bad' bodily discipline, if there is one, is not collective training, but, rather, jogging and body-building as part of the New Age myth of the realization of the Self's inner potentials – no wonder that the obsession with one's body is an almost obligatory part of the passage of ex-Leftist radicals into the 'maturity' of pragmatic politics: from Jane Fonda to Joschka Fischer, the 'period of latency' between the two phases was marked by the focus on one's own body. (Žižek 2004: 78-9)

Žižek's argument comes at the very end of his Afterword ('The Lesson of Rancière') to *The Politics of Aesthetics* by Jacques Rancière. Thus, in a discussion of the body that is ostensibly related to the politics of aesthetics, Žižek identifies a temporal 'passage' from 1960s and 1970s working-class youth and Leftist radicals to contemporary middle-class and middle-age middle-of-the-road vanity and banality. Readers of Žižek will know that this kind of exercise is one of Žižek's favourite activities. In fact, identifying what Hardt and Negri (2001) once called 'symptoms of passage' is evidently Žižek's *drive*. For he regularly repeats this *ad hominem* identification of a temporal transition (from a radical 'once upon a time' to bland and vacuous neoliberal 'now'), and he regularly characterises it as a shift from 'authentic' Leftism to 'postmodernist' identity politics.

For instance, in one exemplary discussion of his favourite *bête noir*, 'cultural studies', Žižek characterises (what he regards as) its *political* decline in terms of the exact same *temporal* passage that we have just seen: once upon a time it was leftist, working class, effective, radical and real. But *now…* etc. However, with cultural studies, Žižek also adds a *spatial* movement too. Namely, Žižek proposes that the decline of cultural studies can be seen most clearly in what he calls 'the shift from English to American Cultural Studies' (2002: 226). Now, despite the decline being linked to a 'shift' to America, it is not simply an anti-American argument; rather, it should be noted that Žižek again presents this decline as taking place in the same 'three decades': late 1960s to late 1980s. So, even through this takes the form of a characteristically dismissive deployment of the word 'America', Žižek is seeking to evoke an *ideological* shift that he perceives as having flourished after the heyday of '60s and

'70s Leftist radicalism. This is a wider transformation that he believes can be inferred from the evidence of the proliferation of cultural studies in the UK and USA through the 1980s and 1990s. Thus, he claims:

> Crucial here is the shift from English to American Cultural Studies: even if we find in both the same themes, notions, and so on, the socio-ideological functioning is completely different: we shift from an engagement with real working-class culture to academic radical chic. (2002: 226)

There is a lot to be explored in such a dense and provocative chiasmus of arguments and assertions (some of which I have discussed elsewhere: Bowman 2006; 2007; 2008). But here, what is to be identified is the way that Žižek uses the same basic tropology in both cases: the trope of temporal decline, or (postmodern) nostalgia. Žižek uses the same trope and the same basic argument in these two (not to mention many other) cases because, to his mind, they are intimately connected. Indeed, the argument about the changing 'political' status of the body, and the argument about the changing political status of cultural studies (which, we might note, is arguably the academic field that came to be most interested in questions about the political status of bodies) are for Žižek basically wedded – indeed welded – together. As we have seen, in both cases, in the 1960s and 1970s, Žižek sees attention to 'genuine working class' issues and 'real working-class culture'; whereas by the 1980s and 1990s, Žižek sees a withdrawal from the genuine and real in the shift to 'academic radical chic'. In fact, this is not just any old argument for Žižek. It is the basis of Žižek's supposedly 'dialectical materialist' argument about the *entirety* of recent history (2001a: 216).

The key date in this argument and in this history is 1968, specifically the social, cultural and intellectual fall-out or discursive reconfigurations in the wake of the widespread political protests and upheavals of that time. The key consequence of 1968 for Žižek is that, 'in Hegel's terms, the "truth" of the student's transgressive revolt against the Establishment [in 1968] is the emergence of a new establishment in which transgression is part of the game, solicited by the gadgets which organize our life as the permanent dealing with excesses' (2001: 24). This *excess*, this *excessiveness* which Žižek focuses on in contemporary capitalism, is what leads to 'the New Age myth of the realization of the Self's inner potentials'. And this, you might recall, is exactly where we began.

Ultimately, in terms of Žižek's theorization of the post-1968 cultural and political world, perhaps the figure of Bruce Lee should not be consigned to the short (parenthetical) position of Žižek's non-list (for, the words 'Bruce Lee, etc.' are *not quite* a list). Indeed, Bruce Lee ought to be regarded as of exemplary importance here because, as Žižek argues:

> The ultimate postmodern irony is thus the strange exchange between Europe and Asia: at the very moment when, at the level of the 'economic infrastructure,' 'European' technology and capitalism are triumphing world-wide, at the level of 'ideological superstructure,' the Judeo-Christian legacy is threatened in the European space itself by the on-slaught of the New Age 'Asiatic' thought, which, in its different guises, from the 'Western Buddhism' (today's counterpart to Western Marxism, as opposed to the 'Asiatic' Marxism-Leninism) to different 'Taos,' is establishing itself as the hegemonic ideology of global capitalism. Therein resides the highest speculative identity of the opposites of today's global civilization: although 'Western Buddhism' presents itself as the remedy against the stressful tension of the capitalist dynamics, allowing us to un-couple and retain inner peace and *Gelassenheit*, it actually functions as its perfect ideological supplement. One should mention here the well-known topic of 'future shock', i.e., of how, today, people are no longer psycho-logically able to cope with the dazzling rhythm of technological develop-ment and the social changes that accompany it – things simply move too fast. Before one can accustom oneself to an invention, it is already sup-planted by a new one, so that more and more one lacks the most elemen-tary 'cognitive mapping'. (Žižek 2001: 12)

Thus, in Žižek's terms, the initial Western interest in Bruce Lee during the kung fu craze in the early 1970s was a 'genuine working class ideology'. By the 1990s, this interest had morphed into its monstrous double, becoming a 'perfect ideological supplement', an exemplary part of 'the hegemonic ideology of global capitalism'. In other words, in Žižek's schema, Bruce Lee iconography *once* worked aesthetico-politically as a (Rancièrean) subjectivating fantasy for the working classes, for 'young-sters whose only means of success was the disciplinary training of their only possession, their bodies'. But *now*, at least to the extent that interest in martial arts has become bound up with the wider ideological tendency to focus on 'the realization of the Self's inner potentials', Bruce Lee and martial arts become disarticulated from 'class' and *therefore* (in Žižek's model) from 'resistance' (2004: 79).

Of course, quite *how* an authentic interest in physical violence (working class or otherwise) amounts to 'aesthetico-political protest' or 'resistance' (2004: 79) is left unsaid by Žižek. Indeed, this is a problem-atic assertion, given that most studies of working-class or indeed underclass pugilism and prize-fighting among 'those who have nothing [but] their discipline' (such as illegal immigrants in the southern USA, for instance) suggest that the ideals and aspirations of those involved are straightforwardly financial, rather than aesthetico-political (Wacquant 1995; Heiskanen 2006). Žižek does not address any of this, or anything like it, at all. Rather, his aim is simply to evoke the way in which the *image*, the *aesthetic*, opens a door in perception which can transform not only a viewer's relation to reality but also lived reality itself.

Unfortunately, what Žižek gives with one hand he takes away with the other. The image *was good*, he suggests, the image *was generative*. But then it *became* warped or perverted – ideologically 'appropriated', 'colonized' or 'hegemonized'. In fact, Žižek's position appears to boil down to something strongly akin to a witty observation once made by the comedian Frank Skinner: the difference between working class men and middle class 'new men' is that although both may be equally interested in fighting, 'new men' go to kickboxing or jujitsu classes three times a week, while working class men *really fight* – in pubs and on the street (Skinner 2002). In other words, for Žižek, if the emergence of the image was a pole of *subjectivating identification*, the future of the image is ideological phantasy.

Taken on the strength of his reading of Bruce Lee alone, then, Žižek's reading of Rancière's *Politics of Aesthetics* – but more importantly, perhaps, his reading of Bruce Lee – appears rather awkward and limited. Nevertheless, his proposition that *something about* Bruce Lee's image has (or had) 'aesthetico-political' potential remains tantalising. This is especially so given the double or *chiasmatic* status that such a figure as Bruce Lee must ineluctably have within Žižek's idiosyncratic ideological cosmology. For if the hegemonic ideology of contemporary capitalism can be seen in 'the strange exchange between Europe and Asia', then we must surely accord a central status to the exchanges facilitated by precisely such figures as the star of 'the first American produced martial arts spectacular', *Enter the Dragon* (1973).

Whether or not one attaches significance to the mythical date of 1968, the fact that Bruce Lee was struggling during the late 1960s to break into the movies and finally managed to become the first Asian male lead in a Hollywood produced film in 1973 should not go unremarked. This fact has been widely noted, and Lee's achievement is often regarded as a major breakthrough in the erosion or deconstruction of monolithic white masculinity in mainstream Western popular culture. To many, Bruce Lee's achievement, cultural place and 'functions' can quite easily be positively assessed in terms of both multiculturalism (the deconstruction of white cultural hegemony) and postcolonial Hong Kong and ethnic Chinese diasporic consciousness and identity. But it also, as Meaghan Morris reminds us, therefore refers us to the wider cultural discourses of 'PC' or 'Political Correctness' (Morris 2001).

Political Correctness (PC) has unappealing and anti-intellectual connotations: the denunciation of PC has for a long time been bound up with right wing battle cries. However, using a reading (of a representation) of Bruce Lee, Meaghan Morris has attempted to reconceive and reconfigure the notion, away from is caricatural and stereotypical form. In doing so, Morris provides an excellent microscopic anatomy of what we might call a Rancièrean moment of political 'subjectivization' (Rancière 1992) that takes place in a film about Bruce Lee. Morris analyses a scene in *Dragon: The Bruce Lee Story* (1993), a film that has the specific virtue of being what Morris calls 'a sanitized as well as hagiographic interpretation of Bruce Lee's life as authorized by his widow' (2001: 180). The film is a simple, formulaic, and generic Hollywood melodrama, and not by any stretch of the imagination conceivable as 'complex', 'challenging' or indeed as 'art'. Nevertheless – or indeed, *because of this* – Morris highlights the way that it offers at least one extremely important lesson about the complexity of film spectatorship, one that links directly, albeit diversely, to philosophical, theoretical and practical issues of politicisation.

Quite unlike Žižek, who elides yet silently relies upon the issue of 'violence', Morris tackles the issue of violence directly. She does so in order to get past it in order to look at Bruce Lee *otherwise* – specifically, in terms of the peculiar importance of *pedagogy* in understanding his significance. Thus, she points out the enduring significance not only of pedagogy in martial arts films, but also the often overlooked importance of remembering that Bruce Lee is perhaps primarily conceived and valued as a kind of teacher. But 'why "fetishize" a *teacher* as the ideal action hero?', she asks. Her answer is that:

> The overwhelming concern with 'the body' in recent cultural criticism can obscure this [pedagogical] aspect of (Western) Bruce Lee worship and

narrow unduly our approach to action cinema in general. Consider the per-
sistence of the training film in Hollywood cinema from John G. Avildsen's *Rocky* (1976) to Ridley Scott's *G.I. Jane* (1997). Hollywood heroes
tend to be self-impelling, their teachers 'family' figures; true friends or an-
tagonists who turn out to be helpers (Mickey in *Rocky,* Master Chief in
G.I. Jane), they are motivators rather than Muses. However, the training
film offers more than a spectacle of fabulously self-made bodies acting out
their masochistic reshaping routines. It also frames and moralizes this
spectacle as a pedagogical experience. Training films give us lessons in
using aesthetics understood as a practical discipline, 'the study of the mind
and emotions in relation to the sense of beauty' – to overcome personal
and social adversity. (Morris 2001: 175-176)

We might note, at this point, that the kind of *looking otherwise* (or *reading differently*) that Morris undertakes here is not deliberately provocative
or controversial. Morris does not seek to offer the kind of reading which
would boil the blood of anti-PC militants of 'common sense'. In fact, although Morris does suggest that 'the technique of "queering" is [the] live-
liest recent manifestation' of a key interpretative drive in film studies, one
that 'can be creative', she actually suggests that queering can also be
'blinkered and narrow in its relentlessness' (2001: 184). So, although
Morris wants to read Bruce Lee beyond the confines of the question of
violence, she does not want to rush headlong into acts of 'queering' or
'othering'. At least not directly. Rather, Morris operates in terms of the
insight that there can only be so many times that looking at Bruce Lee
'otherwise', by for instance revealing the *homo* at the disavowed heart of
the *hetero*, can be regarded as news. In fact, the crux of Morris's entire
article in this regard is that although she sees the grain of truth in Robert
Hughes' caricatural comment that 'the world changes more widely,
deeply, thrillingly than at any moment since 1917, and the American academic left keeps fretting about how phallocentricity is inscribed in Dick-
ens's portrayal of Little Nell' (184); on the other hand, Morris believes
that there has in fact been 'a wide, deep, thrilling change in the world
which Robert Hughes has missed' – namely, that 'fretting over phallocentricity is now a popular occupation' (184).

We may or may not accept Morris' contention that 'fretting over
phallocentricity is now a popular occupation'. (Personally, I do not, although I think that in the mid to late 1990s perhaps it looked like it was
about to become more of 'a popular occupation'; and maybe it did briefly
become slightly more common than it had been, at least journalistically.)
But her conviction that this is so explains why what Morris seeks to

'learn' from Bruce Lee does not relate to the erotic and does not simply relate to issues of patriarchy, phallocentricity, heteronormativity, masculinity, or suchlike. For, everybody with eyes to see can tell that Bruce Lee is *attractive, physical, invincible, Asian,* and hence a particularly compelling and interesting pole of identification, fantasy and desire in any number of ways. Indeed, lesson one of 'Bruce Lee 101' can only be: Look! Bruce Lee is *sexy,* Bruce Lee is *hard,* Bruce Lee kicks white, American, Japanese, Russian, and Fu Manchu-esque villains' asses. Moreover, Bruce Lee does so in a *spectacular* manner, never before (nor, indeed, since) seen. Bruce Lee *exploded.*

Phallocentricity indeed. But also an aesthetic event, emergence or eruption, one that can easily be construed as being of social, cultural and even political importance (Eperjesi 2004). Phallocentricity rearticulated, in fact. First of all, in becoming 'the first Asian male lead' in 'the first American produced martial arts spectacular' (Thomas 2002), Lee disrupted the phallus' erstwhile conflation with whiteness (Chan 2001: 70). For, this film simultaneously re-presented the Asian male *as (being in) the lead* at the same time as presenting an ambiguously homo/heteronormative hyper-masculinity (Jachinson Chan 2000). Thus, the seeds of lesson two are in lesson one: *Bruce Lee is not white.* Get it? Not simply black, of course, but definitely *not white*; so, *black enough* – especially as there never was such a thing as 'simply' black anyway. 'Black' has always fundamentally functioned as a political banner, a prosopopoeic term appealing to all who see themselves as sharing in common an equivalent experience of racism (Hall 1996; 1997). Perhaps because of this, the appeal of Bruce Lee in black communities and cultural contexts has long been acknowledged, too (Brown 1997; Marchetti 2001) – as has his significance for Hong Kong (and) Chinese everywhere, of course (Abbas 1997; Teo 1997; Marchetti 2001; Hunt 2003). Enter the marginal(ized) *and* the dream of a 'cultural China', an unequivocally attractive "Chineseness" (Eperjesi 2004). Diasporas R Us. This much we 'know'.

Morris does not make a meal of any of this, but takes it all as read – or, rather, as *shown,* as *visible, verifiable,* almost *unavoidable.* So, instead of dwelling on such themes, Morris chooses to learn something *else* from Bruce Lee. This is a lesson about learning from cinematic images – or rather about *realising,* becoming aware, being transformed by *experiencing* through cinematic images, and the overall complexity of the experience of films. Furthermore, it relates, as her essay's subtitle adverts, to PC, or political correctness. According to Morris, *Dragon: The Bruce Lee Story* is actually 'one of the more powerful treatments of institutionalized racism in a film *industry* (as well as in film images) that US cinema possesses' (183). However, what Morris would have us learn is actually a lesson about the dubious ethics and orientations of much *film criticism itself*: specifically the tendency of critics to propose that *there is 'an* audience' who receive '*a* message' from a film.

To deconstruct the simplifying tendency of reading as if there is 'one' message for 'one' audience reading 'one' text, Morris isolates a key scene in *Dragon*. This is a scene in which Bruce (played by Jason Scott Lee) and Linda (Lauren Holly), on one of their first dates, end up in a cinema watching *Breakfast at Tiffany's*. (Significantly, they have ended up in the cinema because – for obviously racist reasons – they have been refused entry to a restaurant.) In the cinema scene, we watch them watching the spectacle of Mickey Rooney bumbling around as the slapstick Japanese character, Mr Yunioshi. Morris deftly points out the way that the camera shows us Bruce and Linda watching the same scene *differently*: Linda initially laughs along with the rest of the audience, until she notices Bruce's distinct lack of enjoyment. Then the camera shows us a very significant moment of transformation, or subjectivization. According to Morris, this scene actually shows a viewing subject 'enter into' 'another subjectivity' (181) through the act of viewing (and viewing an other(s) way of viewing and being viewed).

Because of its proximity to the provocative notion of political subjectivization as developed by Jacques Rancière (1992) as well as to that of the political potential of 'aesthetic dissensus' within this process (Rancière 2006: 7), plus its insightful microscopic dissection of the scene (Morris offers a detailed reading which is the polar opposite of the type of generalization one often finds in critics such as Žižek), Morris's reading of this scene deserves to be quoted at some length:

> In the reverse shot a happy, expectant Linda, her face framed by others in similar spirits, leans right to whisper that she 'loves this movie so much'. Bruce winces 'Oh yeah?' in reply; it seems that he, too, has seen 'this movie' before.
> The couple loses unity and abstraction: Linda brightens, Bruce darkens, they part toward opposing edges of the frame. With the audience still in the picture the next shot is of a grossly made-up Mickey Rooney bolting upright in bed to bang his head on his own idiotically positioned lamp.

> The audience then drops out of the image but swells the sound with 'laffs' as we all watch the cartoon 'Oriental' – mammoth buck teeth, raucous voice, singsong 'Ah So' English – fall over his own photographic equipment as he crashes to the door in a slapstick performance of perfect incompetence. An extreme closeup snaps Linda, full face, laughing, nested in the pleasure around her; we share her gaze to the screen as the beautiful Hepburn looks upwards, and we all look with Hepburn at 'Mr. Yunioshi' hideously rasping down the stairwell 'Miss Golightly! I prote-e-e-st!'
>
> The next shot is again of Linda in closeup but holds her face a little longer; she turns right to share her pleasure and her smile suddenly fades. Only then does the camera pan left to reveal the solitude of her partner, who sits unsmiling as Rooney shrieks 'You disturba me! You must have a key made!' When it pans back to Linda, she is still looking in Bruce's direction. Slowly she looks back to the screen, her own face now unsmiling (in a medium closeup which sets her in contrast with those around her) as Rooney screeches: 'I'm an artist! I must have my rest!' When she turns back to Bruce, the couple is framed together for the first time since she declared her love for 'this movie'. They look at each other, and Linda says, 'Let's get out of here'. (Morris 2001: 180)

Morris reads this scene not only as 'a defining moment in the love story organizing *Dragon*' (180), but also proposes that 'with its fluid intercutting of varying "points of view" on *Breakfast at Tiffany*'s this scene is also a rhythmically exact little story about people being differently "moved" […] in the cinema' (180). She goes on to use this insight within her overall argument that 'the scene's affirmation of the diverse collective nature of film experience […] could be said to deconstruct the very idea of *"the* spectator"' (that wishful critical projection) and its attendant generalizing rhetoric about "what really moves *us*"' (180-181).

Thus, her primary target is the way that 'critics' invent and use the 'wishful critical projection' of *'the* spectator'. Her primary point here is *about cinema*. Her argument is that this scene 'promotes the utopian potential of cinematic negotiation' (183). For:

> when Linda suddenly connects the Chinese man beside her, the 'Oriental' on screen, and her pleasure in both, she makes an imaginative leap outside the logic of her own familiar dreams which allows her to experience something new. Putting 'herself' in another's position, she finds that her companion lives a connection between his body and the grotesque parody on screen – one fictionally modeled on a fleeting moment of cinema but relayed and sustained in its everyday life by the gazes (and the voices) of other people. (Morris 2001: 181)

Morris will go on to propose that 'Linda returns to *Breakfast at Tiffany's* with the eyes and ears of a critic, or so I like to think; as a student, she is certainly able to "enter into" another subjectivity…' (181).

But let us hesitate before making such a step ourselves; for, as Rancière (1991) has urged us to notice, an interpretive decision such as this also carries the connotation that becoming 'a critic' amounts to *maturing* into a critic, or, in the case of Linda's (satori-like) moment of revelation, being re-born as an 'enlightened one'. Identifying such a moment of transformation, realisation or 'subjectivization' (Rancière 1992) with an already-instituted institutional category (The Critic) is, in Rancière's argument, to rob it of its subjectively/socio-institutionally transformative potential. Or, as Rancière's sees it, it would be to participate in 'a logic whereby the social critic gains by showing democracy losing' (Ross 1987: xi) – by claiming that the insight, the knowledge, or the wisdom is always and already the property of 'the critic'. For:

> if science belongs to the intellectuals – the masters – and the critique of bourgeois content is reserved for those who already know, then there is only one way for students to criticize their masters' knowledge from the point of view of class, and that is to become their peers. (Ross 1987: xvii)

Rather than this, a Rancièrean approach would be to conceptualise such a moment of aesthetic dissensus as that experienced by Linda and (perhaps) Bruce as one of 'subjectivization', or 'the formation of a one that is not a self but is the relation of a self to an other' through 'a process of disidentification or declassification' (Rancière 1992: 60, 61). Thus, at this point, *Linda* could be regarded as becoming 'an outsider or, more, an *in-between*' (61) by way of what Rancière calls an 'impossible identification' (61). It is 'impossible' because Linda is not that which she has just *realized*; or, in Rancière's terms, Linda's is an identification that cannot be *embodied* by her. As Rancière theorizes it, political subjectification:

> always involves an impossible identification, an identification that cannot be embodied by he or she who utters it. 'We are the wretched of the earth' is the kind of sentence that no wretched of the world would ever utter. Or, to take a personal example, for my generation politics in France relied on an impossible identification – an identification with the bodies of the Algerians beaten to death and thrown into the Seine by the French police, in the name of the French people, in October 1961. We could not identify with those Algerians, but we *could* question our identification with the 'French people' in whose name they had been murdered. That is to say, we could act as political subjects in the interval or the gap between two identities, neither of which we could assume. That process of subjectivization had no proper name, but it found its name, its cross name, in the 1968 assumption 'We are all German Jews' – a 'wrong' identification, an identification in terms of the denial of an absolutely essential wrong. (Rancière 1992: 61)

Comparing the massacre of Algerians in Paris in 1961, or even with the protests of 1968 with the distaste of two fictionalised characters for a piece of slapstick in *Breakfast at Tiffany's* may seem to be a scandalous mismatching of registers or hyperbolising of terms, concepts and realms. But political subjectivization is not a spatially-determined concept (like, say 'the global' in contradistinction to notions like the local or regional, or the technical definition of the difference between, say, an ocean, as distinct from a lake, a pond, or a puddle). It is rather, according to Rancière, 'a heterology, a logic of the other'; and it is so 'for three main reasons':

> First, it is never the simple assertion of an identity; it is always, at the same time, the denial of an identity given by an other, given by the ruling order of policy. [...] Second, it is a demonstration, and a demonstration always supposes an other, even if that other refuses evidence or argument. It is the staging of a common place that is not a place for a dialogue or a search for a consensus in Habermasian fashion. There is no consensus, no undamaged communication, no settlement of a wrong. But there is a polemical commonplace for the handling of a wrong and the demonstration of equality. Third, the logic of subjectivization always entails an impossible identification. (62)

As Meaghan Morris points out in a slightly different way, all of this is present in *Dragon: The Bruce Lee Story*. However, for her, the kind of political subjectivization that takes place in *Dragon* is one which is entirely to be associated with PC. That is, *Dragon* is to be regarded a piece of PC ideology itself, through and through. She notes, for instance, that:

> For some viewers, *Dragon* itself is a provocation to criticism; blurring Lee's overt and distinctive cultural nationalism into a generalized 'reaction against racism' [...], it transfigures a Hong Kong Chinese hero as flexibly 'Asian'-American. Nowhere in the film is this effected more dearly than in the *Breakfast* at *Tiffany's* scene, in which we watch a white American woman empathizing with a Chinese-American man identifying with a *Japanese* stereotype as embodied by an Irish-American actor. (Morris 2001: 182)

Nevertheless, this makes *Dragon* even more appropriate for her ends. This is because Morris' aim is to *redeem* PC from its wider vilification, by trying to re-present it as something quite distinct from its caricatural representation as a tyrannical 'code regulating expression'. Rather, Morris proposes, PC ought to be regarded as 'a spectators' revolt':

> PC is not primarily a code regulating expression but a spectators' revolt. Aesthetically focused but social in resonance, PC is an act or a movement of criticism initiated by groups of people who develop shared responses to particular cultural conventions, and begin to form 'an' audience in the marketing sense: by articulating a collective 'commentary on cinema', they announce themselves as an audience. And they vocally object to the quality of something which cinema provides. Understood this way, PC as a critical formation has less in common with the grim radicals of media bad dreams (real as dreams may be) than with those highly respectable 'consumer movements' which have, through the very same media, powerfully influenced business and advertising practices in recent decades. (181)

This still seems close to Rancière's notions of politics, although with the emphasis now placed on 'political-will-formation', Morris' account moves closer to the type of 'discourse approach' to understanding politics that has been developed by Laclau and Mouffe since the 1980s (Laclau and Mouffe 1985; Bowman 2007). The evocation of the constitution and articulation of 'collective' identities (or demands, or complaints) in the form of a 'spectators' revolt' that is 'aesthetically focused but social in resonance' smacks strongly both of Rancière's notion of 'aesthetic dissensus' (Rancière 2006: 7) and of postmodern politics more generally – especially given that all of this is apparently condensed in and around the rather unexpected figure of Bruce Lee, pioneer and king of the 1970s kung fu craze, Asian-American James Dean, and Einstein of interdisciplinary martial arts training.

However, if we look slightly closer at Morris' formulation of the politics of PC, questions arise about the status of Morris' theory of politics when one tests it against the Žižekian theory of ideology that we encountered earlier. For, on closer inspection, it appears that Morris' notion of politicization boils down to a faith in 'consumer politics' or a belief in the political power of consumers. Such a faith that consumerism can offer a politics really has to be based on a belief in the power of 'demand-side' determination in culture and economics – or, rather (to pre-emptively parry any charge of economistic reductionism) a belief in the determining power of *demand-side cultural production*. For, as Morris has just said: PC 'has less in common with [...] grim radicals [...] than with [...] highly respectable "consumer movements"'. Such a position, then – with its championing of PC, the birth of the reader, the value of queering, as well as with its identification with the institution (the importance of being a critic), and its belief in consumerism and popularity *as* politics, etc. – is arguably the exemplification of everything that Slavoj Žižek construes as being ideologically and politically wrong with the post-1968 'politicized' intellectual discursive formation.

Recall: understood in a Žižekian manner, 'PC' – and a lot more besides – might be read as a short-hand term for a discursive formation which has come to include film-, media-, gender-, queer-, identity-, cultural-, etc.-studies (and their '-politics'); all of which are to be regarded as the shock troops of capitalism's neoliberal ideology of 'tolerance' and 'difference'. In a line of argument similar to Žižek's in this respect, Hardt and Negri have argued that it is possible to construe the dominant form of power today as itself being deconstructive and anti-essentialist in exactly the way that supposedly politicized or radicalized academia has become since the 1960s: Power 'itself', they say, chants along with anti-essentialists and post-modernists, 'Long live difference! Down with essentialist binaries!' (2000: 139) 'Power', they contend, 'has evacuated the bastion [that anti-essentialist intellectuals] are attacking and has circled round to their rear to join them in the assault in the name of difference' (2000: 138).

Thus, herein lies a significant (potential) critique of an intellectual formation that might regard itself as diversely 'radical' but that might actually be pro-, proto- or straightforwardly hegemonic, in the sense of being the avant-garde at the cutting edge of neoliberal ideology, in mis-recognition or disavowal. As discussed, according to this critique, a wide range of approaches and perspectives, including deconstruction, cultural studies, identity studies and so on might be read as ensnared within a diversely shared 'post-1968' problematic. In other words, this might make the declared distances between, say, Derridean deconstruction or Bourdieuian sociology or Rancièrean theory or postmodernism seem rather like the narcissism of small differences rather than fundamental heterogeneity. For, if they might all be lumped together as different points of a discursive constellation thrown up in the same period or milieu, then there is, in Žižekian terms, a question about each orientation's relation to or functioning within 'capitalism'.

But the counter-question – the response to such a charge – is: can such differences really be lumped together and deemed to be equivalent? In what register? For whom? And signifying what? What is the nature of the (academic, theoretical or argumentative) position that sees itself as 'outside' the formation with which it is contemporary, with the implication that it is somehow exempt from or immune to the conditions – not of our own choosing – within which we live and think, learn and act? For, although it is simple to slip and slide, chop and change, from, say, deconstructive terms to Bourdieuian terms, there *are* differences between paradigms. Even though there may be family resemblances or similarities when viewed informally or as if from 'outside', *all* protagonists will insist that deconstruction is not Bourdieuian sociology is not Foucauldian genealogy is not Althusserianism is not Žižekianism is not Hardt and Negrism, etc. Indeed, this consensus about the difference and disagreements between paradigms suggests that in a fundamental sense it is axiomatic that the difference between paradigms, approaches or orientations *makes a difference*: according to all parties, the differences between one's own and other paradigms are differences which make a difference – *differences that matter*.

For instance, despite their apparent proximity, Derrida has characterised Bourdieuian sociology as being an institution that '*clings to the privilege it exposes*' (Derrida 2002: 1-2) – happy with its lot and content in its institutional dwelling, its habitus, with its distinction, with its cultural capital, and so on. Similarly, as Rancière sees it, 'Bourdieu and the new sociology [is to be regarded] as the latest and most influential form of a discourse deriving its authority from the presumed naïveté or ignorance of its objects of study' (Ross 1987: xi). Kristin Ross explains:

> Rancière uncovered a logic whereby the social critic gains by showing democracy losing. It was, for example, all too obvious, he [Rancière] wrote, to say that working-class youth are almost entirely excluded from the university system, and that their cultural inferiority is a result of their economic inferiority. The sociologist attained the level of 'science' by providing a tautology whose systemic workings, veiled to the agents trapped within its grip, were evident to him alone. (1987: xi)

This argument is akin to Barthes' famous deconstruction of the institutional power of the category of 'the Critic', albeit conceptualised in explicitly political terms: for Rancière, that is, the orientation of the institutional '*expert*' is strictly and ineradicably anti-egalitarian, even if, like Bourdieuian sociology, it seeks to redress inequality. According to Rancière, the basic problem is that it *presumes* the inferiority of those 'others' (the poor, the masses, the people) that it purports to care about or wants to work 'for' or speak 'for'. This amphibological short-circuit or re-routing would be a bad enough own goal in strictly academic, methodological, or theoretical terms, but Rancière is ultimately concerned with its sociological or, rather, social implications. For the theoretical inscription of the amphibology (or the 'tragic flaw') that Rancière perceives at the heart of many 'politicised' approaches – as exemplified by Bourdieu and Althusser – has widespread institutional and political ramifications. Again, Kristin Ross has explained Rancière's position concisely. As we have seen, the problem is that if 'science' is regarded as 'belonging' to 'intellectuals', then they become ineluctably regarded as 'masters'. As such, 'there is only one way for students to criticize their masters' knowledge from the point of view of class, and that is *to* become their peers' (Ross 1987: xvii).

In other words, to consider 'the others' to be 'the ignorant' activates an identification with instituted values and procedures which stultifies or 'disciplines' those subject to those institutional values. This, therefore, amounts to a highly conservative force. Rather than this, both deconstruction and Rancière stake a great deal in the premise of the emancipatory potential of the birth of the reader. This is why Meaghan Morris' reading of precisely such a moment of 'birth', as depicted in *Dragon: The Bruce Lee Story*, interests us here.

That being said, the Žižekian critique of contemporary postmodern deconstructive (etc.) thinking – or put differently, the critique of *the hegemony of hegemony* – may nevertheless be regarded as valid and verifiable, in one specific respect at least. This could be represented as an operative consensus (or active premise) in the post-1968 intellectual formation about the *contingent character* and the *ethical and political biases* of *all* cultural and social institutions. From Althusser to all of the Foucauldianisms, from Bourdieuian sociology to the Frankfurt School, the resurgence of Gramscian post-Marxism and to the proliferation of the politicised 'studies'-suffix subjects (cultural-, gender-, queer-, ethnic-, women's-), and way beyond, the shared concern has been with the interpellating, disciplining, and subjectivating work of institutions. This can be formulated even more precisely: What is unavoidably prime here is the matter of the cultural/political work of pedagogical and educational institutions and apparatuses.

This implicit feature of much of the post-1968 discursive formation is something that Rancière's work tackles head on. Yet it remains a largely 'misrecognised', overlooked or under-considered intervention, with the bulk of critical attention having gone to the likes of Bourdieu, the *Tel Quel* group (Barthes, Derrida, Kristeva, etc.) and Foucault. However, there are many differences between Rancière's retheorisation of education and other positions within the formation that he largely takes his distances from: Bourdieuian sociology, deconstruction and a great deal of Foucauldianism, in particular. These differences deserve fuller attention, at least if differences matter. What may still take some by surprise will be the extent to which Bruce Lee will remain an exemplary object – perhaps even *the* exemplary object – of analysis in this context.

Forget Teaching and Learning

This can be seen when we consider Jacques Rancière's analysis of the politics of pedagogy in *The Ignorant Schoolmaster: Five Lessons in Intellectual Emancipation* (1991). This book focuses on the 'adventure' of Joseph Jacotot, an early Nineteenth Century educator who found himself confronted with the task of teaching French to students with whom he did not share a common language. Armed only with a bilingual edition of a novel, he instructed the students to learn the other language by copying, comparing and contrasting the marks on the page with the words they could read. Jacotot was astonished by the level of success the students had:

> He had given no explanation to his 'students' on the first elements of the language. He had not explained spelling or conjugations to them. They had looked for the French words that corresponded to words they knew and the reasons for their grammatical endings by themselves. They had learned to put them together to make, in turn, French sentences by themselves: sentences whose spelling and grammar became more and more exact as they progressed through the book; but, above all, sentences of writers and not of schoolchildren. Were the schoolmaster's explications therefore superfluous? Or, if they weren't, to whom and for what were they useful? (Rancière 1991: 3-4)

This was an epiphany for Jacotot. Until then, says Rancière, 'he had believed what all conscientious professors believe: that the important business of the master is to transmit his knowledge to his students so as to bring them, by degrees, to his own level of expertise' (2-3). Of course:

> Like all conscientious professors, he knew that teaching was not in the slightest about cramming students with knowledge and having them repeat

it like parrots, but he knew equally well that students had to avoid the chance detours where minds still incapable of distinguishing the essential from the accessory, the principle from the consequence, get lost. In short, [he had believed that] the essential act of the master was to *explicate:* to disengage the simple elements of learning, and to reconcile their simplicity in principle with the factual simplicity that characterizes young and ignorant minds. To teach was to transmit learning and form minds simultaneously, by leading those minds, according to an ordered progression, from the most simple to the most complex. (Rancière 1991: 2-3)[13]

However, by removing his own intelligence from the picture – the language barrier meant that Jacotot clearly 'transmitted' nothing – Jacotot discovers that the students forge their own methods and paths. Thus, he concludes:

the intelligence that had allowed them to learn the French in *Télémaque* was the same they had used to learn their mother tongue: by observing and retaining, repeating and verifying, by relating what they were trying to know to what they already knew, by doing and reflecting about what they had done. They moved along in a manner one shouldn't move along – the way children move, blindly, figuring out riddles. And the question then became: wasn't it necessary to overturn the admissible order of intellectual values? Wasn't that shameful method of the riddle the true movement of human intelligence taking possession of its own power? Didn't its proscription indicate above all the will to divide the world of intelligence into two? The advocates of method oppose the nonmethod of chance to that of proceeding by reason. But what they want to prove is given in advance. They suppose a little animal who, bumping into things, explores a world that he isn't yet able to see and will only discern when they teach him to do so. But the human child is first of all a speaking being. The child who repeats the words he hears and the Flemish student 'lost' in his *Télémaque* are not proceeding hit or miss. All their effort, all their exploration, is strained toward this: someone has addressed words to them that they want to recognize and respond to, not as students or as learned men, but as people; in the way you respond to someone speaking to you and not to someone examining you: under the sign of equality. (Rancière 1991: 10-11)

---

[13] Of course, Rancière proceeds to deliver a critique of the politics of pedagogy, as he continues immediately with the counter-Bourdieuian argument that: 'By the reasoned appropriation of knowledge and the formation of judgment and taste, a student was thus elevated to as high a level as his social destination demanded, and he was in this way prepared to make the use of the knowledge appropriate to that destination: to teach, to litigate, or to govern for the lettered elite; to invent, design, or make instruments and machines for the new avant-garde now hopefully to be drawn from the elite of the common people; and, in the scientific careers, for the minds gifted with this particular genius, to make new discoveries. Undoubtedly the procedures of these men of science would diverge noticeably from the reasoned order of the pedagogues. But this was no grounds for an argument against that order. On the contrary, one must first acquire a solid and methodical foundation before the singularities of genius could take flight. *Post hoc, ergo propter hoc*' (Rancière 1991: 3).

Herein consists the kernel of Rancière's entire theory of politics and of pedagogy. What is of most pertinence to our discussion is the radical reconceptualisation of institutions, of institutional relationships such as those of pedagogy, and in particular of the 'teacher's' relationship to the 'student'. As Rancière proposes, the true radicality of this may boil down to acknowledging that the 'shameful method' of trying to solve riddles is in actual fact the essence of learning. Educators have tried to deter this independence, argues Rancière, because it will rob them of their cultural capital. Yet, despite the extent to which educators, reformers and masters try to deter such 'intellectual emancipation', the solving of what appear at first as riddles may amount to 'the true movement of human intelligence taking possession of its own power'.

Talk of 'riddles' in this context, of course, calls out for a return to the riddles most strongly associated with Bruce Lee: the riddle of his death, of course; the riddle of 'fighting without fighting'; and the riddle of the finger pointing away to the moon. Each of these have become inter-linking coordinates of the mythopoetic fantasy construct that is Bruce Lee, metonym of martial arts and, indeed, of an entire martial arts symbolic order or discursive constellation. Perhaps the primary 'riddle' deployed and capitalized upon by Bruce Lee was that of the 'finger pointing to the moon', which he delivered without explication in *Enter the Dragon*, on the TV show *Ironside*, in notebooks and in 'Liberate Yourself from Classical Karate'. (It is equally noteworthy that Rancière's own interests in *The Ignorant Schoolmaster* and beyond can be encapsulated in the word 'emancipation', which is certainly not very far removed from the word 'liberation'. Indeed, the proximity between Lee and Jacotot/Rancière here is striking.)

Is this riddle philosophical? Is it a meaningless cliché? What is its significance? Is it akin to Miller's verdict on what Bruce Lee's idea for a TV show called *The Warrior* finally became? Miller writes:

> Lee's story idea eventually became the Kung-fu TV series, which in the dubious tradition of Fu Manchu, Charlie Chan and Mr Moto, starred Caucasian non-martial artist David Carradine, who, week after week, shuffled across deserts and through cow-towns in varying states of consciousness. Tan says of the series, 'What was passed off as Taoism and Buddhism were writers' childhood Torah teachings filtered through West Coast big bucks and pseudo-hippie aesthetics'. (Miller 2000: 118)

Such capitalization is undoubtedly present. Yet, can it be written off as such? For, the history of the finger-pointing 'lesson', even if it is also a cliché, does have some quite persuasive credentials. In an essay on the pedagogy of Buddhism, for instance, Eve Kosofsky Sedgwick quotes Walter Hsieh:

> Employing speech as a skilful means, the Buddha spoke many sutras, which should only be taken as 'the finger that points to the moon', not the moon itself. The Buddha said, 'I have not taught a single word during the forty-nine years of my Dharma preaching'. (qtd. in Kosofsky Sedgwick 2003: 170)

Sedgwick chases the interpretation of the finger-moon riddle through the archives of Zen Buddhist writings; for the 'implication of the finger/moon image is that pointing may invite less misunderstanding than speech, but that even its non-linguistic concreteness cannot shield it from the slippery problems that surround reference' (2003: 170). In our exploration of this in Chapter Two, we arrived at a point not dissimilar to that at which Sedgwick arrives: 'Perhaps the most distinctive way Mahayana Buddhism has tried to negotiate the "finger pointing at the moon" issue is through the ostentive language of thusness or suchness' (170), she argues. As we saw in Chapter Two, however, ostention, indexicality, acts of reference, and suchlike, produce a 'resonant double movement' (171), which Sedgwick prefers to approach through the terms and poetics of Buddhism itself. This preference allows her to propose that 'finally, in the view of thusness, even the distinction between finger and moon dissolves, and with it perhaps the immemorial injunction against confusing them':

> As a contemporary Zen abbot notes, 'The finger pointing to the moon is the moon, and the moon is the finger. . . they realize each other' (...). A koan commentary elaborates: 'When the monk asked about the meaning of "the moon", the master [Fa Yen] answered "to point at"; when someone else asked about the meaning of "to point at" the master replied 'the moon': Why was it so? The deepest reasoning, probably, was in the Enlightened mind of the Ch'an master, where there was no distinction between what the ordinary mind called "to point at" and "the moon": To him, the relation between the two was similar to the relation of an ocean to its waves'. (Sedgwick 2003: 171)

Rather than allowing the 'double movement' of acts of pointing, designating, referring, showing, and teaching to 'dissolve', however, in this study I have sought to draw attention to the constitutive character – and doubleness – of such acts. This has inevitably involved an element of approaching Bruce Lee otherwise, through various double movements. But this is at least doubly called for. For, as we have seen, there are at least two lessons of Bruce Lee, and in one respect they are utterly contradictory. One takes place in the cinematic oeuvre of Bruce Lee, and it boils down to the interruptive and reorganising effects of the explosive entrance of the dragon: the revelatory introduction of the amazing new, never before seen Chinese fighting art of kung fu to the western popular cultural imaginary, and the rearticulation of a Chinese imaginary. The other lesson relates to Bruce Lee's own experiments, teaching, writings and innovations in martial arts practice, which he ultimately considered to be a set of principles – not a *style* and not an *institution*, but a set of *principles* – that he called *jeet kune do*, or 'way of the intercepting fist'. The contradictory relationship of these two lessons can be seen in the fact that Lee's films depict a kung fu that is (supposedly) eminently traditional and ethnically 'Chinese', while Lee's work under the heading of jeet kune do is adamantly pragmatic, interdisciplinary, anti-institutional, egalitarian, verificationist, and avowedly non-traditional. Bruce Lee would take anything that worked and teach anyone who would work, irrespective of culture or ethnicity.

However, nothing ever stops at two. Thesis and antithesis demand synthesis. The dialectical synthesis of these apparently diametrically opposing 'lessons' of Bruce Lee (the traditionalism and nationalism of the 'lesson of the celluloid Lee' versus the pragmatic, egalitarian inter- and antidisciplinary 'lesson of JKD') can be found in what might be called a certain 'spirit'. This can be seen to be subtending, infusing and suffusing (if not simply sublating) 'both' lessons of Bruce Lee. This spirit is often too quickly represented as the spirit of Zen – a putatively timeless, 'transcultural' spirit. However, such a spirit surely can and should be historicized. According to Sedgwick:

> In the United States it seems to have fallen to the twentieth-century popularizers of Zen, after World War II, to begin to articulate the centrality in many forms of Buddhism of [a] radical doubt that a basic realization can be communicated at all. After all, if Zen practice cannot promise to bring one methodically over the high learning threshold of satori ['awakening', 'realization'], it at least offers distinct practices, such as wrestling with koans, for dramatizing and perhaps exhausting the impossibility of methodical learning. Furthermore, the anti-scholasticism of Zen and the often anti-intellectualism of the counterculture merged in a durable consciousness of the limits of verbal articulation. The 1960s heyday of these explorations [...] was one when a critique of school institutions became the ve-

hicle of almost every form of utopian investment; if Buddhist explorations were peripheral to the student movement, they nonetheless both enabled and were enabled by it. (172)

Quite how one ultimately judges the value and lasting effects of such a movement remains to be decided. What is clear is the central place of Bruce Lee within this movement, as expression and agency, bringing many elements of the cultural and political margins right to the centre of global popular culture. Indeed, Bruce Lee arguably provided what Rancière calls 'the aesthetic dimension of the reconfiguration of the relationships between doing, seeing and saying that circumscribe the being-in-common [which] is inherent to every political or social movement' (2000: 17). Of course, Rancière adds quickly, 'this aesthetic component of politics does not lead me to seek the political everywhere that there is a reconfiguration of perceptible attributes in general. I am far from believing that "everything is political"'. Yet, he quickly adds: 'On the other hand, I believe it's important to note that the political dimension of the arts can be seen first of all in the way that their forms materially propose the paradigms of the community' (17). This is not to suggest that Bruce Lee was a herald and trailblazer of a PC utopia. However, it is to locate Bruce Lee firmly at the shifting centre of enduring intercultural and cross-ethnic representation:

a process in which the acceleration and intensification of contacts brought by technology and commerce entail an acceleration and intensification of stereotypes, stereotypes that, rather than simply being false or incorrect (and thus dismissable), have the potential of effecting changes in entire intellectual climates... (Chow 2002: 63)

Works Cited and Consulted

Abbas, Ackbar (1997), *Hong Kong: Culture and the Politics of Disappearance*, University of Minnesota Press: Minneapolis and London.

Adorno, Theodor (1984), *Minima Moralia*, London: Verso.

Adorno, Theodor, and Horkheimer, Max, (1972), *Dialectic of Enlightenment*, London: Herder & Herder. Online at http://sfs.scnu.edu.cn/blogs/linghh/uploadfiles/2007314215657614.pdf

Althusser, Louis (1971), *Lenin and Philosophy*, New York: Monthly Review Press.

Barthes, Roland (1972), *Mythologies*, Paladin: London.

Barthes, Roland (1977), *Image – Music – Text*, Fontana, London.

Barthes, Roland (1989), *The Rustle of Language*, Berkeley: University of California Press.

Benjamin, Walter (1999), *Illuminations*, London, Pimlico.

Bewes, Timothy (2001) 'Vulgar Marxism: The Spectre Haunting Spectres of Marx', *parallax* 20, July-September 2001, pp. 83-95.

Bolelli, Daniele (2003), *On the Warrior's Path: Philosophy, Fighting, and Martial Arts Mythology*, Berkeley, Ca.: Blue Snake Books.

Bourdieu, Pierre (1990), *The Logic of Practice*. Translated by Richard Nice. Stanford: Stanford University Press.

Bowman, Paul (2006), 'Cultural Studies and Slavoj Žižek', Gary Hall and Claire Birchall, eds., *New Cultural Studies: Adventures in Theory*. Edinburgh: Edinburgh University Press.

Bowman, Paul (2006a), 'Enter the Žižekian: Bruce Lee, Martial Arts and the Problem of Knowledge', *Entertext*, Volume 6, Number 1, Autumn. (http://arts.brunel.ac.uk/gate/entertext/issue_6_1.htm)

Bowman, Paul (2007), *Post-Marxism Versus Cultural Studies: Theory, Politics and Intervention*. Edinburgh: Edinburgh University Press.

Bowman, Paul (2007a), 'The Tao of Žižek', Paul Bowman and Richard Stamp, eds., *The Truth of Žižek*, Edinburgh: Edinburgh University Press.

Bowman, Paul (2008), *Deconstructing Popular Culture*, London: Palgrave.

Brown, Bill (1997), 'Global Bodies/Postnationalities: Charles Johnson's Consumer Culture', *Representations*, No. 58, Spring, pp. 24-48.

Brown, Terry (1997), *English Martial Arts* Anglo-Saxon Books: Frithgarth, Norfolk.

Butler, Judith (2000), 'Competing Universalities', Butler, Laclau, Žižek, *Contingency, Hegemony, Universality: Contemporary Dialogues on the Left*, London: Verso.

Chan, Stephen (2000), 'The Construction and Export of Culture as Artefact: The Case of Japanese Martial Arts', *Body & Society*, Vol. 6(1): 69–74.

Chan, Jachinson W. (2000), 'Bruce Lee's Fictional Models of Masculinity', *Men and Masculinities*, Vol. 2 No. 4, April 2000 371-387.

Clarke, J. J. (1997), *Oriental Enlightenment: the Encounter Between Asian and Western Thought*, London: Routledge.

Chow, Rey (1991), *Woman and Chinese Modernity*, Minnesota and London: University of Minnesota Press.

Chow, Rey (1993), *Writing Diaspora: Tactics of Intervention in Contemporary Cultural Studies*, Bloomington, Indiana: Indiana University Press.

Chow, Rey (1995) *Primitive Passions*, New York: Columbia University Press.

Chow, Rey (1998), *Ethics After Idealism*, Bloomington, Indiana: Indiana University Press.

Chow, Rey (2002), *The Protestant Ethnic and the Spirit of Capitalism*, New York: Columbia University Press.

Chow, Rey (2006), *The Age of the World Target*, Durham and London: Duke.

Chow, Rey (2007), *Sentimental Fabulations: Contemporary Chinese Films*, New York: Columbia University Press.

De Man, Paul (1978), 'The Epistemology of Metaphor', Sheldon Sacks, ed., *On Metaphor*, Chicago: Chicago University Press.

Debord, Guy (1967/1992), *The Society of the Spectacle*, London: Verso.

Debord, Guy (1988), *Comments on the Society of the Spectacle* (http://www.notbored.org/commentaires.html).

Derrida, Jacques (1962/1978) *Edmund Husserl's Origin of Geometry: An Introduction*, New York and Brighton: Harvester.

Derrida, Jacques (1974), *Of Grammatology*, Baltimore and London: Johns Hopkins University Press.

Derrida, Jacques (1978), *Writing and Difference*, London, Routledge & Kegan Paul.

Derrida, Jacques (1981), *Dissemination*, trans. B. Johnson, Chicago and London: University of Chicago Press.

Derrida, Jacques (1982), *Margins of Philosophy*, London: Harvester Wheatsheaf.

Derrida, Jacques (1987), *The Truth in Painting*, Chicago: University of Chicago Press.

Derrida, Jacques (1992), 'Mochlos; or, The Conflict of the Faculties', *Logomachia: The Conflict of the Faculties*, in Richard Rand (ed.), Lincoln and London: University of Nebraska Press.

Derrida, Jacques (1992a), 'Canons and Metonymies: An Interview with Jacques Derrida', *Logomachia: The Conflict of the Faculties*, Rand, R. (ed.), Lincoln and London, University of Nebraska Press.

Derrida, Jacques (1994), *Specters of Marx: The State of the Debt, the Work of Mourning, & the New International*, London: Routledge.

Derrida, Jacques (1995), *The Gift of Death*, Chicago and London: University of Chicago Press.

Derrida, Jacques (1995a), *Points...: Interviews, 1974-1994*, Stanford, California: Stanford University Press.

Derrida, Jacques (1996), 'Remarks on Deconstruction and Pragmatism', Chantal Mouffe (ed.) *Deconstruction and Pragmatism*, London: Routledge.

Derrida, Jacques (1997), *Politics of Friendship*, London: Verso.

Derrida, Jacques (1998), *Resistances of Psychoanalysis*, Stanford, Ca.: Stanford University Press.

Derrida, Jacques (1998a), *Monolingualism of the Other; or, the Prosthesis of Origin*, Stanford, Calif., Stanford University Press.

Derrida, Jacques (2002), *Who's Afraid of Philosophy?: Right to Philosophy 1*, Stanford, Calif., Stanford University Press.

Dickinson, John (1976) *A Behavioural Analysis of Sport*, London: Lepus.

Downey, Greg (2002), 'Domesticating an Urban Menace: Reforming Capoeira as a Brazilian National Sport', *The International Journal of the History of Sport* 4, December, 1-32.

Downey, Greg (2006), '"Practice without Theory": The Imitation Bottleneck and the Nature of Embodied Knowledge', unpublished manuscript.

Eperjesi, John R. (2004), 'Crouching Tiger, Hidden Dragon: Kung Fu Diplomacy and the Dream of Cultural China', *Asian Studies Review*, Vol. 28, 25-39.

Ferraris, Maurizio (2001), 'What is there?', in Jacques Derrida and Ferraris, *A Taste for the Secret*, Polity: Cambridge.

Feyerabend, Paul (1993), *Against Method: Outline of an Anarchistic Theory of Method* (3rd Edition), London: Verso.

Foucault, Michel (1988) *Power/Knowledge: Selected Interviews and Other Writings, 1972-1977*. Random House: London.

Foucault, Michel (1978), *The History of Sexuality: Vol. 1*, London: Penguin.

Foucault, Michel (1988), *Power/Knowledge: Selected Interviews and Other Writings, 1972-1977*, London: Harvester Press.

Freud, Sigmund (1899), 'Screen Memories', *The Standard Edition of the Complete Psychological Works of Sigmund Freud, Volume III (1893-1899): Early Psycho-Analytic Publications*, 299-322.

Funakoshi, Gichin (1975), *Karate-Dō: My Way of Life*, Tokyo, New York and London, Kodansha International.

Gilbert, Jeremy, and Pearson, Ewan (1999), *Discographies: Dance Music, Culture and the Politics of Sound*, Routledge, London.

Giroux, Henry A. (2000), *Impure Acts: The Practical Politics of Cultural Studies*, London: Routledge.

Giroux, Henry A. (2002), *Breaking into the Movies*, London: Blackwell.

Godzich, Wlad (1987), 'Afterword: Religion, the State and Post(Al) Modernism', in Sam Weber, *Institution and Interpretation*, Minneapolis: University of Minnesota Press.

Hall, Stuart (1980), 'Encoding/Decoding', *Culture, Media, Language: Working Papers in Cultural Studies, 1972-79*, ed. Stuart Hall, Dorothy Hobson, Andrew Lowe and Paul Willis, London: Routledge.

Hall, Stuart (1992), 'Cultural Studies and Its Theoretical Legacies', in Lawrence Grossberg, Cary Nelson, Paula Treichler (eds.), *Cultural Studies*, New York and London: Routledge.

Hall, Stuart (1996), 'On postmodernism and articulation: an interview with Stuart Hall', David Morley and Kuan-Hsing Chen, eds., *Stu-*

art Hall: Critical Dialogues in Cultural Studies, London: Routledge.

Hall, Stuart (1996a) 'New Ethnicities', in *Stuart Hall: Critical Dialogues in Cultural Studies*, ed. David Morley and Kuan-Hsing Chen, London: Routledge.

Hall, Stuart (1997), 'Minimal Selves', *Studying Culture*, ed. Jim McGuigan, London: Arnold.

Hardt, Michael, and Negri, Antonio (2000), *Empire*, Cambridge, Ma. and London: Harvard University Press.

Harland, Richard (1987) *Superstructuralism*, Methuen: London.

Heath, Joseph and Potter, Andrew (2005), *The Rebel Sell: Why The Culture Can't Be Jammed*, Capstone: Chichester.

Hegel, G. W. F. (1977), *Phenomenology of Spirit*, Oxford: Oxford University Press.

Heidegger, Martin (1971), 'A Dialogue on Language: Between a Japanese and an Inquirer', *On The Way To Language*, New York: Harper Collins.

Heiskanen, Benita (2006), 'On the ground and off: The theoretical practice of professional boxing', *European Journal of Cultural Studies*, Volume 9, No. 4, 481-496.

Hunt, Leon (2003), *Kung Fu Cult Masters: From Bruce Lee to Crouching Tiger*, London: Wallflower.

Inosanto, Dan (1980), *Jeet Kune Do: The Art and Philosophy of Bruce Lee*, Los Angeles: Know How Publishing.

Kennedy, Brian and Guo, Elizabeth (2005), *Chinese Martial Arts Training Manuals: A Historical Survey*, Berkeley, Ca.: North Atlantic Books.

Kosofsky Sedgwick, Eve (2003), *Touching Feeling: Affect, Pedagogy, Performativity*. Duke: Durham and London.

Krug, Gary J. (2001), 'At the Feet of the Master: Three Stages in the Appropriation of Okinawan Karate Into Anglo-American Culture', Cultural Studies: Critical Methodologies, Volume 1 Number 4, 2001 395-410, Sage Publications, 395-410.

Laclau, Ernesto, and Mouffe, Chantal, (1985), *Hegemony and Socialist Strategy: Towards A Radical Democratic Politics*. London: Verso.

Laclau, Ernesto (1989) 'Preface', in Slavoj Žižek, *The Sublime Object of Ideology*, London: Verso.

Laclau, Ernesto (2000), *Contingency, Hegemony, Universality: Contemporary Dialogues on the Left*, London: Verso.

Laplanche, Jean, and Pontalis, J.-B. (1988), *The Language of Psychoanalysis*, London: Karnac.

Bruce Lee (1963/1987), *Chinese Gung-fu: The Philosophical Art of Self-Defense*, Santa Clarita, California: Ohara Publications.

Lee, Bruce (1971) 'Liberate Yourself from Classical Karate' (Black Belt Magazine, September 1971).

Lee, Bruce (1975), *The Tao of Jeet Kune Do*, Santa Clarita, Ca., Ohara Publications.

Lee, Bruce (2001), *Bruce Lee, Artist of Life: The Essential Writings*, compiled and edited by John Little, Boston: Tuttle.

Lee, Bruce (n/d), http://www.fightingmaster.com/masters/brucelee/

quotes.htm

Little, John (1996), *Bruce Lee: A Warrior's Journey*, McGraw Hill Contemporary.

Longxi, Zhang (1992), *The Tao and the Logos: Literary Hermeneutics, East and West*, Duke: Durham and London.

Lui, Elizabeth (2005), *The Travels of Lao Ts'an*, Yi Lin Chu Ban She.

Lyotard, Jean-François (1984), *The Postmodern Condition: A Report on Knowledge*, Minneapolis: University of Minnesota Press.

Lyotard, Jean-François (1988), *The Differend: Phrases in Dispute*, Manchester: Manchester University Press.

Marchetti, Gina (2001), 'Jackie Chan and the Black Connection', in Matthew Tinkcom and Amy Villarejo, eds., *Keyframes: popular cinema and cultural studies*, London: Routledge.

May, Reinhard (1996), *Heidegger's Hidden Sources: East-Asian Influences on His Work*, London: Routledge.

Miller, Davis (2000), *The Tao of Bruce Lee*, Vintage: London.

Montague, Erle, (1993), *Dim Mak: Death Point Striking*, New York: Paladin.

Morris, Meaghan (2001), 'Learning from Bruce Lee', in Matthew Tinkcom and Amy Villarejo, eds., *Keyframes: popular cinema and cultural studies*, London: Routledge. Pp. 171-184.

Mowitt, John (1992), *Text: The Genealogy of an Antidisciplinary Object*, Durham and London: Duke.

Mowitt, John (2002), *Percussion: Drumming, Beating, Striking*, Duke: Durham and London.

Mowitt, John (2003), 'Cultural Studies, in Theory', in Paul Bowman, ed., *Interrogating Cultural Studies: Theory, Politics and Practice*, London: Pluto.

Musashi, Mayamoto (1994), *The Book of Five Rings*, trans. Thomas Cleary, Boston and London: Shambala.

Peters, Michael A. (2001), *Poststructuralism, Marxism and Neoliberalism: Between Theory and Politics*. London: Rowman and Littlefield.

Preston, Brian (2007), *Bruce Lee and Me: A Martial Arts Adventure*, London: Penguin.

Protevi, John (2001), *Political Physics: Deleuze, Derrida and the Body Politic*, London, Athlone.

Rancière, Jacques (1987/1991) *The Ignorant Schoolmaster: Five Lessons in Intellectual Emancipation*, Stanford: Stanford University Press.

Rancière, Jacques (1992), 'Politics, Identification, and Subjectivization', *October*, Vol. 61, *The Identity in Question*. (Summer), pp. 58-64.

Rancière, Jacques (2000), 'Jacques Rancière: Literature, Politics, Aesthetics: Approaches to Democratic Disagreement: interviewed by Solange Guénoun and James H. Kavanagh', *Substance*, 92, 3-24.

Rancière, Jacques (2006), 'Thinking Between Disciplines: An Aesthetics of Knowledge", *Parrhesia*, Vol. 1, No. 1, 1-12.

Rancière, Jacques (2006), *The Politics of Aesthetics*, London: Continuum.

Rayns, Tony (1984), 'Bruce Lee and Other Stories', in Lau Shing-hon (ed.), *A Study of Hong Kong Cinema in the Seventies*, Hong Kong: Hong Kong International Film Festival/Urban Council, 26-9.

Rojek, Chris (2003), *Stuart Hall*, London: Polity.

Ronell, Avital (2004), 'Koan Practice or Taking Down the Test', *parallax*, Vol. 10, No. 1, 58–71.

Ross, Kristin (1987/1991), 'Translator's Introduction' in Jacques Rancière *The Ignorant Schoolmaster: Five Lessons in Intellectual Emancipation*, Stanford: Stanford University Press.

Royle, Nicholas (2000), 'What is Deconstruction?', *Deconstructions: A User's Guide*, Basingstoke and New York: Palgrave.

Said, Edward (1978) *Orientalism*, London: Vintage.

Sandford, Stella (2003), 'Going Back: Heidegger, East Asia and 'The West'', *Radical Philosophy*, 120, 11-22, July/August.

Silverman, Kaja (1983), *The Subject of Semiotics*, Oxford University Press: Oxford.

Silverman, Kaja (1992), *Male Subjectivity at the Margins*, London: Routledge.

Skinner, Frank (2002), *Frank Skinner*, Arrow Books: London.

Smith, Damon (2006), 'Tai Chi Ch'üan', Yongquan Martial Arts Association (http://www.xingyi.org.uk/html/tai_chi_chuan.html).

Smith, Robert W. (1999), *Martial Musings: A Portrayal of Martial Arts in the 20th Century*, Erie, Pennsylvania: Via Media.

Smith, Huston and Novak, P. (2003), *Buddhism*, London: Harper Collins.

Spivak, Gayatri Chakravorty (1976), 'Translator's Preface', in Jacques Derrida, *Of Grammatology*, Baltimore: Johns Hopkins University Press.

Spivak, Gayatri Chakravorty (1988), 'Can the Subaltern Speak?', *Marxism and the Interpretation of Culture*, Chicago: University of Illinois Press.

Spivak, Gayatri Chakravorty (1999), *A Critique of Postcolonial Reason: Toward a History of the Vanishing Present*, Cambridge Ma., and London: Harvard University Press.

Teo, Stephen (2008), *Hong Kong Cinema: The Extra Dimension*, London: British Film Institute.

Thomas, Bruce (1994/2002), *Bruce Lee: Fighting Spirit*, Basingstoke and Oxford, Sidgwick & Jackson.

Thompson, Geoff (1993), *Real Self Defence*, G. Thompson, Chichester: Summersdale.

Thompson, Geoff (1993a), *The Pavement Arena: Adapting Combat Martial Arts to the Street*. Chichester: Summersdale.

Tierney, Sean M. (2006), 'Themes of Whiteness in *Bulletproof Monk, Kill Bill*, and *The Last Samurai*', *Journal of Communication*, 607-624.

Toch, Hans (1972), *Violent Men: an inquiry into the psychology of violence*, Harmondsworth: Penguin.

Unknown (1971), *Secrets of Shaolin Boxing*, Taipei: Zhonghuawushu Press.

Wacquant, Loic (1995), 'The pugilistic point of view: how boxers think and feel about their trade', *Theory and Society*, Volume 24, No. 4, 489-535.

Watts, Alan (1957), *The Way of Zen*, London: Penguin.

Weber, Sam (1982), *The Legend of Freud*, Minneapolis: University of Minnesota Press.

Weber, Sam (1987), *Institution and Interpretation*, Minneapolis: University of Minnesota Press.

Wile, Douglas (1996), *Lost T'ai-chi Classics from the Late Ch'ing Dynasty*, New York: State University of New York Press.

Xu, Jian (1999), 'Body, Discourse, and the Cultural Politics of Contemporary Chinese Qigong', *The Journal of Asian Studies*, 58, no. 4, 961-991, November.

Yamamoto, Tsunetomo (1979), *Hagakure: The Book of the Samurai*, Translated by William Scott Wilson, Kondansha International.

Yu, Cheng (1984), 'Anatomy of a Legend' in Li Cheuk-to (ed.) *A Study of the Hong Kong Martial Arts Film*, Hong Kong: HKIFF/Urban Council, 149-50.

Žižek, Slavoj (1998), 'A Leftist Plea for "Eurocentrism"', *Critical Inquiry* 24 (2), pp. 988-1,009.

Žižek, Slavoj (2000), *Contingency, Hegemony, Universality: Contemporary Dialogues on the Left*, Butler, J., Ernesto Laclau and Slavoj Žižek (ed.), London, Verso.

Žižek, Slavoj (2001), *On Belief*, London: Routledge.

Žižek, Slavoj (2001a), *Did Somebody Say Totalitarianism? Five Interventions in the (Mis)use of a Notion*. London: Verso.

Žižek, Slavoj (2002), *Revolution at the Gates: Selected Writings of Lenin from February to October 1917*, London, Verso.

Žižek, Slavoj (2004), 'The Lesson of Rancière', Afterword to Jacques Rancière's *The Politics of Aesthetics*, London: Continuum.

Žižek, Slavoj (2005), *Interrogating the Real*, ed. Rex Butler and Scott Stephens, London and New York: Continuum.

Filmography

A Beautiful Mind (2001) Ron Howard
A Clockwork Orange (1971) Stanley Kubrick
Austin Powers: International Man of Mystery (1997) Jay Roach
Batman (1966-8) Bob Kane, William Dozier
Billy Jack (1971) Tom Laughlin Frank
Blade (1998) Stephen Norrington
Braveheart (1995) Mel Gibson
Breakfast at Tiffany's (1961) Blake Edwards
Bridget Jones' Diary (2001) Sharon Maguire
Buffy The Vampire Slayer (1997-2003) Joss Whedon
Bulletproof Monk (2003) Paul Hunter
Crouching Tiger, Hidden Dragon (2000) Ang Lee
Dances With Wolves (1990) Kevin Costner
Dragon: The Bruce Lee Story (1993) Rob Cohen
Dr No (1962) Terence Young
Enter the Dragon (1973) Robert Clouse
Friends (1994-2004) David Crane, Marta Kauffman
Fight Club (1999) David Fincher
Fist of Fury (1972) Lo Wei
Game of Death (1973/1978) Bruce Lee
Ghost Dog: The Way of the Samurai (1999) Jim Jarmusch
Gladiator (2000) Ridley Scott
Goldfinger (1964) Guy Hamilton
Hero (2002) Zhang Yimou
Hidalgo (2004) Joe Johnston
How to Get Ahead in Advertising (1989) Bruce Robinson

Kill Bill, Vol. 1 (2003) Quentin Tarantino
Kill Bill, Vol. 2 (2004) Quentin Tarantino
Kung Fu (1972-75) Ed Spielman, Jerry Thorpe, Herman Miller
M. Butterfly (1993) David Cronenberg
Napoleon Dynamite (2004) Jared Hess
No Retreat, No Surrender (1986) Corey Yuen
Once Upon a Time in China (1991) Tsui Hark
Rashomon (1950) Akira Kurosawa
Saving Private Ryan (1998) Steven Spielberg
Star Wars (1977) George Lucas
Sunshine (2007) Danny Boyle
The Big Boss (1971) Lo Wei
The Bourne Identity (2002) Doug Liman
The Bourne Supremacy (2004) Paul Greengrass
The Bourne Ultimatum (2007) Paul Greengrass
The Crow (1994) Alex Proyas
The F Word (2008) Channel 4
The Fifth Element (1997) Luc Besson
The Green Hornet (1966-7) William Dozier
The Karate Kid (1984) John G. Avildsen
The Karate Kid, Part II (1986) John G. Avildsen
The Last Emperor (1987) Bernardo Bertolucci
The Last Samurai (2003) Edward Zwick
The Man From U.N.C.L.E. (1964-68) Norman Felton
The Matrix (1999) Larry and Andy Wachowski
The Mechanic (1972) Michael Winner
The Octagon (1980) Eric Karson
The Silent Flute (1980) Richard Moore
Warriors (1979) Walter Hill
Way of the Dragon (1972) Bruce Lee

Index